New Literacies and
Teacher Learning

Colin Lankshear and Michele Knobel
General Editors

Vol. 74

The New Literacies and Digital Epistemologies series
is part of the Peter Lang Education list.
Every volume is peer reviewed and meets
the highest quality standards for content and production.

PETER LANG
New York • Bern • Frankfurt • Berlin
Brussels • Vienna • Oxford • Warsaw

New Literacies and Teacher Learning

Professional Development and the Digital Turn

Edited by Michele Knobel and Judy Kalman

PETER LANG
New York • Bern • Frankfurt • Berlin
Brussels • Vienna • Oxford • Warsaw

Library of Congress Cataloging-in-Publication Data

Names: Knobel, Michele, editor. | Kalman, Judy, editor.
Title: New literacies and teacher learning: professional development
and the digital turn / edited by Michele Knobel, Judy Kalman.
Description: New York: Peter Lang, [2016].
Series: New literacies and digital epistemologies; vol. 74 | ISSN 1523-9543
Includes bibliographical references and index.
Identifiers: LCCN 2015047353 | ISBN 978-1-4331-2912-4 (hardcover: alk. paper)
ISBN 978-1-4331-2911-7 (paperback: alk. paper) | ISBN 978-1-4539-1823-4 (e-book)
Subjects: LCSH: Teachers—In-service training. | Computer literacy.
Classification: LCC LB1731.N373 2016 | DDC 370.71/1—dc23
LC record available at http://lccn.loc.gov/2015047353

Bibliographic information published by **Die Deutsche Nationalbibliothek**.
Die Deutsche Nationalbibliothek lists this publication in the "Deutsche
Nationalbibliografie"; detailed bibliographic data are available
on the Internet at http://dnb.d-nb.de/.

Contents

Acknowledgments

First up, we want to thank our authors for their contributions to this book. We know they all lead busy and demanding lives, and we are deeply appreciative of their generosity with their time, work and goodwill.

Heather Lotherington, Stephanie Fisher, Jennifer Jenson and Laura Mae Lindo would like to thank parents and students at Joyce Public School for their participation in their project and for granting permission to use the video image shown in Figure 4.1. Christina Cantrill and Kylie Peppler would like to acknowledge Kim Douillard's generosity in letting us use images she took during a National Writing Project e-Puppetry workshop.

Any book that involves ten sets of authors in seven different countries and two editors miles apart from each other is, by definition, a big project! Just keeping the records straight in terms of where everybody is in their chapter writing and revisions, in following through on questions and answers, or completing small but necessary tasks like organizing bio blurbs or initially formatting the text required dedication, time, and pristine organization. So here is a big shout out to Ali Zeidan and Melissa Collucci for helping us get through all of this!

Special thanks are also due to Chris Myers, Stephen Mazur, Sophie Appel and Bernadette Shade at Peter Lang for their enthusiasm about and support for our book. Many thanks also go to Benjamin de Buen for his thoughtful translation from Spanish of Chapter 2.

From the start, putting this book together has been a truly collaborative project, and the editors hope readers will learn as much from this book about teaching, learning, new literacies and the digital turn as they did.

CHAPTER ONE

Teacher Learning, Digital Technologies AND New Literacies

MICHELE KNOBEL AND JUDY KALMAN

Right now, "improving teachers" is a trending topic internationally. Interestingly, the last time teachers were so fixed in the crosshairs of national policy makers, international cooperation agencies, and initiative funders was the 1970s. This was a time when education pundits around the world called for the "rationalization of teaching and learning" (Novoa 2008: 49) and teachers were "trained" to teach by developing lesson plans based on very specific learning objectives. Then, during the 1980s, the epicenter of attention shifted away from teachers to focus on curricular reform, while in the 1990s, school (re)organization became the priority (Novoa 2008). Organizations such as the World Bank, the United Nations Scientific and Cultural Organization (UNESCO), and the Organization for Economic Cooperation and Development (OECD), among others, persuaded national governments to invest time and resources in curriculum reform and school reorganization efforts. While teachers were asked—if not required—to put many of these organizations' specific guidelines and directives into action, teachers themselves were not leading players during this period. It seemed government bodies and other organizations alike assumed that changing the curriculum or organizing schools differently would necessarily result in improvements in student learning and this, in turn, would ultimately contribute directly to social benefits like "poverty alleviation," economic development, and social equality.

However, disappointing outcomes from these efforts have pushed the pendulum back towards widespread focus on teachers and what goes on in classrooms, especially from 2000 onwards. Robalino Campos (2005: 8)—an education specialist with UNESCO—argued, for example, that "evidence coming from studies on the quality and equity of education contribute to the general perception that neither education nor the reforms carried out have produced coherent and sufficient changes in regard to the societal, economic, political, and scientific demands of the 21st century." She also emphatically identified teachers as "central to school improvement efforts" (Robalino Campos 2005: 1). This position is indicative of what was already a growing seachange in education reform foci. Indeed, the past fifteen years have seen a surge in policies closely targeting teachers and teaching—with Robalino Campos (2005: 1) going so far as to problematize disappointing student test results in terms of "the teacher question" whereby blame for poor student results is placed squarely on teachers' shoulders. Indeed, as recently as 2014, Bokova—Director General of UNESCO—claimed that an "education system is only as good as its teachers" (Bokova 2014: 1). As evidenced by a proliferation of publications, programs and approaches, teachers now are considered by many policymakers and pundits to be "the single most influential and powerful force for equity, access and quality in education" (Bokova, quoted in UNESCO 2015a: 1). In 2008, for example, the Organization of Iberoamerican States—a regional agency focused on Spain, Portugal and their former colonies in the Americas—published two volumes relevant to our discussion here: one specifically on teacher professional development and the other on information and communication technologies (ICT) take-up in education (de Medrano and Vailant 2008; Toscano and Diaz 2008). Both volumes include a heavy focus on teacher change. Similarly, a recent World Bank document titled *System Approach for Better Education Results (SABER): What Matters Most in Teacher Policies? A Framework for Building a More Effective Teaching Profession* declared that "[p]rofessional development and on-the-job support for teachers are an essential component of teacher policies" (World Bank 2012: 7).

These same international organizations claim that student learning outcomes are less than optimal for current national needs and that schooling has proved itself incapable of keeping up with the fast pace of social, economic, and technological change. They cast teachers as key to addressing these two issues. The 2005 OECD publication, *Teachers Matter: Attracting, Developing and Retaining Effective Teachers*, for example, notes that teachers are "the most significant and costly resource in schools" (OECD 2005: 1) and need to "deal effectively" (OECD 2005: 2) with student diversity, use new technologies, and keep up with ongoing changes in academic disciplines. This report also places much of the responsibility for how students fare at school squarely on teachers' shoulders, claiming that "[t]here is now substantial research indicating that the quality of teachers and their teaching are the most important factors in student outcomes" (OECD 2005: 9). Collectively these agencies call for actions such as "reinforcing teacher training institutions and teacher educators," "peer-coaching or collaborative activities with expert input" (UNESCO 2012: 2, 5), "improving teacher quality by developing standards for teachers," (UNESCO 2015b: 1) and the more standard "[t]raining, training, training" (Hawkins 2002: 42).

As such, ongoing learning and professional growth for teachers has been a hot-button topic within—and outside—education, especially over the past 10 years. In the U.S. at present, commercial professional development companies and publishing houses like Kagan, Learners Edge, The Master Teacher, Pearson, and others are the new "big players" in training teachers. They loudly tout their products and services in terms of "capacity-building support for your teaching effectiveness initiatives" (Pearson 2015: 1) and "provid[ing] practical, evidence-based strategies that enhance teachers' instruction and students' learning" (Landmark School Outreach Program 2015a: 1). These offerings focus on things like the Common Core Standards, particular commercial reading program packages, reading skills, teaching English language learners, teacher autism training [sic], and so on. Many of these services comprise an "outside expert" coming to the school and delivering an intensive, short-term presentation on some topic or program (see critiques in Darling-Hammond et al., 2009; Gulamhussein 2013). This especially appears to be the case where digital technologies are concerned. Companies like SMART Technologies (2015) offer short workshops or self-paced online tutorials on how to use their SMART Boards or apps on their SMART Tables; Landmark School Outreach offers a 5-day graduate course focused on assistive technologies for supporting students with special learning needs (Landmark School Outreach Program 2015b: 1); or class sets of iPads or Chromebooks appear in schools and teachers are given a short introduction to the machine side of things (cf. criticisms in Carpenter and Krutka 2014).

And yet, a long history of research into teachers' professional development suggests teachers gain most from professional development experiences that are *not* delivered by expert-outsiders and that are *not* one-size-fits-all, one-shot sessions on how to do something better (Carpenter and Krutka 2014; Hardy and Rönnerman 2011; Lawless and Pellegrino 2007). Instead, research suggests what works includes things like sustained and supported opportunities to learn something new or to learn about something familiar more deeply, learning opportunities that are grounded in immediate teaching contexts, encouragement to change classroom and school practices in innovative ways, enacting social theories of learning to shape collaboration among fellow teachers, fluid leadership and expert roles within a professional learning group or space, and a conviction that what's being learned is going to be useful or beneficial to students (see, for example, Carpenter and Krutka 2014; Lawless and Pellegrino 2007; Opfer and Pedder 2011; Patton, Parker and Tennehill 2015). But even with a well-established and ample list of characteristics for substantively defining "effective" professional development for teachers, formal professional development experiences still tend to be criticized by the very teachers for whom they were designed and by scholars working in this field. Opfer and Pedder argue that a good deal of the problem is due to professional development in schools still emphasizing "specific activities, processes, or programs in isolation from the complex teaching and learning environments in which teachers live" (2011: 377). For Opfer and Pedder, there is too little attention paid to the complex systems within which teachers work in relation to designing and delivering professional development experiences and too much emphasis on quick fixes.

Recognizing the complexity of teaching and its *situatedness*—in classrooms, in schools, and in communities—is a key factor driving this edited collection. For us, professional development is not just concerned with teacher learning and improvement but with contributing to and enriching professional *practice*. Professional practice, in this sense, refers to a thoroughly social understanding of what it means to "be a teacher" (cf. Gee 2013). That is, understanding that teaching as a social practice comprises sets of beliefs, ways of doing things, ways of using resources, configurations of physical spaces, and ways of speaking (to students, to colleagues, to parents, to administrators, etc.). Furthermore, it includes sets of ideas about the nature and purpose of schooling, a body of knowledge, particular orientations towards students and their well-being, skills and tools that are socially recognized as part and parcel of teaching and learning (e.g., content area knowledge, classroom management, effective teaching approaches etc.), and so on. As such, we wanted to bring together in one place depictions of how different people have approached professional development with a close eye to professional *practice* and teacher *learning* as something that's complex, highly situated, deeply collaborative and participatory, and that takes into consideration the thoroughly social nature of "being a teacher." Added to this, we also were deeply interested in gathering and circulating accounts of professional development experiences that engaged teachers in using or learning about a range of literacies and digital technologies in creative, meaningful, and fruitful ways. This was prompted by a sense that the academic literature to date has been dominated by "education technology" accounts of "upskilling" teachers to use particular digital devices, software programs or apps, or online services and then leaving it to teachers to find things to do with these devices and software in their literacy teaching (Kalman 2013). This body of work has tended to place digital technology itself at the heart of the professional development experience rather than examine how digital technologies can become part of deep, useful and ongoing literacy learning experiences for teachers and students alike (cf. similar critiques in Guererro 2013; Hutchison 2011; *Language Arts* 2012).

THE DIGITAL TURN AND NEW LITERACIES

Teacher educators and academics talk about "turns" that signal large-scale, even paradigmatic shifts in thinking and practice within a field of study. These kinds of "turns" are often transdisciplinary in nature and can reshape or reconstruct "the objects of research" or generate new research objects or foci (Runnel et al. 2013: 7). The idea of a "turn" usefully captures how a change in direction and focus isn't necessarily wholesale within a field and that original trajectories and ways of doing things continue, while the shift itself nonetheless becomes relatively well established and recognized. Literacy studies and education can lay claim to a number of "turns" in the past few decades (e.g., the postmodern turn: Green 1995; McLaren and Lankshear 1993; Poynton 1993; the social turn: Barton, Hamilton and Ivanič 2005; Gee 1999; Street 2003).

Currently, it's easy to argue that there is a "digital turn" in a range of fields and disciplines (e.g., architecture, communications and media studies, art). This particular turn is not only about acknowledging and investigating the proliferation of digital devices, services and networks in many people's everyday lives around the world. It also includes sustained academic interest in developing ways of understanding changes in, and new practices concerning how people make, share and take up meanings and resources that are digitally mediated or produced (cf. Mills 2010; Runnel et al. 2013).

The study of "new literacies" is one such response to this digital turn within education and literacy studies. The idea of new literacies has been developed since the early 1990s, with the aim of providing insights into understanding and responding to some of the deep changes evident during recent decades that have impacted many people's everyday lives, and, in turn, education in most countries. In many ways, "[n]ew literacies researchers and scholars seek to explore and understand continuities and differences between the ways people in societies like our own produced, distributed, shared, and negotiated meanings during an era that entered transition from the 1950s, and the ways people have increasingly produced, distributed, shared, and negotiated meanings from, say, the 1980s" (Knobel and Lankshear 2014: 97). A good deal of this research is interested in "anticipat[ing] beyond the present and envisag[ing] how best to educate *now* in order to enhance learners' capacities for effective meaning-making and communication in the foreseeable future" (ibid.).

In a nutshell, "new literacies," when considered from a sociocultural-New Literacy Studies orientation, can be thought about along two dimensions: technically/technologically and in terms of a different "ethos" (Lankshear and Knobel 2011: Ch. 3). New literacies do not presuppose use of digital technologies and media (e.g., writing with video remixes predates digital times), although our focus here is on those that do. In terms of technical "stuff," new literacies differ fundamentally from conventional print literacies in that their inscriptions are rendered—at least initially—by means of digital code rather than by material means (whether printed and illustrated/imaged/diagrammed by hand, typewriter or press). Consequently, "new" kinds of texts often are seamlessly multimodal rather than involving distinct processes for different modes (text, image, sound), or they exist nowhere and everywhere because collaborative cloud-based interfaces mean multiple authors can work on a literacy "text" simultaneously. Facebook is a good example of this, where the interface enables users to post text, emoticons, images, sounds and video clips, where friends can write on one's "feed" or "timeline" or share photos, videos and songs, where users can "like" others' posts, join groups, follow popular pages or celebrity profiles, etc. with few people knowing where or how their personal information is stored because Facebook isn't on their "hard drive" per se. Electronic networks that span computers, tablets and smartphones also mean that these new literacy practices and the "texts" they produce can be shared with others or accessed on a vast scale with just the click of a mouse.

As social practices characterized by a new "ethos," Colin Lankshear explains how

> new literacies are more participatory, collaborative, and distributed, and less "published," less "author-centric" and less "individual" than conventional literacies. Typically, although— regretfully—not universally (Gee and Hayes, 2013), engaging in social media sites, affinity spaces (Gee 2013), and within environments and practices of participatory cultures (Jenkins, et al. 2006), involves deep interactivity, openness to feedback, sharing of resources and expertise, and a will to collaborate and provide support that is writ large into myriad contemporary everyday practices. Participants in new literacy practices actively seek out memberships and peers in areas of affinity and interest and pursue different kinds of relationships between "authors" and "audiences" from those characterizing many conventional literacy practices. They generally value attending to the interests and knowledge of others, recognize that quality is judged by groups rather than appointed experts, welcome diversity of opinion in decision-making, and so on. This broad "ethos" of new literacies sets them apart from simply being conventional literacies in digital form. (in Knobel and Lankshear 2014: 98)

A deliberately in-common thread running across the chapters in this book is an interest in teachers taking up new literacies in their classrooms in ways that do not strip these new literacies of their newness or that colonize them to existing classroom practices. Forcing a class of students to use a private discussion board to post their thoughts about a book they were required to read is not a new literacy practice, for example. While this task does include some new technical procedures, it certainly does not embody the new "ethos" stuff of new literacies, and the same task could be achieved just as well with pencil and paper or in-person dialogue. The professional development projects described in the following chapters take both dimensions of new literacies very seriously. Teachers are engaged in producing complex, high-quality "memory" videos that cast them as both storytellers and story*makers*; one teacher works with special-needs students to produce a polished remix video that retells a significant event from the point of view of a minor character in a story; two teachers and their students in very socioeconomically and culturally distinct schools collaborate virtually and in person on a set of online newspapers that engage with each community's previously unexamined assumptions about the other; and so on. There are no pre-packaged lesson plans, subject area software, or class sets of iPads in any of these accounts.

THE DIGITAL TURN AND TEACHERS' PROFESSIONAL DEVELOPMENT

As indicated above, the digital turn can be seen in two ways. On one hand, the term signals an academic interest in documenting and interpreting changes in how people experience and act on their world when digital technologies become part of the mix. On the other hand, and especially when we look at teachers' professional development in schools, the term often can have a mechanistic meaning that's best described as a "turn to the digital (device)" with high hopes riding on an assumed causal relationship between installing computers plus internet connections in classrooms and improved student learning outcomes and standardized test scores.

Indeed, taking up digital technologies in classrooms is a leading component of the ongoing push to "improve" teachers, with information and communication technologies especially invoked by international agencies and policy makers on national and local levels as a way to "improve the quality of education" and to "force and support necessary changes in education practices to meet the societal demands of the twenty first century" (Cabrol and Servin 2010: 1, authors' translation; see also Hernández 2015). Yet little thought has been given to the kinds of challenges teachers face when figuring out what these "necessary changes" might be or how to accomplish them. Apparently it is "assumed that teachers will somehow naturally transition to using these artifacts" (Kalman and Guerrero 2013: 261). Furthermore, it seems policy makers' and service providers' expectations for teachers, digital technologies and professional development outcomes vary considerably from place to place. Coll (2008), for example, identifies three dominant sets of expectations he sees shaping conceptions of and approaches to teachers' professional development and digital technologies. In some cases, administrators' and practitioners' expectations are restricted to the specific goal of training teachers to use the computer and to navigate the internet, with an eye on introducing computers as a new subject area. Here, a key assumption is that teachers will explicitly teach their students how to use various digital resources like word-processing software or keyboards, and, in doing so, will contribute directly to students' success at school and beyond. A second set of popular expectations for professional development is that teachers will become more efficient when digital technologies are added to their classrooms; that is, they'll be doing what they have always done, but better. This orientation emphasizes teacher productivity, teachers developing requisite skills and mastery of digital teaching materials such as specialized subject area software (e.g., Geometer, Descartes' Cove, Accelerated Reader), and pre-packaged lesson plans and activities designed to help teachers "engage" students in using digital technologies while they learn (e.g., webquests, using PowerPoint for traditional classroom presentations). A third set of expectations sees digital technologies as a catalyst for transforming or reconceptualizing classroom teaching and learning in some way. Coll (2008: 124) notes that within this set of expectations, "it's not about using ICT to do the same but better, faster or easier or even more efficiently, [it's about] doing different things, about initiating teaching and learning processes that would not be possible in the absence of ICT" (authors' translation). More to the point, within this third set of expectations, digital technologies and digital practices are regarded as just one element of developing teaching approaches that center-stage collaborative and social learning, realign relationships between teachers and students, shift how learning is distributed and taken up, reconceptualize knowledge as "unfixed" and constructed, and open up possibilities for tinkering with and remixing learning projects so that the learning and production process itself is foregrounded rather than taking a back seat to a particular kind of pre-approved end product.

The authors in this book collectively offer different takes on how this third set of expectations can play out in real-life, complex, shared and productively messy learning experiences. Their work with teachers or within their own classrooms embodies a new ethos of collaboration, distributed practice, and participation. Their approaches are also very much grounded in the digital turn—both in the sense of developing research insights into what it means to "be more digital" and in working through ways of taking up digital technologies meaningfully within teachers' professional lives and teaching contexts.

THE IMPORTANCE OF SOCIAL LEARNING

Education isn't the only field interested in *professional* learning or development. The growing ubiquity of ready internet access, possibilities for tapping into distributed online and offline networks of shared expertise and knowledge, and opportunities for working collaboratively with a range of people on projects and ideas has seen fields like business studies, media and marketing, product development, medicine, resource management, and the like become more interested in how people learn to be good at what they do (cf. Bingham and Conner 2015; Brown and Adler 2008; Thomas and Brown 2011). What soon becomes clear when we look beyond schools is that learning—and especially professional learning—is often enacted in thoroughly *social* and *participatory* ways.

The idea of learning as a social phenomenon isn't new, and it is typically defined in terms of a close connection between learning and shared activity grounded in social contexts and meaningful, authentic purposes. This version of social learning therefore closely associates learning with social practice, and knowledge with using mental and material tools, acquiring and employing skills, and drawing on forms of existing understandings, know-how, skills, processes and the like in socially recognizable (albeit adaptable) ways (Kalman 2003; Lankshear and Knobel 2011). Early conceptions—building directly on work by Vygotsky and Bandura—grounded learning in the physical world and in face-to-face interactions (cf. Brown, Collins and Duguid 1989; Lave and Wenger 1991; Rogoff 1990). Social learning in a digital and networked world, however, blurs the distinction between physical and virtual contexts, and opens up a whole range of relatively new ways of learning about something or learning to do something well. Studies of children and young people learning to do something that involves some dimension of new literacy (e.g., play a massively multiplayer online game, remix anime videos) or be someone (e.g., a game modder, an online fan fiction writer) show time and again that they learn to do and be by means of following up on their interests and by hanging out in online spaces with others who share the same interest. They also are documented sharing ideas and insights with others (especially with strangers) on discussion boards, microblogs like Twitter, or in dedicated chat sessions; collaborating on projects across time zones and physical locations; providing feedback on others' work; drawing resources and troubleshooting guides as needed from resource websites or wikis; refining their own skills and knowledge; and so on, usually while engaging in the very practice that they're learning rather than preparing themselves with a study period or just-in-case know-how (see accounts in Gee 2012; Ito 2010; Thomas and Brown 2011). Professionals in all manner of fields are engaging in social learning in very similar ways. Scientists, archaeologists, biologists, astronomers, physicists, designers, artists, musicians, sociologists, anthropologists, IT workers, doctors, nurses, and so on are taking advantage of this new scale of access to resources, networks, and other people's knowledge to hone their own understandings and contributions to their respective fields (Bingham and Conner 2015; Hagel and Brown 2012; Surowiecki 2005).

This kind of collaborative, networked, distributed learning is made possible not just by physical digital devices, networks and services but by shifts in social relationships and digital affordances best described in terms of "participatory culture." A participatory culture is one characterized by low barriers to being able to "join in" (the practice, the activity, the discussion, artistic expression, etc.) and sustained support for "creating and sharing one's work" (Jenkins 2009: 5). It also includes some kind of mentorship that may be quite fluid and distributed across a number of people and that enables novices to tap into expertise and experts to share their knowledge and skills with novices and to perhaps learn something more in the process (ibid.; see also Haythornewaite 2014). Importantly, a participatory culture is one in which "members believe their contributions matter, and feel some degree of social connection with one another" (Jenkins 2009: 6). One classic example is fan fiction writing, where fans of a television show, movie, book, or other popular phenomenon write narratives that build on or recognizably reimagine the original storyline, characters, setting etc. These narratives can be posted to hosting sites like Fanfiction.net that are free to join and require low internet bandwidth to access. The fan fiction community tends to readily welcome others' narratives—as long as these new narratives respect the original source material and other people's enjoyment of it (Black 2008). Sites like Fanfiction.net have review functions built in so that readers can provide feedback on authors' work and where authors can respond directly to reviewers' comments. Studies of fan fiction suggest that authors who receive feedback on their work feel their writing matters to others, and this sense of "being appreciated" often plays a direct role in authors continuing to write and to improve their writing (cf. Black 2008; Curwood 2013).

Participatory culture isn't confined to popular culture but can be a hallmark of inclusive, interactive and supportive professionally oriented pursuits, too. For example, Carpenter and Krutka (2014) surveyed 494 educators who used Twitter for education-related professional development purposes. Findings suggested that these teachers valued the "personalized, immediate and interactive nature" of Twitter (Carpenter and Krutka 2014: 8). Respondents variously described how using Twitter for professional development purposes gave them access to others who "shared worthwhile information and knowledge" as well as tips on trends and new developments. They also reported how Twitter helped them establish connections with others—often forging important, new personal relationships—especially within dedicated participation threads (e.g., #edchat). Key activities included resource and idea sharing, collaborating on something, giving and receiving emotional support, and giving and sharing ideas for classroom teaching (Carpenter and Krutka 2014: 9).

In short, learning to be or do something outside schools often involves deep interactivity, openness to feedback, sharing resources and expertise, a willingness to try, and an openness to collaborating with and providing support to others that is writ large into myriad contemporary everyday practices. Thomas and Brown (2011) go so far as to argue that we're now in a time marked by a "new culture of learning." This new culture of learning, as they see it, has two key elements that capitalize on the social and participatory nature of learning in a digital world:

> The first is a massive information network that provides almost unlimited access and resources to learn about anything. The second is a bounded and structured environment that allows for unlimited agency to build and experiment with things within those boundaries. (Thomas and Brown 2011: 19)

Their first element has been discussed above. Their second element captures the importance of recognizing that "good" learning occurs within a specific context that has, we argue, "borders" marked out by a specific social practice that sets in place what is generally recognized by others as belonging to that practice. This is to say that for "good" social learning to take place, it's not a matter of anything goes, but that learning itself is informed and shaped by the values, content, and quality standards attached to the practice (all of which are decided by those who fully engage in this practice regularly, which makes these features somewhat fluid over time). For example, a young person learning to create anime music remix videos soon learns that cheesy transitions between video clips—such as the checkerboard effect—won't pass muster with aficionados of the practice. Boundaries also are set by one's profession and professional interests; biologists focus on matters of biology, historians focus on matters of history, architects on matters of design, human requirements, and structure. It is possible, of course, to move beyond the boundaries of one's interests or profession to other spheres and "bring back" ideas, resources and knowledge to share with others or use oneself—but these will only be taken up more widely as part of the practice if they sufficiently "fit" or extend this practice in recognizable or valuable ways. Thomas and Brown regard "boundaries" (2011: 35) to be usefully constraining because they spur "the imagination to become more active in figuring out novel solutions within the constraints of the situation or context."

In sum, it makes sense to attend to how people are learning to do things well in the everyday world when thinking about and planning robust approaches to teachers' professional development, especially when digital technologies are part of the mix. While we recognize that a good many teachers around the world do not have easy access to digital devices or networks (e.g., Shaheen, Walsh, Power and Burton 2013; Traxler and Leach 2006), the *principles* to be gained from looking outside schools are still useful and important in a wide range of schooling circumstances (cf., Guerrero 2013; Guerrero and Kalman 2011; Junqueira and Buzato 2013; Kalman and Rendón 2014). These principles include professional learning organized around supportive and sustained collaboration on meaningful projects, ensuring low barriers to participation and that people feel their contributions are valued, moving fluidly among expert and novice statuses, learning to do and be within a social practice, access to and sharing distributed knowledge and resources, to name a few. The chapters in this book thoroughly embody these principles in a range of ways, from teachers working collaboratively with their students to develop participatory cultures within their own classrooms (Bostock and colleagues) to working collaboratively over extended periods of time (Lotherington and colleagues; Kupiainen and colleagues; Hernández Razo and colleagues; Strong-Wilson and colleagues; Erstad) to accessing distributed expertise (Biddolph and Curwood) through to engaging teachers in learning by doing (Cantrill and Peppler; Jacobson; Dussel). All of these chapters describe projects where teachers felt immensely valued and engaged, even when things didn't go quite to plan, and where expertise certainly was not the sole province of the professional development leaders. The digital technologies in these professional development projects were not designed to be ends in themselves or to facilitate administrative efficiency (cf. Coll 2008) but rather were part of these teachers' learning and a resource in their teaching.

Thomas and Brown's point about boundaries is deeply relevant to the work of this book, too. Any focus on teacher professional development necessarily invokes distinct boundaries, whether they are local or larger ones. The chapters in this book collectively show not only what can be done with social and participatory approaches to professional development but engage directly with how this can be done within bounded, situated and complex systems and contexts that inform and shape teachers' practices. The key purpose of this book is to showcase professional development that makes sensible and meaningful uses of new literacies and digital technologies to enhance or contribute to *real* learning and then to call for more.

A CLOSER LOOK AT THE CHAPTERS IN THIS BOOK

The chapters in this book speak to a broad range of situations, grade levels, activities, scales and even national contexts. Authors hail from Argentina, Australia, Canada, Finland, Mexico, Norway, and the U.S., with projects taking place with educators who teach in Grade 1 classrooms through to adult literacy education and university contexts. As such, the chapters collectively provide insight into different approaches to teachers' professional development in a range of countries, across different grades, and to taking up new literacies and digital technologies within these learning contexts. Despite these differences, authors in this book nonetheless share several important ideas. One common thread is that while they all mention different aspects of using various digital resources like movie editing software, wikis, or YouTube; employing digital devices like tablets and laptops; searching for multimodal digital resources; and the like, they agree that digital "stuff"—while important—is not of central concern. Whether it be in classroom projects with young learners or in spaces for teacher professional learning, the pedagogical orientations, collaborative and maker learning theories, the complexities of teachers' workplaces, among many other contributing factors, are what's foregrounded in discussions about using new literacies and digital technologies in the classroom. In this sense, a key premise within these chapters is that teaching and learning are about deep engagement; representing meanings in a range of ways; relationships and knowledge; thinking critically about events, phenomena and processes; and about participating in valued social and cultural activities. And, as these chapters illustrate, this kind of learning doesn't simply occur in a one-off session but takes time, commitment, and multiple opportunities to interact with others, to explore, play, make mistakes, and get it right. Hernández,

Rendón and Kalman's chapter describes a distributed project involving middle school teachers in Mexico City learning how to engage students in thinking about history in connected and contextualized ways through using probing questions, infographics and digital timelines. Bostock, Lisi-Neumann and Collucci, working in the U.S., describe an upcycling project that was largely developed by students and that remixed a popular "entrepreneurial pitch" television show with learning about caring for the environment. This chapter also describes how one early-year's teacher blurred in-school and out-of-school lines for students and parents alike in order to enhance students' reading experiences. Lotherington, Fisher, Jenson, and Lindo present a whole-school project based in Canada that involved a teacher and her special-needs students creating a video that remixed an original story to retell it from a minor character's perspective. Erstad recounts several projects that focus on teachers developing innovative learning projects for their high school students in Norway, including inter-community newspapers that aimed at scrutinizing unexamined assumptions about people living in each community; teachers and students reconfiguring their traditional roles and relationships while examining environmental issues (and which included knowledge sharing with a school in Spain); and a digital storytelling project focused on accounts of being young in the past and in the present and which blurred personal and "academic" narratives in interesting creative ways. Kupiainen, Leinonen, Mäkinen and Wiseman describe a multi-school professional development initiative in Finland that aimed at replacing primary school teachers' reliance on textbooks with digital literacy approaches to student learning through collaborative pedagogy. Strong-Wilson, Mitchell and Ingersoll map out a multidirectional memory project with school and university educators based in Canada. Jacobson reports on several adult literacy educators' professional development initiatives in the U.S. Biddolph and Curwood analyze Twitter as a professional development space for literacy and English subject area teachers in Australia. Cantrill and Peppler describe a number of initiatives housed with the U.S.'s National Writing Project, including having teachers create hand puppets from felt and electronic circuits as an activity and a context for thinking about learning. Finally, Dussel provides a warts-and-all account of what didn't work so well in two classrooms within the ambit of a massive-scale digital literacies project in Argentina.

Authors in this collection draw on a wealth of different theoretical framings for thinking about new literacies, learning and digital technologies, too. This includes: Thirdspace theory (Bostock, Lisi-Neuman, and Collucci), connected learning theory (Cantrill and Peppler), Actor Network Theory (Dussel), sociocultural theory (Hernández, Rendón and Kalman; Biddolph and Curwood), Freirian theory (Jacbobson), multidimensional memory theory (Strong-Wilson, Mitchell and Ingersoll), New Literacy Studies and multimodality theory (Erstad; Lotherington, Fisher, Jenson and Lindo), and multiliteracies (Kupiainen, Leinonen,

Mäkinen and Wiseman). These different orientations collectively recognize the interrelated, historical, complex character of learning and participating in a variety of domains of social life—such as work, art, recreation, and school. And, while the framings for each chapter have somewhat different takes on "the social," all of them, without exception, theorize learning as a social process in a way that challenges theoretical versions of learning as an individual mental act. Authors collectively emphasize the complexities of learning in context while interacting with other people and while constructing different ways of meaning, understanding, and symbolic encoding. In multiple, albeit often unpredictable, continuous processes, different artifacts and material goods come into play and *mediate* activity and meaning and knowledge making in a variety of ways. Digital technologies across the board, however, are just one example of the kind of mediators drawn on by authors.

The digital turn within formal schooling reinvigorates old discussions about learning and inequity in school: Why is it that despite multiple education reforms, many students, particularly marginalized and minority children and youth, continue to struggle at school? What can we do to make school more interesting and engaging? Or, to borrow Peppler and Cantrill's question in this volume: How can we help youth to develop powerful ways of seeing and acting in the world? Aware of the shortcomings of teaching and learning based on highly controlled, hierarchical and "monitored learning environments" (see Lotherington, Fisher, Jenson and Lindo, this volume), the authors in this collection focus on how teaching, learning, and new literacies are conceptualized and practiced rather than on how technology can "fix" education. Given that when used in creative and innovative ways, digital technologies, resources and networks of people offer innovative avenues for learning, the chapters in this book point out how teachers are caught in the middle of policy statements hawking the importance of deep changes in the way we do "teaching" and education pundits lamenting the slow pace of change in schooling when, in fact, educational systems do not typically reward change (see Erstad, this volume). All too often, as Erstad notes, "teachers have been blamed for the lack of change and innovation in educational practices using digital media."

This raises the issue of what it is that teachers need to know and know how to do, and the ways in which they can they come to know these things. Teachers cannot be expected to "naturally" transition towards using digital technologies in their classrooms (see Hernandez, Rendón and Kalman, this volume). Research strongly suggests that effective professional development must be collaborative so that teachers have a voice in shaping their learning experiences and in making these experiences relevant to the work they do in classrooms (see Bostock, Lisi-Neuman and Collucci, this volume). While there is no prescription that can fit every bill, the chapters in this book offer a series of examples and experiences that can usefully inform teachers' and administrators' decision making with regard to how to approach their own situated learning and development needs, along with examples of some of the possible pitfalls to look out for or to factor in (see Dussel, this volume).

Writing about contexts that range from high schools in Argentina to adult education in the U.S., from new mobilities in Norway to junior high schools in Mexico, there are four prominent themes that run across all the chapters: collaboration, risk taking, play, and remixing the curriculum. Shared by many of the chapters, if not by all, there is ongoing discussion of the shift from teacher professional development to teacher learning as a pivotal point in the ongoing debate over how teachers might learn to "change up" their teaching. One of the central ideas of the chapters is that teachers' and students' learning is greatly enhanced by working together. Collaboration here refers to finding a common cause and demonstrating a willingness to listen to each other, to work through sometimes difficult situations, and to generate collective solutions and where "leadership" within the collaborative activity is fluid and porous. In this sense, collaboration is starkly different from cooperation where everyone contributes a stand-alone piece that is cobbled into a "whole." The authors in this book describe and analyze how teachers and students (and, at times, parents and community members) mutually support each other and participate in completing projects. Authors also speak to how roles within their project groups shift back and forth between teacher and learner. It's worth noting here, too, that eight out of eleven chapters in this volume have more than one author, which speaks to the collaborative nature of many of the projects reported in this volume.

A second theme in common across all chapters is the recognition that learning is a risky business. Providing teachers with opportunities to try innovative and unknown approaches is a key feature of teacher learning, but with each intent comes the possibility—if not probability—of making mistakes and missing the mark the first time around. Creativity and change require an ability to brave the unknown and a willingness to try, rethink, and redo. Learners—be it teachers or young people—learn when they are given opportunities to develop their knowledge and know-how and have some choice and control over what they learn and how they learn it. While it is widely recognized that failure is an integral part of learning, it is often not welcome or ignored in professional development contexts and classrooms. Teachers have to be at ease with mistakes and taking risks when trying to learn something new; they're also well served by appreciating what making mistakes and trying to correct them means for their students. Placing teachers in the learners' seat is as much a part of their professional development as is theorizing education, critiquing policy, or analyzing practices. As Cantrill and Peppler (this volume) note, risk taking "when supported in a shared community of mutual benefit, allows for further risk-taking and change."

Trying to do new things, trial-and-error processes, rethinking and redoing are invitations to experiment and play. In sustained teachers' learning endeavors, the possibility of shifting focus from the outcomes to the process, and from closely following pre-determined steps to imagining what might be is not only liberating, but helps create a "sense of discovery" in teachers (Cantrill and Peppler, this volume). Encouraging teachers to "muck around" in a low-risk environment and follow a hunch, even if it does not work out in the end, helps them take more control over their learning and the choices they make and to take an experimental stance toward learning firsthand. They can take this experience back to their classrooms and use it to guide their students through the unknown. Furthermore, playing, experimenting and mucking around help develop a critical stance towards taken-as-normal assumptions about the world and how it "works," and such experiences give teachers something to compare and contrast against over-standardized, textbook-driven, content-centered, transmissive pedagogies. This kind of open-ended exploration is time consuming and somewhat erratic but usefully opens up space for important questions about curriculum and lesson planning, deep learning, and conceptions of learning as linear, controllable and measurable. The accounts by authors in this collection show multiple ways in which this can be achieved.

This book is about the digital turn, new literacies, teacher professional development, and teachers' learning. The authors and editors aim to contribute to understanding that education can and should be about more than idealized, staged progressions of learning and standardized achievement. The historical outcomes of this version of schooling are all too well known: too many students are forced out, stigmatized, classified as being "at risk," or just out and out declared failures (at school and at life). While the contributors to this book see the potential of using digital technologies in schools as a way of making classrooms more inclusive, creative, and supportive of learning and personal and collective expression, we also recognize that good teaching and effective teacher development have so little to do with digital technologies alone.

REFERENCES

Barton, D., Hamilton, M. and Ivanič, R. (eds) (2005). *Situated Literacies: Reading and Writing in Context*. London: Routledge.

Bingham, T. and Conner, M. (2015). *The New Social Learning: A Guide to Transforming Organizations Through Social Media*, 2nd edn. Alexandria, VA: American Society for Training and Development.

Black, R. (2008). *Adolescents and Online Fan Fiction*. New York: Peter Lang.

Bokova, I. (2014). Foreword. In P. Rose (ed), *Teaching and Learning: Achieving Quality for all. EFA Global Monitoring Report*. Paris, France: UNESCO, 3–4. Available: http://unesdoc.unesco.org/images/0022/002256/225660e.pdf. Downloaded 8 October, 2015.

Brown, J. and Adler, R. (2008). Minds on fire: Open education, the long tail and Learning 2.0. *Educause Review*. 43(1): 17–32.

Brown, J., Collins, A. and Duguid, P. (1989). Situated cognition and the nature of learning. *Educational Researcher*. 18(1): 32–42.

Cabrol, M. and Servin, E. (2010). TICs en Educación: Una Innovación Disruptiva. *Banco Interamericano de Desarollo Educación* [ICTs in education: A disruptive innovation. Interamerican Bank of Education Development]. Washington, DC: Banco Interamericano de Desarollo. Available: https://publications.iadb.org/handle/11319/3123?locale-attribute=es. Downloaded 8 October, 2015.

Carneiro, R. Toscano, C. and Díaz, T. (2008). *Los Desafíos de las TIC para el Cambio Educativo* [Technology challenges for educational change]. Madrid: Organización de Estados Iberamericanos y Fundación Santanilla. Available: http://www.oei.es/metas2021/LASTIC2.pdf. Accessed 8 October, 2015.

Carpenter, J. and Krutka, D. (2015). Engagement through microblogging: Educator professional development via Twitter. *Professional Development in Education*. 41(4): 707–728.

Coll, C. (2008), Aprender y enseñar con las T.I.C.: Expectativas, realidad, y potencialidades. In R. Carneiro, J. Toscano and T. Diaz (eds), *Los Desafíos de las TIC para el Cambio Educativo*. Madrid, Spain: Organización de Estados Iberomericanos. 113–126.

Curwood, J. (2013) Fan fiction, remix culture, and the Potter Games. In V. Frankel (ed), *Teaching with Harry Potter*. Jefferson, NC: McFarland, 81–92.

Darling-Hammond, L., Wei, R., Andree, A., Richardson, N. and Orphanos, S. (2009). *Professional Learning in the Learning Profession: A Status Report on Teacher Development in the United States and Abroad*. Palo Alto, CA: National Staff Development Council and The School Redesign Network at Stanford University.

Gee, J. (1999). The future of the social turn: Social minds and the new capitalism. *Research in Language and Social Interaction*. 32(1–2): 61–68.

Gee, J. (2012). *Social Linguistics and Literacies: Ideology in Discourses*, 4th edn. New York: Routledge.

Gee, J. (2013). *Good Video Games and Good Learning: Collected Essays on Video Games, Learning and Literacy*. New York: Peter Lang.

Green, B. (1995). Post-curriculum possibilities: English teaching, cultural politics, and the postmodern turn. *Journal of Curriculum Studies*. 27(4): 391–409.

Guerrero, I. (2013). Technology and literacy: Towards a situated comprehension of a Mexican teacher's actions. In J. Kalman and B. Street (eds), *Literacy and Numeracy in Latin America: Local Perspectives and Beyond*. London: Routledge, 167–183.

Guerrero, I. and Kalman, J. (2011). Matices en la inserción de tecnologia en el aula: posibilidades de cambio en las prácticas docentes [Nuances in inserting technology in the classroom: Possibilities for change in teachers' practices]. *Cuadernos Comillas*. 1: 84–104.

Gulamhussein, A. (2013). *Teaching the Teachers: Effective Professional Development in an Era of High Stakes Accountability*. Alexandria, VA: Center for Public Education.

Hagel, J. and Brown, J.S. (2012). *The Power of Pull: How Small Moves, Smartly Made, Can Set Big Things in Motion*. New York: Basic Books.

Hardy, I. and Rönnerman, K. (2011). The value and valuing of continuing professional development: Current dilemmas, future directions and the case for action research. *Cambridge Journal of Education*. 41(4): 461–472.

Hawkins, R. (2002). Ten lessons for ICT and education in the developing world. In G. Kirkman, P. Cornelius, J. Sachs and K. Schwab (eds), *Global Information Technology Report 2001–2002: Readiness for the Networked World.* New York: Oxford University Press, 38–43.

Haythornewaite, C. (2014). New media, new literacies, and new forms of learning. *International Journal of Learning and Media.* 4(3–4): 1–8.

Hernández Razo, O. (2015). *Trabajo, estudio y canto: actividades cotidianas y la apropiación de prácticas digitales en una comunidad suburbana de la ciudad de México.* [Working, studying and singing: Everyday activities and the appropriation of digital practices in a marginalized community in Mexico City]. Doctoral thesis. Departamento de Investigaciones Educativas, Center for Research and Advanced Study of the IPN, Mexico D.F.

Hutchison, A. (2011). Literacy teachers' perceptions of professional development that increases integration of technology into literacy instruction. *Technology, Pedagogy and Education.* 21(1): 37–56.

Ito, M. (2010). *Hanging Out, Messing Around and Geeking Out: Kids Living and Learning with New Media.* Cambridge, MA: MIT Press.

Jenkins, H. (2009). *Confronting the Challenges of Participatory Culture: Media Education for the 21st Century.* Cambridge, MA: MIT Press.

Junqueira, E. and Buzato, M. (eds) (2013). *New Literacies, New Agencies? A Brazilian Perspective on Mindsets, Digital Practices and Tools for Social Action In and Out of School.* New York: Peter Lang.

Kalman, J. (2003). El acceso a la cultura escrita: la participación social y la apropiación de conocimientos en eventos cotidianos de lectura y escritura. *Revista Mexicana de Investigación Educativa,* Enero-Abril, Vol. VIII, Número 17 Consejo Mexicano De Investigación Educativa México, 37–66.

Kalman, J. and Guerrero, E. (2013). A social practice approach to understanding teachers learning to use technology and digital literacies in their classrooms. *E-Learning and Digital Media.* 10(3): 260–275.

Kalman, J. and Rendón, V. (2014). Use before know-how: teaching with technology in a Mexican public school. *International Journal of Qualitative Studies in Education.* 27(8): 974–991.

Knobel, M. and Lankshear, C. (2014). Studying new literacies. *Journal of Adolescent and Adult Literacy.* 58(2): 97–101.

Landmark School Outreach Program (2015a). *Professional Development. Landmark School Outreach Program: Professional Development for Educators.* Available: http://landmarkoutreach.org/profes sional-development. Downloaded 14 September, 2015.

Language Arts (2012). Special Theme Issue: "Professional Development in the Age of Nick.com." *Language Arts.* 89(4).

Lave, J. and Wenger, E. (1991). *Situated Learning: Legitimate Peripheral Participation.* Cambridge, UK: Cambridge University Press.

Lawless, K. and Pellegrino, J. (2007). Professional development in integrating technology into teaching and learning: Knowns, unknowns, and ways to pursue better questions and answers. *Review of Educational Research.* 77(4): 575–614.

McLaren, P. and Lankshear, C. (2003). Critical literacy and the postmodern turn. In C. Lankshear and P. McLaren (eds), *Critical Literacy: Politics, Praxis, and the Postmodern.* Albany, NY: State University of New York Press, 379–419.

de Medrano, C. and Vailant, D. (eds) (2008). *Aprendizaje y Desarrollo Profesional Docente* [Learning and Teacher Professional Development]. Madrid, Spain: Organización de Estados Iberoaméricanos.

Mills, K. (2010). A review of the "digital turn" in the New Literacy Studies. *Review of Educational Research*. 80(2): 246–271.

Novoa, A. (2008). Profesores: ¿el futuro aún tardará mucho tiempo? [Teachers: How long will the future take to get here?] In C. de Medrano and D. Vailant (eds), *Aprendizaje y desarrollo profesional docente* [Learning and Teacher Professional Development] Madrid, Spain: Organización de Estados Iberoaméricanos, 49–56.

OECD (Organization for Economic Cooperation and Development) (2005). *Teachers Matter: Attracting, Developing and Retaining Effective Teachers. Overview*. Washington, DC: OECD Publishing. Available: http://www.oecd.org/edu/school/34990905.pdf. Downloaded 11 October, 2015.

Opfer, V. and Pedder, D. (2011). Conceptualizing teacher professional learning. *Review of Educational Research*. 81(3): 376–407.

Patton, K., Parker, M. and Tannehill, D. (2015). Helping teachers help themselves: Professional development that makes a difference. *NASSP Bulletin*. 99(1): 26–42.

Pearson (2015). Capacity-building support for your teaching effectiveness initiatives. *Instructional Resources*. Available from: http://www.pearsonschool.com/index.cfm?locator=PS1sAj. Downloaded 14 September, 2015.

Poynton, C. (1993). Grammar, language and the social: Poststructuralism and systemic-functional linguistics. *Social Semiotics*. 3(1): 1–21.

Robalino Campos, M. (2005). Passive bystanders or active participants? The dilemmas and social responsibilities of teachers. *PRELAC Journal*. Theme: Regional Education Project for Latin America and the Carribean. 1(1): 7–13.

Rogoff, B. (1990). *Apprenticeship in Thinking: Cognitive Development in Social Context*. New York: Oxford University Press.

Runnel, P., Pruulmann-Vengerfeldt, P., Viires, P. and Laak, M. (eds) (2013). *The Digital Turn: User's Practices and Cultural Transformations*. Frankfurt am Main, Germany: Peter Lang.

Shaheen, R., Walsh, C., Power, T. and Burton, S. (2013). *Assessing the impact of large-scale teacher professional development (TPD) in Bangladesh: English in Action (EIA)*. Paper presented to the American Educational Research Association, 27 April-01 May 2013, San Francisco, California. Available: http://bit.ly/1PkkqOv. Downloaded 8 October, 2015.

Street, B. (2003). What's "new" in New Literacy Studies? Critical approaches to literacy in theory and practice. *Current Issues in Comparative Education*. 5(2): 77–91.

SMART Technologies (2015). Training for Education. *SMART Education*. Available from: http://smarttech.com/Home%20Page/Resources/Training/TrainingforEducation. Downloaded 18 September, 2015.

Surowiecki, A. (2005). *The Wisdom of Crowds*. New York: Anchor Books.

Thomas, D. and Brown, J.S. (2011). *New Culture of Learning: Cultivating the Imagination for a World of Constant Change*. Lexington, KY: CreateSpace.

Traxler, J. and Leach, J. (2006). Innovative and sustainable mobile learning in Africa. *Wireless, Mobile and Ubiquitous Technology in Education, 2006. Fourth IEEE International Workshop*. Available from: http://r4d.dfid.gov.uk/PDF/Outputs/TechDistLearn/JTraxlerJLeach2006-WMUTE.pdf. Downloaded 19 September, 2015).

UNESCO (United Nations Scientific and Cultural Organization) (2012). UNESCO Strategy on teachers (2012–2015). Policy statement. UNESCO. Paris. Available: http://goo.gl/32EFWm Downloaded 8 October, 2015.

UNESCO (United Nations Scientific and Cultural Organization) (2015a). Teachers. *UNESCO*. Available: http://en.unesco.org/themes/teachers. Downloaded 16 September, 2015.

UNESCO (2015b). Education: UNESCO Teacher strategy: Supporting teachers for quality learning (2012–2015). Available:www.unesco.org/new/en/education/themes/education-building-blocks/teacher-education/strategy/. Downloaded October 2, 2015.

World Bank (2012). *System Approach for Better Education Results (SABER): What Matters Most in Teacher Policies? A Framework for Building a More Effective Teaching Profession*. Washington, DC: World Bank. Available at: https://openknowledge.worldbank.org/bitstream/handle/10986/11926/688640REPLACEM0rk0paper000701102012.pdf?sequence=1. Downloaded: 8 October, 2015.

CHAPTER TWO

Accompaniment: A Socio-Cultural Approach FOR Rethinking Practice AND Uses OF Digital Technologies with Teachers

OSCAR HERNÁNDEZ RAZO, VICTOR RENDÓN CAZALES
AND JUDY KALMAN
Translated from Spanish by Benjamín de Buen

INTRODUCTION

In the year 2000, Mexico started to develop nationwide programs aimed at incorporating digital technology into public elementary schools. Although these were not the first programs to equip schools with computers and an internet connection, they were the first attempts to reach a massive and national student body. The 2000–2006 administration rolled out the *Enciclomedia* program looking to provide every fifth and sixth grade classroom with a computer, an electronic blackboard, and internet connection. Later, during the Calderón government (2006–2012), *Habilidades Digitales para Todos* [Digital Skills for Everyone] replaced the *Enciclomedia* program and focused on developing learning materials to support academic subjects in schools, which were made available online. In a parallel effort, state governments received federal funds intended for teacher training opportunities and, finally, devices were distributed to a number of previously identified pilot schools (Zorrilla et al. 2009). The current government, which will remain in office from 2012 until 2018, has substituted *Habilidades Digitales para Todos* with *Mi Compu MX* [My Computer MX] and is providing fifth- and sixth-grade students with laptops or tablets (SEP 2013) in accordance with the one-child-one-device model (Area 2011; Severín and Capota 2011).

Through current educational policy, curricular guidelines, learning materials, and other official documents and directives, all teachers in Mexico are now required to include digital technology in the classroom and compelled to transform their teaching to be based less on rote learning and more on "constructivism," described as interactive, exploratory, and collaborative (Navarro 2011; Santiago and Sosa 2012). However, studies have shown that programs for incorporating technology usually focus on providing schools with equipment but have offered teachers scarce guidance on how to integrate technology into their practice (Cuban 2003; Kalman and Rendón 2014; Sunkel 2006; Warschauer 2002). It appears that teachers are expected to transition "naturally" towards using digital technology in the classroom and, in the process, discover new teaching approaches (Kalman and Guerrero 2013).

The Laboratory for Education, Technology and Society (LETS), located in Mexico City,[1] has designed a professional development program from a sociocultural perspective. Since 2009 we have been organizing work groups with teachers where they collaborate with researchers in planning, implementing, and revising learning activities that include using digital technology in their classroom. The participating teachers have always been volunteers, and in most cases, they have heard about our work groups from another teacher or through a written invitation we send to their school principals. For the project reported here, we received a grant from the National Council of Science and Technology in Mexico (CONACYT) for researching teachers' appropriation of technology and its use in the classroom over a three-year period. While our grant covered many aspects of our study, it did not provide funds for purchasing additional equipment for the teachers or their students, so we worked within the boundaries of what the schools provided for them, typically dedicated computer laboratories that did not always have enough computers for each student to use (i.e., no class sets of tablets, etc.) or did not have a reliable internet connection. This chapter describes LETS professional development program and introduces the notion of "accompaniment" as a guiding concept for working with teachers and important to keep in mind when designing programs. We present a case study, which provides empirical evidence to support and illustrate our ideas. Our professional development methodology has used the introduction of technology in schools as an opportunity for teachers, researchers, and graduate students to imagine, design, and implement learning activities; introduce different modes of representation; and question standing classroom relationships and practices. Together we explore and develop teaching approaches that seek to place students in the center of curricular-based learning activities and academic subject matter articulated with current public, economic, and community issues (The New London Group, 1996).

TRAINING TEACHERS TO USE DIGITAL TECHNOLOGY IN MEXICO AND LATIN AMERICA

Much like the rest of Latin America, Mexico has tried for the last ten years to include the use of digital technology in basic education (i.e., preschool, elementary, and middle school) while assuming that equipment in and of itself will help close the digital divide, transform teaching practices, and carry the nation into the so-called knowledge and information society (SEP 2013). As of 2000, the federal government has made an effort to bring schools and digital technology together, and—as indicated earlier—programs for introducing computers into basic education have become increasingly prominent in Mexico's public policies (Santiago and Sosa 2012). Since 2000, the federal government has implemented programs nationwide in an attempt to incorporate technology with education. State governments have endeavored to complement these efforts by imitating them on a smaller scale. Previous to the year 2000, a number of initiatives brought computer labs, VCRs, and satellite dishes to some schools while also developing materials and digital learning projects for classrooms. Over the years the Mexican government has ushered in technology-in-schools programs that, for the most part, are tool focused.

Many of these efforts were criticized from day one. Teachers often complained about the way the federal government, through its *Enciclomedia* program, had equipped fifth-, sixth-, and seventh-grade classrooms with electronic blackboards, computers, and digitized textbooks,[2] yet failed to offer any training on how to use the equipment (Loredo, García and Alvarado 2010). Pre-installed software on government-funded computers included Microsoft's *Encarta Encyclopedia* and interactive materials developed during previous initiatives, especially for mathematics and science. But during *Enciclomedia's* six-year lifespan, infrastructure, properly built schools (complete with walls, windows, doors, a roof and bathrooms with running water), electricity and internet connections remained widely unavailable. In some cases, security conditions to prevent the equipment from being stolen were also non-existent which ultimately proved problematic in terms of schools even being able to use their equipment: often principals and teachers preferred to lock their computers in a storage area rather than risk theft.

Mexico has recently joined the latest wave of Latin American countries that are creating programs for incorporating technology into schools and classrooms by distributing computers and tablets directly to students and teachers that they can use at home and school (Severín and Capota 2011). Some of the assumptions underlying this approach are that, unlike other programs where a number of students share equipment placed in computer rooms at school, if each student has their own device, it will help close the digital divide by providing other family members with the opportunity to become familiar with the computer or tablet as well. Furthermore, it also is assumed that this will bring greater educational benefits by transforming teaching practices, increasing achievement, and enhancing student learning. All in all, it is believed that equipping students with digital devices they can use at home and school will offer students better preparation for their future.

Even though countries in the region have had one-student-one-device programs for a short period of time, recent evaluations and research findings coincide in that official programs have mostly overlooked teachers' professional development, even when this important aspect is highlighted in policy statements as one of the fundamental pillars necessary for promoting the appropriation and use of technology. If transforming traditional teaching and learning practices into more progressive approaches is also a desired outcome of using digital technology, as Marchesi (n/d), former president of the Organization of Iberian States suggests, teachers undoubtedly will need opportunities for professional development (Area 2011; Guerrero and Kalman 2011; Kalman and Guerrero 2013; Linne 2014; Severín and Capota, 2011; Valiente 2011).

While teacher development programs in Latin America are fairly scarce, those that do exist usually follow one of two tendencies. First are programs that address instrumental and technical aspects of using technology by means of teaching specialized terminology that is foreign to teachers' and officials' experience (Fischman and Ramírez-Romero 2008); these courses focus on using electronic devices "correctly" and separate the ability to handle the tools from any considerations regarding their classroom "application" (Gutiérrez 2008). Other courses promote technology as one of the many learning resources that complement a teacher's repertoire in the classroom. Teachers are given opportunities to develop abilities, such as how to use specific educational software packages, how to handle information, and how to evaluate the relevance and reliability of information found on the internet (Chumpitaz 2012; Robalino and Körner 2005).

Kalman and Rendón (2014) have pointed out that, specifically in Mexico, while there are some courses available for teachers to learn about using the computer in the classroom, most programs promoting technology use in the classroom relegate professional development to a personal matter that is up to teachers to solve on their own time. For the most part, and despite the national policy rhetoric, institutions provide few development opportunities for teachers to help them through the process of learning to teach with technology. In other words, programs are largely unavailable and those that are offered to teachers follow the same tendencies as those described above.

Even though programs are few and far between, many authors have hypothesized and speculated about the ways professional development programs might encourage classroom teachers to use digital resources and transform their teaching practices (Area 2011; Severín and Capota 2011). According to different proposals, teachers learning how to use technology in education should study "basic" computer abilities, how to use hardware and software, how to navigate the Web, use social media, and benefit from Web 2.0 platforms such as blogs and wikis. Programs, according to these pundits, should also include ways for teachers to use these tools with their students (Area 2011; Severín and Capota 2011; Valiente 2011).

In some instances, the transformation of traditional teaching practices, defined as those that privilege the transmission and repetition of academic content, is a simultaneous goal of introducing technology. Therefore, many posit that teacher training should include opportunities for learning new teaching practices through activities such as "problem-based learning," "collaborative learning," and learning by projects such as "webquests" (Area 2011; Pantoja and Covarrubias 2013; Rojas-Drummond, Mazón, Littleton and Vélez 2012). However, this approach for promoting the use of digital technology tends to emphasize procedures and overlooks teachers' local working conditions: the type of students at their schools, teachers' relationship to official professional organizations such as their trade union,[3] and finally, any school-based traditions or institutional demands underlying many of their teaching practices.

The LETS group in Mexico City has worked with local teachers to explore how they might include technology in their practice while trying to gain insight into what it means for them to be guided through this process. Our latest program ran over a full school year and included 25 junior high school teachers (Grades 7 to 9) and entailed teachers working directly with us in 12 workshops, in addition to visiting and observing them in their own classrooms. We believe that "teachers' use of digital technology (or lack thereof) is a social construction where multiple processes—the realities of their workplace, their understanding of digital technologies and the internet, as well as their long standing beliefs about teaching and learning—coincide to shape their classroom practices" (Kalman 2013: 99). We use the notion of *accompaniment*—in a sense similar to a pianist accompanying a singer—to create ways of reflecting, imagining, and designing classroom situations with the use of digital devices so that the process addresses teachers' specific needs, problems, and characteristics in a situated, collaborative way rather than a top-down, expert-driven way.

LETS WORK: TOWARDS A DEFINITION OF THE GUIDANCE APPROACH FOR TEACHER TRAINING AND THE USE OF DIGITAL TECHNOLOGY

LETS has developed a working methodology that encourages teachers to reflect on their activities in relation to their beliefs about teaching, learning, and school while considering ways to include technology in their classrooms. Teachers are encouraged to change some of their more traditional approaches through the collective construction of new practices. In the process, we have developed our understanding of what we ourselves mean by accompaniment: parallel to what a pianist does for a singer, we stay in the background, articulating themes and harmonies, and encourage the teachers to carry the melody, so to speak. Together we—the LETS collective and participating teachers—make decisions about innovations and changes; what to keep and what to revise.

Our concept of accompaniment is built upon five interrelated aspects: continuity, collaboration, reflection, construction, and working in the classroom. The first, continuity, refers to working with teachers several times throughout the entire school year and entails keeping track of the activities they develop with other teachers and with students. We also try to develop interrelated activities (such as approaches to giving students feedback or how to analyze different types of data in a text) and promote ongoing communication among participants.

Second, collaboration is understood as a form of commitment through mutual support (Lave and Wenger 1991). Within our program, guided participation and participatory appropriation (Rogoff 1995) are inseparable processes where people communicate and coordinate their efforts and transform their ways of involvement through the experience of using digital technology in the classroom. Third, we promote reflection through dialogue, asking teachers to speak about their practice, expectations, and beliefs. In the LETS approach, reflection is a collective activity rather than a process of individual introspection. For example, as part of our ongoing activities, some teachers provided photo and video samples of their classroom activities and of their students' classwork for the rest of the group to collectively review and provide feedback on. We found this to be a way of promoting reflection on how different groups of students respond to different activities, interpret instructions, and participate and how teachers adapt activities as they take place in their particular classrooms. The fourth aspect of our approach involves collective construction of possible activities, cultural products, and processes that relate to teaching practices, which include digital options. Finally, we encourage teachers to look at their work with others through different analytic lenses by revisiting the activities they design and put into practice using technology in the classroom.

Accompaniment largely takes place through the creation of Pedagogical Research Groups [*Grupos de Investigación Pedagógica* in Spanish], which are made up of teachers and LETS members (typically 15 to 20 people per group) who partake in a number of activities throughout the school year. We give it this name as a way of signaling to teachers that throughout the project they are part of a working group rather than trainees. These activities are based on a sociocultural perspective of learning. That is, digital technologies are seen as part of learning environments where design tools and resources converge with information and communication options in such a way that it is possible to represent concepts and phenomena in a dynamic and multimodal fashion (Kress 2010; Jewitt 2006). For us, social interaction plays an important role in learning with and by digital technology. While working with others, individuals appropriate and construct common social meanings and representations of knowledge. They also encounter the opportunity to share and participate with others in a context of purposeful, situated technology use (Lave 2011). This is not an automatic outcome of using the computer or searching for information on the internet; rather, it is the result of purposefully engaging teachers in activities where this can take place.

Our work with teachers happens in three main stages. First, we invite teachers to a meeting where we establish a series of initial agreements and commitments regarding their participation in the program. While their participation is voluntary, we explain that they are expected to attend workshop sessions throughout the school year, report on classroom activities, collect samples of students' classwork, bring samples of material they developed for their students, and provide pictures or other audiovisual testament of their practice in the classroom. Finally, we ask them to give their consent for their materials to appear in potential academic products.

The second stage comes after the pedagogical research group has been established. An intensive workshop takes place over six different consecutive face-to-face sessions known as Installation Week [*Semana de Instalación* in Spanish]. Thus, during the week prior to the beginning of the school year, teachers participate in a series of activities orchestrated by LETS that promote forms of collaborative participation, critical and constructive reflection, and the configuration of cultural products within digital environments. The main purpose of the first week's activities is to lay the groundwork for teachers to subsequently attend monthly sessions with a common understanding of teaching and technology use for academic purposes. A LETS member who is in charge of providing guidelines for the day's activities also introduces each session. S/he leads activities, describes expected outcomes, discusses student assessment alternatives such as matrices or rubrics, and hands out materials previously designed by LETS for the session. Handouts include, for example, descriptions of possible activities and technical guides for using Google Maps, Movie Maker or building a timeline in Excel. Teachers then focus on the main activity for the day (e.g., creating a video, analyzing student work) while alternating between individual and collective tasks using different technological tools (e.g., Google Docs or Bookmarkers). Finally, the day's progress is examined within the context of a group discussion, where participants talk about how they carried out the activities, any difficulties they encountered, and the solutions they came up with. They also talk and exchange ideas about their way of handling curricular content, how they interact with students, and which classroom situations might benefit most from digital resources.

The third stage of our program consists of monthly meetings that we call Follow-up Meetings [*Reuniones de Seguimiento* in Spanish]. Over a total of ten follow-up meetings, teachers discuss the activities they designed and implemented for their classes, show some of the samples they brought from their own classrooms, and partake in additional activities orchestrated by LETS for each of these sessions. Monthly meetings encourage teachers to reflect with their peers on their experiences with their students, schools, and digital activities, as well as on their teaching roles and methods. During the final two months of the program, teachers are asked to develop a final project where they design and implement a learning activity in their own classrooms. The aim is to try a new way of teaching a section of curricular content in their classrooms. At this point, weekly online sessions take place between teachers and LETS members via Google Hangouts, which allows for up to ten participants to communicate via instant messaging or even meet in a videoconference. Videoconferences usually include three or four teachers plus a moderator from LETS. Hangouts are a place for teachers to share their proposed activities and their latest progress, discuss any difficulties they encountered, as well as celebrate their achievements. The rest of the group provides suggestions and ideas for improving the activity under discussion, enquire into details that are unclear, and share their own experiences.

It is difficult to write about a program that is simultaneously carefully designed and responsive to teachers' interests and needs. So while the content and focus of each monthly meeting was carefully planned and resourced, this content and focus grew directly out of what we were observing in classrooms and in our ongoing interactions with participating teachers. For example, on multiple occasions we noticed that the participating teachers commented on their students' work only in very generic ways. This prompted us in the next monthly follow-up meeting to pose the question, "What kind of feedback do students need to improve their work?" We developed a workshop session around commenting on students' written and multimodal productions by presenting the teachers with samples to collectively critique. We then developed some guidelines for developing feedback and for including revisions in activity planning, making second (and sometimes third) versions part of student projects.

During the meetings and online sessions, we have found a number of variations in teachers' approaches to the program and rationales for the activities they design, which are signals of changes in their thinking, their practice, and their understanding of digital culture. We have observed transitions from a teacher-centered practice, where the goal is to transmit content to students, to a more horizontal approach, where students are much closer to the center of learning activities. A telling sign of this new approach to pedagogy is that teachers begin to see learning as a continuous process: they begin to ask students to work on projects over longer periods of time, they include more coaching on intermediate assignments rather than simply giving instructions or waiting for students' work to be handed in, and then grading it with no mentoring or response on their part during the process. They began to go beyond pronouncing the official discourse regarding "constructivism" and started to show signs of including specific approaches in their teaching that supported knowledge construction processes, such as asking students to analyze how they created a video or what types of decisions they made. Such transitions also demonstrate a shift in the way teachers understand technology: they began to look past its purely instrumental use and begin to think about it in a way that is consonant with a digital culture based on collaboration, communication, purposeful content production, connectivity, and the creation of communities (Buckingham 2007; Gere 2012; Jenkins 2009; Lankshear and Knobel 2007).

In the remaining half of this chapter, we highlight some examples of the ways in which teachers are involved in accompaniment processes as part of integrating digital technology to their practice. We describe specific episodes and look at a case study involving Francisca, a teacher who participated in the 2012–2013 Pedagogical Research Group. We chose to analyze her participation because her case illustrates how transitions in teaching appear (cf. Kalman 2013).

THE CASE OF FRANCISCA

Francisca teaches Mexican history in four different ninth-grade classrooms at a public school located in Mexico City's south. At age 49, she holds a degree in social sciences and reports to have been a teacher for 27 years. When Francisca joined our project, she—like many of the participating teachers—had minimal experience using digital technologies. Francisca was a self-professed newcomer to computers and the internet.

The transitional moments we describe in Francisca's practice, as well as our analysis of the episodes that display examples of accompaniment, are based on data obtained from her contributions during group discussions, from her recollections of classroom activities, from photographic documents, and from her responses in interviews and questionnaires that took place throughout the workshop. We present two dialogues that were transcribed from videotapes and which we organized according to Gee's methodology (2005) for fragmenting transcribed speech.

The Accompaniment Process and the Appropriation of Digital Possibilities in the Classroom

Through the activities and interactions we promoted in each session, Francisca became familiar with different ways of using the computer and internet. She also started thinking about some of the possible ways her students could use digital technology in their own work. During this process, Francisca also began to change the way she understood her teaching, and it was evident in the adjustments she made at school when she reworked some of the activities we previously designed collaboratively in a session so that her students could do them without requiring digital technology at all. Francisca maintained the activity's intent and form but used other tools and resources or used digital resources in different ways from what was proposed originally.

As part of Installation Week activities, Francisca and her colleagues designed a digital infographic using Microsoft's PowerPoint as the design software and images and information collected from internet sources. The activity gave Francisca bearings for something she could later adapt within her specific class-room. We introduced the idea of an infographic as a way of presenting results and different types of data obtained through documentary research, and shared online examples for participating teachers to consider. We asked them to work in small groups to create their own infographic then and there but did not provide much insight or many instructions on how to do it. The point was to give them a chance to develop a production process while creating their infographic. Each group was asked to come up with a question and an outline of the content, look up sources, select resources, and organize everything on a vertical PowerPoint slide to produce an infographic poster (we chose PowerPoint deliberately for this activity because it is something that does not require the computer to be online all of the time, because the software comes pre-installed on school computers, because it also is available on machines in cyber cafés, and because we wanted to take something that is often quite hackneyed in how it gets used in classrooms and show how to re-use or remix it to serve new purposes).

The infographic as a product and as a design process was one of the workshop activities that most interested Francisca. During the first follow-up meeting, Francisca explained how she incorporated a selection of resources she had first learned about during the LETS activity by transferring them to her own teaching conditions, where during the month of September, computers were not available at her school. She also later told us that she did not feel very confident with the idea of showing students how to use the computer and was content with the idea of recreat-ing the infographic activity with physical materials such as sheets of paper, cutouts, handwritten text, printed text, drawings, handmade maps, and images that students had printed out. In adapting the activity, Francisca made sure that these groups of students used some of the same modes of representation that she developed with her team during the first week at LETS: maps, a timeline, written information, and drawings. She also ensured that they followed a production process similar to the one developed in her session at LETS. Francisca shared one of her students' paper-based infographics. It showed two maps, one of the world with the crossing of the Bering Straits marked in and the other of Mexico, showing the location of different pre-Hispanic cultures. Around the maps the students placed pictures of "primitive peoples" cut out from "*monografías*" (i.e., one-page information sheets sold at stationery stores that are popular among Mexican primary and middle school students). They printed a couple of small texts (most likely at home or in a cybercafé) from the internet, cut them out, and pasted them among the pictures. The map of Mexico clearly had an infographic quality to it; the students glued pictures of different pre-Hispanic cultures around the edges, drew arrows from their geographic location to the illustrations. They also wrote in the names of cultures and places by hand. To the right of the map of Mexico, the students wrote the question, "How was the American continent populated and what were the consequences?" and provided an answer. At the bottom of the sheet they placed a time line composed of three brightly colored papers cut out and glued together to form an arrow. Each color was assigned to an era of pre-Hispanic cultures (pre-classic, classic, post-classic) and labeled with the different civilizations (Olmec, Teotihuacan, Mayan, etc.) Below the time line they listed several bibliographic references as to where they obtained their information and definitions that were displayed on their infographic.

During Installation Week, we suggested Francisca and other teachers pursue complex questions—rather than a yes/no or one-word-answer question—as a way to launch the infographic. A strong question would double as a guide in students' searches for information and the design of their work. During this particular workshop, teachers discussed and reflected on the possibility of students themselves generating such questions as a way of involving them in research activities. It would allow them to articulate curricular content, explore relationships, and produce more elaborate answers that would stem from a problem or interest they found on their own. They also discussed and reflected on the differences between these kinds of questions and others that ask only for hard facts—dates, names, or definitions—and which are very common in middle school and secondary classrooms in Mexico.

Francisca's activity and her students' work reveal another transition: instead of Francisca defining and determining content, she encouraged students to formulate their own research question within a broad topic (e.g., history) and then present the answer in an infographic that required multiple ways of representing information. Thus, students were the ones who had to search, select, and analyze any findings obtained through investigation. This is unusual in Mexican classrooms due to the dominance of the teacher-directed pedagogical traditions. Students became engaged in their work and seemed to enjoy what they were doing in school more.

ARTICULATING INTERESTS AND BUILDING ACCOMPANIMENT AS A COLLECTIVE

Aspects of accompaniment are evident in the first infographic activity that Francisca and her colleagues completed during Installation Week. Their digital infographic was about slavery and started with a researchable question (e.g., "What are the forms of slavery present in pre-Hispanic Mexico?") It took this group of three teachers nearly three sessions to settle on a question because they revised and rewrote it as they looked for information on the internet and in printed materials. This activity alone enabled moments of collective reflection, too. For example, Francisca and her team discussed what they wanted to research and hypothesized about how their students might react to composing their own questions and doing similar activities in class. Below is an exchange transcribed from a video recording that shows how this group of teachers was able to design a complex research question. The episode relates to the first group session, which brought three history teachers together in one team: Anita and Gerardo were there with Francisca. Once the teachers looked over their curriculum they came up with an initial complex question and commented as follows:

Table 2.1:

Codes Key (Coates, 1996; Dyson, 2006; Gumperz, 1982):
=
signifies latching (when one speaker finishes another's sentence)
- - -
signifies overlapping speech
…
indicates a pause and
:::
signifies extended syllables
<u>Underlining indicates</u> printed text read out loud by speaker.
Line by line numbers refer to original transcriptions.

4415. **Anita:** Let's see, say it again (asks Gerardo to repeat the question)

4416. **Gerardo:** (reads question) <u>What are the differences between slavery in pre-Hispanic Mesoamerican civilizations</u>

4417. **Anita:** Yes

4418. **Gerardo:** (Reads) <u>And the type [of slavery] imposed by colonizers?</u>

4419. We can then establish that the Mexicas[4] had slavery

4420. when sometimes there were, um:::actions against the Mexica State

4421. **Anita:** There we can also start with-

4422. remembering that **concepts** are important

4423. here we would have to explore what is it they (the students) understand as slavery

4424. don't you think?

4425.	**Gerardo:** Uh-huh (agrees)
4426.	**Anita:** I am thinking, what is their **understanding** of slavery?
4427.	**Gerardo:** Uh-huh (agrees)
4428.	**Anita:** With that we could lead the way into what is
4429.	what slavery was like? In-
-----	-----------------------------------
4430.	**Anita:** and based on that we could lead into how slavery was during =
4431.	**Gerardo:** =During the Mesoamerican age and what the Spaniards imported
-----	-----------------------------------
4432.	**Gerardo:** because it is about establishing the difference
4433.	**Francisca:** That's right, establishing the differences
4434.	and if a student finds, for example, the words,
4435.	concepts as you say,
4436.	well in… in the colonial era they used other words, other concepts
4437.	but at the end of the day well they're going to compare (Anita listens to Gerardo and Francisca)

After their initial attempt to construct a research question, the three teachers discussed possible situations they and their students could encounter when faced with the question: *What is the difference between the types of slavery in pre-Hispanic Mesoamerican civilizations and those imposed by colonizers?* Gerardo thought their question could lead to analyzing specific items from curricular content; for example, different types of slavery within Mexica culture (lines 4419 and 4420). On the other hand, one of Anita's comments suggests that she was thinking about ways to answer this question with her students. She thought they could study a series of important concepts in class while requesting that students express their own understanding of "slavery" (lines 4421 to 4425) as a way to start answering the question. At this point, through complementary conversational turns, we can identify how Anita and Gerardo are imagining where the activity might take them when engaging with their students (4430–4431). It also shows how they articulate Gerardo's interest in covering curricular content and Anita's interest in thinking about how her students might come up with a question in the context of trying to articulate it with her colleagues.

In line 4432, Gerardo contributes to the simultaneous conversation about students and the construction of their question by saying how important it is for students to recognize the differences between one type of slavery and another (comparing slavery in pre-Hispanic and Spanish cultures and political systems). After introducing the idea of recognizing the differences, Francisca participates in the conversation by agreeing with Gerardo's comments and adds another element she finds relevant: a comparison between the different names for slavery. As she puts it: "in the colonial era they used other words, other concepts, but at the end of the day [...] they are going to compare" (4436–4437). These lines show how Francisca articulates her interests and expectations involving the activity, specifically in regards to developing a research question. From their experiences and their knowledge, and with their students in mind, these teachers collaboratively constructed a research question that made sense to all three of them, both in terms of the content it covers as well as the way they imagined future activity in the classroom.

Learning to Use a Computer through Accompaniment and Teacher-Teacher Collaboration

During several workshop sessions, we also promoted collaboration among participating teachers by asking them to share their knowledge of how the computer and other digital resources might be used. Here, collaboration is understood as a common effort for accomplishing a shared goal. Examples of collaboration were evident during different points in teachers' conversations with each other, when their dialogue laid foundations of trust between them and provided a safety net to support their venture into new areas of knowledge and action. Throughout the sessions, there were moments of guided participation ("involvement between people as they communicate and coordinate efforts") and participatory appropriation ("how individuals change through their involvement in one or another activity;" Rogoff 1995: 142); that is, how people communicate with each other and coordinate their efforts, as well as how they change through their involvement in activity. In addition, we deliberately encouraged teachers to use their (growing) knowledge of digital resources in a situation where experimenting and making mistakes did not lead to negative outcomes or sanctions. The following example shows the relationship between guided participation and participative appropriation within a context of collaboration.

During the fourth Installation Week session, Francisca asked Anita, the most technologically savvy teacher in the history team, how to cut text from one place to paste it into another. Then, after being guided through this process on a number of occasions by Anita, Francisca had the opportunity to turn around and guide one of her other colleagues through a similar procedure: the steps needed for copying files directly from a USB memory stick to the computer screen. In this example, Gerardo is sitting in front of his own computer and has control of the mouse. Francisca points to different places or icons on the screen as she talks.

Table 2.2:

291	**Anita:** (To Gerardo) Move what you have on the memory (to the computer)
292	you can drag it or copy and paste it
293	you know how (to Francisca who approaches Gerardo's seat)
294	**Francisca:** (To Gerardo) This one, let's see, there it goes, the memory, where do you keep your USB?
295	**Gerardo:** There
296	**Francisca:** Open (Instruction)
297	**Gerardo:** I have to copy it
298	**Francisca:** First you copy then you paste, right? (To Anita)
299	**Anita:** Yes, control C copy and control V paste (she says it, looks at Francisca and Gerardo, and then returns to work on her laptop)
300	**Gerardo:** ¿Control E?
301	**Anita:** Yes, it's control V
302	**Gerardo:** Control E
303	**Anita:** No, control C and control V
304	**Francisca:** <u>First</u> you do control C over the image (points to the image of the computer on the screen)
305	yes, control C
306	**Gerardo:** With copy, cut, too? Can you do it that way too?
307	**Francisca:** Yes
308	**Gerardo:** And then?
309	**Francisca:** On your USB, ... paste (returns to her seat)
310	**Gerardo:** No, (Anita takes Gerardo's computer and turns it around)
311	.... let's see once more. I've got it, I'll just click here (speaking to Anita)
312	**Anita:** Uh-huh, control C,
313	**Gerardo:** Do I click or just do this?
314	**Anita:** All of this, put it on the memory (points to Gerardo's screen)
315	everything because...with everything
316	**Gerardo:** Ah, everything?
317	**Anita:** Yes
318	**Gerardo:** Professor Francisca, give me a hand please
319	**Francisca:** I don't know much
320	but let's have a look

In this example, Anita asks Gerardo to transfer files from the USB drive to the computer where the infographic is being made. Since Gerardo is not familiar with this procedure, Anita asks Francisca to explain it to him. Anita knows that Francisca can help Gerardo, because in previous sessions Francisca had repeatedly asked Anita for help with similar tasks. Here, Francisca transitioned from being someone who asked for help to someone who could assist others. As a result, Francisca explained the process to Gerardo even though she still asked for confirmation from Anita (line 298), who was attentive to their questions and gave them the necessary answers (lines 299–303) as they progressed. In lines 304 and 305, Francisca summarized the process that Anita had taught her about the copy-and-paste command. In line 309 she showed Gerardo how to finish the process. When he was unable to complete the final step, Gerardo asked for Anita's guidance despite Francisca being right there beside him, but Anita repeated what Francisca had already explained ("control C"), thus validating Francisca's instruction (line 312), which led Gerardo to return to her guidance (line 318). In this episode, collaboration required teachers to participate in an activity, ask for assistance, offer each other support, and be guided by whoever had greater expertise in that moment and for a given task (this proved to be a fluid role across all the teachers for the duration of the program). Francisca's transition from being guided by a colleague to being a guide for another colleague happened in a context of collaboration and trust, where involvement and mutual support were present during interactions and task accomplishment.

Accompaniment as a way of Reflecting and Redefining an Activity

Our final example of times when others accompanied Francisca occurred during the Google Hangout sessions that were part of the program and where teachers met via video chat and spoke about designing and carrying out activities that involved technology for their students. Hangout sessions were a collective space where classroom activities were constructed and developed. It was also the place where teachers shared activity ideas for their own students, expressed doubt, offered suggestions, studied possibilities, and discussed their progress. This enabled them to collaborate on planning specific aspects of their projects and discuss pertinent decision making while planning their classroom activities. Francisca's case is an example of how interaction in a Hangout group (made up of two other teachers and one research assistant from LETS) helped her design an activity that started out as a vague idea and, when finished, was an implemented and adapted activity that was tried and tested in her classroom.

During the first Hangout, Francisca expressed her early doubts. She focused on how to develop an activity in which her students could elaborate a digital infographic and became confident that she could guide them through the use of the computer to accomplish this but was worried about how to "manage" setting up this task for students. She also was unsure about how she might assess this activity. Regarding her first concern, Francisca could not decide whether to develop the research question herself for her students or if this was a task for her students to do. In response, others in the Hangout suggested that it should be the students who came up with the question, but maybe she could show them a few examples. During that session, Francisca decided to use PowerPoint for the infographic activity. She decided the topic would be an analysis of the different groups involved in the Mexican Revolution and their respective ideologies.

During the third online session, after two class periods with her students, Francisca presented her advances in planning and decision making to the rest of her Hangout group. She showed samples of her students' work, sparking a discussion among the participants about what had been completed up to that point. One of the strongest observations that emerged during this conversation was that instead of an infographic, Francisca's students had created PowerPoint presentations that displayed information over several slides in a sort of monographic format: a stark contrast with Francisca's initial expectations and instructions. This led the other teachers to recommend modifications that would help the activity recover its original purpose: a digital poster on a single slide. The research assistant from LETS showed her a photograph of one of the infographics that her students produced on a large sheet of paper earlier in the school year and, with the other teachers, they discussed with her some of its characteristics: the use of just one poster-sized page, the distribution of space, the different modes of representation (e.g., brief written texts, pictures, maps, a time line, colors, arrows) and a list of references. Anita suggested that she look for some infographics online using phrases such as "history infographics" and "infographics for the [Mexican] Revolution" to show to her students.

Following this conversation, Francisca retooled the activity with her students the next day by re-explaining what an infographic was and how it looked, hoping they could build on their earlier work. She began by showing her students a few samples of infographics online as her colleague had suggested, giving them a better idea of the outcome she expected. As such, even though not physically present in her classroom, Francisca's peers nonetheless accompanied her in this first attempt at designing a complex activity involving a digital end product. It soon became a collective effort that was facilitated by the Hangout group as a whole. During this process, Francisca made several adjustments to her instructions to students and gradually reconfigured the activity to achieve her desired outcomes.

The Hangout sessions provided a space for participating teachers to talk about activities, students, and resources and also helped create a sense of how to design educational activities. Suggestions from the Hangout group were taken back to classrooms, but it was expected that activities would often vary depending on the available resources, on the specific school's conditions, and on the ongoing context created through the teacher's interaction with her students. The process of reconfiguration and digital appropriation took time. It merely began with the possibility of participating in activities in a workshop setting. It also required gaining (new or renewed) confidence in the school subject being taught and the new pedagogical approach being learned by participating teachers. This example highlights how appropriation and the use of technology in teaching is a gradual process that requires on-the-spot adjustments—just in time, just in place—and *sustained* interaction with others (Lankshear and Knobel 2011). In short, we argue it is a process of remaking (Kress 2000), that is, reassembling teachers' understandings, contextual factors, and beliefs (Latour 2005) and adapting teachers' learning needs to sync with their classrooms and students.

CONCLUSION: WHAT WE HAVE LEARNED ABOUT ACCOMPANIMENT AND TEACHER PROFESSIONAL DEVELOPMENT

Our experience with junior high school teachers has placed the concept and practice of *accompaniment* at the center of our proposal for professional development for teachers. It articulates our understanding and actions for helping teachers transform their practice while learning to use digital technology in their teaching. The previous examples offer evidence that using technology in innovative ways goes beyond learning how to operate the computer or navigate the internet. Accompaniment, as we understand it, means creating the time, the space, and the conditions for teachers to reflect on what they do in the classroom and their relationships with their students. Accompaniment enables teachers to design learning activities in which students use digital technology as a resource for searching, designing, representing, and communicating ideas and meanings as part of learning and understanding academic subject content.

As we have developed it, accompaniment requires working with teachers over an extended or sustained period of time. Within our program and during our tenure together, we seek to establish a rapport with participating teachers and create trusting relationships. We encourage new dialogue channels among participating teachers but also between teachers and researchers. Therefore, our notion of accompaniment is not available for programs that promote crash courses or quick training that only tries to teach "computer basics." As we stated earlier in the chapter, digital technology in teaching is more than simply learning to operate a computer. It is an opportunity to reflect on long-standing "business as usual" school practices (Lankshear and Knobel 2011). Using technology in innovative ways requires working with teachers to broaden their understanding of teaching, of the role students play in becoming agents of their own learning, as well as the way digital technology can help transform their work with learners.

Another lesson from working with these teachers is that professional development requires time to explore, create, and review activity designs for the classroom. Approaches to teaching curricular content through technology depend largely on teachers' professional experience, their willingness to experiment and take risks, their handling of technology, and even the specific conditions they face at school (Kalman 2013). Interacting with others—especially other teachers—is key to revising their thinking. With the infographic example, Francisca was not able to use the computer lab with her students and chose instead to attempt the activity on paper and then on the screen; the first experience allowed her to add new elements to her practice without having to use unfamiliar technology. Likewise, in their first attempt on the computer, her students created separate slides without keeping the infographic design on a single display. In response, she suggested they review their work, which led them to create the infographic on a single digital display and keep its poster-like qualities. During the LETS workshops that took place over the course of a whole school year, Francisca obtained firsthand experience in the ongoing process involved in working with drafts and making adjustments to activities that were unfolding over an extended timeframe. This helped her approach her students in a similar fashion when guiding them through the activity.

Over extended periods of time, accompaniment allows teachers to sit in the apprentice chair while in a context of support that nurtures opportunities for ongoing feedback from colleagues and researchers. During the exploration of content and analysis of artifacts such as infographics, maps, tables, and charts, we promoted the idea that revision and re-elaboration is an integral part of the learning process and that several drafts often were necessary. Accompaniment is also comfortable with small, incremental changes that are aimed at addressing specific key issues such as commenting on student work, sharing responsibility with students, engaging students in constructive criticism or developing complex questions rather than with hankering after major paradigm shifts in how teachers think about and approach student learning. This is important because, all too often, policies and professional development providers seem to assume that change can be achieved by decree and forget that new practices must be constructed with teachers over time.

Rapport is essential for teachers (and researchers) to be able to work together. In order to reconsider learning activities, relate to their peers and students, work with curricular content, and represent knowledge, teachers need to be able to experience it themselves before taking it to their classrooms.

Such is the purpose of accompaniment: providing time to reflect, creating new ways of teaching and doing in school, while helping and being helped through collaboration with others. For us, accompaniment as a guiding concept and principle for designing teachers' professional development helps researchers and teachers to work together to reconfigure outmoded, one-size fits all approaches to "teaching" teachers.

REFERENCES

Area, M. (2011). Los efectos del modelo 1:1 en el cambio educativo en las escuelas. Evidencias y desafíos para las políticas iberoamericanas [The effects of the 1:1 approach on changing education in schools: evidence and challenges for policy in Latin America]. *Revista Iberoamericana de Educación*. 56(1): 49–74.

Buckingham, D. (2007). *Beyond Technology: Children's Learning in the Age of Digital Culture*. London: Polity Press.

Chumpitaz, L. (2012). La formación de docentes de educación básica en el uso educativo de las TIC y la reducción de la brecha digital [Training basic education teachers in the use of ICT for learning purposes and closing the digital gap]. *Educación*. 16(31): 29–41.

Coates, J. (1996) *Women Talk: Conversation Between Women Friends*. Oxford, UK: Blackwell Publishers.

Cuban, L. (2003). *Oversold and Underused: Computers in the Classroom*. Cambridge, MA: Harvard University Press.

Dyson, A. (2006). On Saying It Right (Write): "Fix-Its" in the foundations of learning to write. *Research in the Teaching of English*. 41(1): 8–42.

Fischman, G. and Ramírez-Romero, J. (2008). Tecno-esperanzas y educación pública en América Latina [Techno-hopes and public education in Latin America]. *Profesorado: Revista de Currículum y Formación del Profesorado*. 12(1): 1–19.

Gee, J. (2005). *An Introduction to Discourse Analysis: Theory and Method*, 2nd edn. New York: Routledge.

Gere, C. (2012). *Community Without Community in Digital Culture*. London and New York: Palgrave Macmillan.

Guerrero, I. and Kalman, J. (2011). Matices en la inserción de tecnologia en el aula: posibilidades de cambio en las prácticas docentes [Nuances of inserting technology in the classroom: possible changes in teaching practices]. *Cuadernos Comillas*. 1(1): 84–104.

Gumperz, J. (1982): *Discourse Strategies*. Cambridge: Cambridge University Press.

Gutiérrez, A. (2008). Las TIC en la formación del maestro: "Realfabetización" digital del profesorado [The role of ICT in teacher training: New digital literacies for teachers]. *Revista Interuniversitaria de Formación de Profesorado*. 63(22): 191–206.

Jenkins, H. (2009). *Confronting the Challenges of Participatory Culture: Media Education for the 21st Century*. Cambridge, MA: MIT Press.

Jewitt, C. (2006). *Technology, Literacy and Learning. A Multimodal Approach*, 1st edn. New York: Routledge.

Kalman, J. (2013). Beyond common explanations: Incorporating digital technology and culture into classrooms in Mexico. *Digital Culture & Education*. 5(2): 98–118.

Kalman, J. and Guerrero, E. (2013). A social practice approach to understanding teachers' learning to use technology and digital literacies in the classroom. *E-Learning and Digital Media*. 10(3): 260–275.

Kalman, J. and Rendon, V. (2014). Use before know-how: teaching with technology in a Mexican public school. *International Journal of Qualitative Studies in Education.* 27(7–8): 974–991.

Kress, G. (2000). Multimodality. In B. Cope and M. Kalantizis (eds), *Multiliteracies. Literacy Learning and the Design of Social Futures.* London: Routledge, 149–158.

Kress, G. (2010). *Multimodality. A Social Semiotic Approach to Contemporary Communication.* Oxon: Routledge.

Lankshear, C. and Knobel, M. (2007). Sampling "the New" in New Literacies. In C. Lankshear and M. Knobel (eds), *A New Literacies Sampler.* New York: Peter Lang, 1–24.

Lankshear, C. and Knobel, M. (2011). *New Literacies: Everyday Practices and Social Learning*, 3rd edn. New York: Open University Press.

Latour, B. (2005). *Reassembling the Social.* Oxford: Oxford University Press.

Lave, J. (2011). *Apprenticeship in Critical Ethnographic Practice.* Chicago: The University of Chicago Press.

Lave, J. and Wenger, E. (1991). *Situated Learning: Legitimate Peripheral Participation.* Cambridge, UK: Cambridge University Press.

Linne, J. (2014). Adolescents from low-income sectors: the challenge of studying in a time of digital environments. *International Journal of Adolescence and Youth.* 19(4): 434–443.

Loredo, J., García, B., & Alvarado, F. (2010). Identificación de necesidades de formación docente en el uso pedagógico de enciclomedia [Identifying needs in teacher training for the use of enciclomedia in the classroom]. *Sinéctica.* 34(1): 1–16.

Marchesi, A. (2015). Preambulo. In R. Carneiro, J. Carlos Toscano and T. Díaz (eds), *Los Desafíos de las TIC Para el Cambio Educativo.* Madrid: Fundación Santillana y OEI, 7–10.

Navarro, A. (2011) Formación de agenda en la transición del programa enciclomedia hacia habilidades digitales para todos [Creating the transitional agenda from the enciclomedia program to the digital skills for all program]. *Revista Mexicana de Investigación Educativa.* 16(50): 699–723.

New London Group. (1996). A pedagogy of multiliteracies: Designing social futures. *Harvard Educational Review.* 66(1): 60–93.

Pantoja, J. and Covarrubias, P. (2013). La enseñanza de la biología en el bachillerato a partir del aprendizaje basado en problemas (ABP). *Perfiles Educativos.* 35(139): 93–109.

Rogoff, B. (1995). Observing sociocultural activity on three planes: Participatory appropriation, guided participation, and apprenticeship. In J. Wertsch, P. del Rio, and A. Alvarez (eds), *Sociocultural Studies of Mind.* Cambridge, UK: Cambridge University Press, 139–164.

Rojas-Drummond, S., Mazón, N., Littleton, K. and Vélez, M. (2012). Developing reading comprehension through collaborative learning. *Journal of Research in Reading.* 37(2): 138–158.

Robalino, M., and Körner, A. (2005). *Experiencias de Formación Docente Utilizando Tecnologías de Información y Comunicación.* [Experiences in Teacher Training Through Information and Communication Technology]. Santiago de Chile: ORELAC/UNESCO.

Santiago, G. y Sosa, N. (2012). Recomendaciones para la reformulación de políticas de incorporación de las TIC en la educación básica en México. Desafíos y decisiones estratégicas [Recommendations for recreating ICT incorporation policies in Mexican schools. Challenges and strategic decisions]. *Revista Latinoamericana de Estudios Educativos.* 42(4): 15–31.

Secretaria de Educación Pública (SEP). (2007). *El Uso del Pizarrón Interactivo en la Escuela Secundaria (Primera).* [Using Interactive Blackboards in Secondary Schools (First)]. Mexico City: Secretaria de Educación Pública.

Secretaria de Educación Pública (SEP). (2013). *Mi Compu.mx. Dotación de Equipos de Cómputo Portátiles Para Niños de Quinto y Sexto Grados de Escuelas Primarias Públicas. Documento Base* [Mi

Compu.mx: Providing Computer Portable Computer Equipment for Fifth and Sixth Grade Children in Public Schools. Base Document]. Mexico City: Secretaria de Educación Pública.

Severín, E. and Capota, C. (2011). La Computación uno a uno: Nuevas perspectivas [One to one computers: New perspectives]. *Revista Iberoamericana de Educación*. 56(1): 31–48.

Sunkel, G. (2006). *Las Tecnologías de la Información y la Comunicación (TIC) en la Educación En América Latina. Una Exploración de Indicadores* [Information and Communication Technologies in Education in Latin America: An Exploration of Indicators]. Santiago de Chile: CEPAL, UNESCO.

Valiente, Ó. (2011). Los modelos 1:1 en educación. Prácticas internacionales, evidencia comparada e implicaciones políticas [The 1:1 approach to education: International practice, compared evidence and political implications]. *Revista Iberoamericana de Educación*. 1(56): 113–134.

Warschauer, M. (2002). Reconceptualizing the great divide. *First Monday*. 7(7). Online. Available: http://firstmonday.org/ojs/index.php/fm/article/view/967/888/. Downloaded 26 October, 2015.

Zorrilla, J., Dehesa, N., ÁLvarez, A., Lampón, D., González, M. and Tenorio, L. (2009). *Informe final de la Evaluación Externa 2009 en Materia de Diseño. Programa Habilidades Digitales para Todos* [Final Report From the 2009 External Evaluation of the Digitial Tools for All Program Design]. Available: http://www.sep.gob.mx/es/sep1/habilidades_digitales_para_todos#.VLOx7oqG-IQ. Downloaded 26 October, 2015.

NOTES

1. The authors of this chapter are all members of LETS, and over the last seven years, they have worked with junior and senior high school teachers, supporting and accompanying them in the use of digital technologies in the classroom, particularly for the social sciences and the language arts.

2. Translator's note: Each school year, the Mexican government prints and distributes free personal copies of textbooks to all K-9 basic education students as part of its *Libro de Texto Gratuito* policy in place since 1959. Digital textbooks were electronic versions of the print editions with hyperlinked activities, videos, maps, and other complementary materials.

3. Translator's note: In Mexico, the teachers' union is a powerful organization that influences much of what goes on in education, even at the classroom level.

4. Translator's note: The Mexicas, also known as the Aztecs, were the inhabitants of central Mexico who founded the city of Tenochtitlan, where Mexico City is now located.

CHAPTER THREE

Doing-It-Ourselves Development: (Re) defining, (Re)designing AND (Re)valuing THE Role OF Teaching, Learning, AND Literacies

SUSI BOSTOCK, KATHLEEN LISI-NEUMANN AND
MELISSA COLLUCCI

A NOTE TO THE READER

This chapter has been written collaboratively by three educators, two of who are completing (Melissa Collucci) or have recently completed doctoral studies (Susi Bostock) and one who is a published author in the area of literacy and family involvement (Kathleen Lisi-Neumann). The professional learning described and analyzed in this chapter draws on the classroom work of Susi Bostock and Kathleen Lisi-Neumann to illustrate how these two teachers have taken charge of their own professional learning in order to address their commitment to deep learning for their students.

INTRODUCTION

As schools in the U.S. today face many challenges—from working with an increasingly diverse population of students to integrating new technology in the classroom, from working with limited resources to implementing national Common

Core standards—administrators continue to require teachers to participate in professional development workshops that ostensibly are designed to help them become more knowledgeable and enhance their classroom instruction. Unfortunately, however, many professional development opportunities continue to comprise only one-day workshops or short sessions that focus on learning how to use specific digital tools rather than focusing on authentic curriculum improvements such as curricular integration of new technologies (cf. Hutchinson 2012). Although studies suggest that professional development courses and workshops play an important role in educating teachers and keeping them informed (McNeill and Knight 2013; Scull and Kupersmidt 2010), reflecting on our own experiences in the classroom has led us to consider a new paradigm for professional development, one that takes place inside the classroom in direct collaboration with students and interested others.

A PARADIGM SHIFT: FROM PROFESSIONAL DEVELOPMENT TO PROFESSIONAL LEARNING

"Professional development" for teachers, typically referred to as activities such as continuing education, study groups, or in-service workshops designed to enhance professional growth, helps teachers to not only learn new teaching approaches but also develop new insights into pedagogy and their own practice. Oftentimes, professional developers identify the desire to "change" (Guskey 2002; Stein and Wang 1988) or "transform" (Ingersoll, Merrill, Stuckey 2014) teachers and their practice, as though there is "something lacking" in teachers or something needing to be "improved" in how they understand and do things. Recent research in the field, however, offers additional suggestions regarding ways to foster the authentic continuing education of teachers so that opportunities for teacher learning are directly relevant to teachers and their classrooms and, therefore, more effective.

To add a sense of authenticity to the professional learning experiences, research strongly suggests that effective professional development must be collaborative so that teachers have a voice in shaping their learning experiences and in making them relevant for the work they do in the classroom (Ball and Cohen 1999; Goodman et al. 2009). Kopcha (2010), Plair (2008), and Wright (2010) explain that professional development today should focus less on "how-to" workshops and more on pedagogy that will support teachers in designing meaningful learning experiences for their students. For example, Kopcha (2010) suggests professional development for teachers regarding the inclusion of technology that begins with a mentor who assists teachers by negotiating some of the barriers often faced, such as beliefs about technology, time, access to computers, and school culture. Over time, the mentor provides support and modeling that is situated in the context of teachers' classrooms. This collaboration helps teachers better understand how to develop learning activities that will be engaging and meaningful for their students. Such mentoring can be extended to the students, too, thereby creating a culture of teaching *and* learning for everyone in the classroom community.

Under such collaborative and supportive conditions, teachers are more likely to invest in expanding their pedagogical practices (Polly and Hannafin 2010) and work with students and colleagues to generate ideas that extend beyond the prescribed curriculum mandated by school districts and Common Core Standards (Casbon, Shagoury and Smith 2005). Indeed, Easton (2008) argues that "educators today must become learners, and they must be self-developing" (p. 755). This body of research and Easton's claim regarding the importance of do-it-ourselves professional development shape our own approach to meaningful learning and teaching and our view of ourselves as advocates of learning in our classrooms and schools. This orientation calls for a shift in mindset from professional development to *professional learning*.

Professional learning is an *ongoing* process that requires a shift in attitudes about teaching and learning and is especially relevant to current times as the educational landscape continues to change at a rapid pace: new curriculum initiatives, implementation of Common Core State Standards, and relevant practices that continue to develop and evolve with the use of technology. Much of the decision-making power regarding professional learning resides within each teacher and is, therefore, relevant to their current resources and needs. We (Susi and Kathy) have found that engaging in such professional learning requires an investment in our own education and personal growth in order to remain current in terms of pedagogy and practices as 21st-century educators.

PROFESSIONAL LEARNING AND TEACHING IN THE 21ST CENTURY

Our current work to improve the educational opportunities of our students strongly resonates with the suggestions of Ball and Cohen (1999), whose reframing of professional learning emphasizes that "[t]eachers [need] opportunities to reconsider their current practices ... as well as to learn more about the subjects and students they teach" instead of "being told to do so" (p. 3). Ball and Cohen (1999) usefully explain that teachers' professional learning requires, among other dispositions and skills, the ability "to combine intellectual aggressiveness and a willingness to take risks with a humility about the incompleteness and uncertainty of their own ideas" (p. 27). Such an orientation toward professional learning is challenging, at times daunting, but to us worth every bump in the road, because the impact is ours. Although our cases discussed below differ in terms of goals, participants, and content, they similarly reflect our willingness to probe with "intellectual aggressiveness" deeply into our practices with humble uncertainty intent on improving the education of our students. To teach in 21st-century classrooms requires time, exploration, practice, and reflection in an environment where teachers feel safe, valued, and supported. Specifically, teachers need opportunities to explore transitional practices in supportive environments in order to be able to re-define and re-design current curriculums and construct new approaches to teaching and learning in the digital age (Bostock 2012) in linguistically and culturally diverse classrooms.

SUSI AND KATHY CONCEPTUALIZE THIRDSPACE THEORY AND PEDAGOGY

Over the last few years, we have come to understand that our professional learning and evolving practice as 21st-century teachers are the results of working side by side with our students and colleagues in what has been termed the "Thirdspace" (Brooke, Coyle and Walden 2005; Gutierrez 2008; Soja 1996). According to Gutierrez (2008), this space lies between two unique and readily identifiable spaces (a.k.a. the Firstspace and the Secondspace). These two unique spaces could be the classroom and the home (Gutierrez 2008); city infrastructure and formal plans for urban development (Soja 1989,1996); or, as in our case, the typical expectations and roles within a classroom and the imagined/theorized ideas for how to improve education (Brooke, Coyle and Walden 2005). For it is "'between' the real [our classroom expectations and roles] and imagined spaces [theories of new literacies, funds of knowledge, and second language learning]" that we develop our own unique Thirdspaces (Brooke, Coyle and Walden 2005: 368). In our work, we purposefully have chosen to spell Thirdspace in this way—one word, capital T—because our classroom work aligns closely with the sentiment of Brooke and colleagues (2005) and Edward Soja (1996) in that embracing this complicated theory in the practical world of the classroom means we work tirelessly towards creating metaphorical and actual "spaces" for learning that extend beyond typical classroom mandates and expectations.

Taking into account these theoretical positions on Thirdspace and putting central ideas and concepts that work for us (and our students) into practice, we have found that the evolution of a Thirdspace supports the inclusion of languages, discourses/Discourses, knowledge, experiences, resources, funds of knowledge, and individuals not often "welcome" in schools.

Our own particular "take" on Thirdspace is shaped by two bodies of academic work: Gee's theory of discourse/Discourse and Moll and colleague's conception of "funds of knowledge." Gee best defines discourse/Discourse (1990), explaining that discourses/Discourses are "ways of being in the world" which are "much more than language alone" (Lankshear and Knobel 2011: 19–20). It is important to differentiate between what Gee (1990) refers to as Discourse (with a big D) and discourse (with a little d), as these differences directly impact interactions within the Thirdspace. While individuals belong to multiple Discourses (for example, Kathy, Melissa and Susi are all teachers, wives, mothers, authors), we and our students each belong to a respective primary discourse within which we each use a distinctive language in socially patterned ways and "which shapes who and what we initially are as persons" (Lankshear and Knobel 2011: 20). We are first and foremost *Susi* and *Kathy* and *Melissa*—our core selves, just as our students are. Taking into account Gee's idea of multiple Discourses, we are most concerned with the ways in which Thirdspaces can support the use of discourses/Discourses that often "don't belong" in school such as home languages and technological literacies.

"Funds of knowledge" as a conceptual framework for understanding and valuing a wide range of knowledge and know-how is similar in many ways to discourse/Discourse theory but is more explicitly focussed on an individual's lived experiences and home life. "Funds of knowledge" is defined by Gonzales, Moll and Amanti (2005: 133) as the "historically accumulated and culturally developed bodies of knowledge and skills essential for household or individual functioning and well-being." For some, these funds of knowledge may be related to childcare or work outside the home such as carpentry. For others, their funds of knowledge may be grounded in language or technical knowhow that support the prosperity of their home (Gonzales, Moll and Amanti 2005; Moll and Greenberg 1992). Funds of knowledge can be drawn from several lived and shared experiences that are quite unique in comparison to classroom and school knowledge and not typically embraced by the educators and valued in a classroom. Bringing together discourse/Discourse theory and "funds of knowledge" has helped to flesh out our understandings of Thirdspace and our practices within it.

And in doing so, embracing Thirdspace theory has contributed to our own professional learning, helped us to refine our own professional work, and directly enhanced our students' learning.

PROFESSIONAL LEARNING AT THE FOREFRONT: THEORIZING "THIRDSPACE" WITH A FOCUS ON "WAYS OF BEING" AND KNOWLEDGE

This combination of compatible theories regarding knowledge, "ways of being," and everyday lived experiences has led us to re-think our own professional learning and our students' learning, in turn enabling the evolution of our particular approach to Thirdspace work. By taking such a stance we embrace the metaphorical need to find space that better serves our students (as well as our own professional learning) and create a reality that works for each of us and our students. As will become evident in the cases we share below, there are no set expectations for what student and/or family knowledge includes and how such knowledge is brought to the Thirdspace. Such Thirdspace work allows students to "reconceive who they are and what they might be able to accomplish academically and beyond" with the help of us, their teachers (Gutierrez 2008: 148). From this perspective, traditional social roles and power structures that situate students in a subordinate position in the classroom (Davidson 2011; Rogoff 2003) are replaced by classroom communities where the role of the teacher and student, novice and expert all intersect, thereby "creating the potential for authentic interaction and learning to occur" (Gutierrez, Baquedano-Lope and Turner 1997: 372). As we work within our own Thirdspaces, we welcome and nurture all voices, discourses/Discourses, languages, and funds of knowledge as we embrace the authenticity of what develops between the real and imagined spaces. Although unique, the two cases presented in this chapter highlight the benefits of developing an authentic Thirdspace for learning by inviting others to be equal collaborators and by welcoming ideas often marginalized by those who develop traditional school curriculum.

SUSI BOSTOCK: FOURTH-GRADE TEACHER

Several years ago while teaching Grade 1, I engaged in what was, for me, a truly transformative learning experience in the Thirdspace of my classroom (Bostock 2012). This experience unfolded at a time when I myself was learning about digital technologies and tools along with developing an understanding of digital literacies. I sat side by side with my students as they performed as digital text participants and guided me in developing my own technological prowess. This inspired my interest in and research into teaching and learning in the digital age—work that is far more complex than simply using a computer or providing students with access to tablets. Now, just a few years later, I am teaching Grade 4, and my own desire to encourage possibilities and creative alternatives by means of a Thirdspace classroom has provided rich learning experiences for me and my students that extend beyond a set curriculum and enable shared learning and teaching among us. In the following story, I describe how my fourth-grade students and I engaged Thirdspace teaching and learning while investigating a science unit about the ways in which humans impact the environment.

Nurturing Organic Ideas

Reflecting on the work I (Susi) do in my classroom is an ongoing process of my professional learning. I have found that learning in my classroom is most meaningful when it flows from collaboratively agreed-upon, "organic ideas"—those born out of my students' curiosities that often unfold *as* they are learning. As my class and I engaged in a research project learning about ways in which humans impact the environment, we drew on a rich range of news articles, books, videos, and websites to identify ways in which humans negatively impact the environment, as well as—most importantly—how we can make positive changes.

Before I could plan for what might come next, I wanted to tap into the students' passions and curiosities to facilitate the development of critical literacy in practice (cf. Vasquez 2004). Critical literacy in practice enables opportunities for students to question ideas and roles of power, explore and shift identities, and engage in social action that helps develop other identities of their own (Coffey 2015). Classrooms where critical literacy practices are in action require that teachers and students remain cognizant of their work together and relate to the larger community. Viewing literacy in this way welcomes ideas, discourses/Discourses, and knowledge often overlooked or unexplored in classrooms, all of which are welcome in our (always evolving) Thirdspace classroom. As such, I deliberately encouraged my Grade 4 students to investigate social and political issues and use their own knowledge and insights to challenge these issues in their local communities and the larger world. Thus, like Vasquez (2004), I tried in this environmental study to create spaces where my students engage in literacy practices that are intended to contribute to positive social change, no matter if this is only on an intensely local scale.

Soon the students made observations about our classroom environment and became aware of the abundance of empty plastic bottles in our recycling bin. One student suggested we all use refillable sports bottles, and we all agreed that was an easy and positive solution. Other project ideas began to develop. One student proposed creating public awareness posters to educate others about water pollution on Long Island (New York State) emphasizing the economic impact as well as the quality-of-life impact of dirty water. Another student suggested showcasing an idea read about in the news magazine *New York State Conservationist for Kids*: "upcycling." We learned that upcycling happens when an item deemed trash or ready for recycling is instead turned into something new and once again useable, such as glass jars repurposed to hold pencils or plastic soda pop bottles crafted into birdfeeders. I asked this student to explain what he was envisioning, and he suggested, "We can make an upcycled product at home then bring it in to present to the class... We can just look through stuff at our house—like in the recycling bin or other stuff that we don't use anymore and figure out something else to do with it". This idea resonated with the class; students started cheering! Caught up in their excitement, I blurted out, "Let's do a Shark Tank presentation!"

Shark Tank is a reality competition television series, where entrepreneur-contestants make business presentations to a panel of investors (sharks) in hopes of brokering a deal to help them develop their product or business. *Shark*

Tank was a frequent conversation in our classroom, because most of my students watched it at home, as did I. More cheering from the students let me know they were interested and excited with this proposed presentation format, so we outlined the project requirements together. Because this current project would be individualized for each student, we titled the project "Do-it-yourself upcycling." Collectively, we decided the upcycled product had to have a clear purpose for its use and needed to use materials from a recycling bin to create something new or re-purpose an existing item or material for another use. Although I was excited about this project and believed the project was useful in drawing students' attention to an environmental problem, I had no idea where it would take our learning. For me and my students, a Thirdspace developed in our classroom.

In the sections that follow, I highlight how my students and I re-defined and re-designed learning together in the Thirdspace of our classroom. To ensure I was keeping up with the district curriculum, I made some adjustments in the current classroom schedule. For the next two weeks our forty-minute English Language Arts period would be designated for any related lessons or learning related to the "upcycling" project. I set this time period knowing that students would be writing persuasive introductions for their presentations. Additionally, this time would be used for learning about and creating "brand" names for products, analyzing YouTube media clips, and rehearsing presentations—all of which encompass the language arts standards. Week three would be reserved for the presentations. Below I share some meaningful learning opportunities that transpired due to our willingness to work within our Thirdspace together.

Ideas Become Upcycled Products

As the upcycled products arrived, our classroom was abuzz with excitement as students spent time viewing and examining each other's creations. There were puzzles, games, candle holders, craft supply organizers, a bird hotel, an animal tent, tote bags, a broom made from plastic water bottles, plant holders, and even an outdoor lamp! My mind flooded with questions. "*Where did they get these ideas? Were they original ideas based on some material they re-imagined in some way? Did they google ideas? Did they search for ideas on the internet and then redesign an existing idea with their own personal touch?*" Because this project largely was student driven, I had not anticipated what would ensue once the upcycled projects entered the classroom. Many of the projects were reflections of each student in terms of who created them and how the original "trash" was re-designed to include identity presentation. For example, Chloe, a self-described "nature lover," repurposed a small wooden container into a planting container decorated with hearts, peace signs, and stars (some of Chloe's favorite doodles). Chloe explained that the heart represented "I love plants" and the peace sign was meant to symbolize peace to the environment. As I marveled at Chloe's "planting container" and the other upcycled projects, I wanted to expand this learning experience and prompt them to think even more deeply about their own work as designers, creators, and critical thinkers.

New Opportunities for Teaching and Learning

The students demonstrated how they could make positive changes through what they had learned about human impact on our environment, but I saw another opportunity for meaningful learning. Before presenting authentic *Shark Tank*-worthy products, the students needed to think more critically about the products they had created. As students continued to peruse the display of projects, I took a few minutes to create a "product information sheet." It required them to list the type of product they created (e.g., a checkers game), the product's category/purpose (e.g., game, household item, organization, outdoor item, art-decor, apparel/accessories.), target market (e.g., adults, children, both, other), upcycled materials used, and estimated cost of product if purchased at a store such as Target or Walmart. Key to this deep thinking were their reflections about overall design and purpose in creating "brand" names to market their products. I gave an example of a marketing name using the classroom SMART Board. I suggested brainstorming a list of words related to their product and exploring alliteration or wordplay. Students worked in pairs and small groups to brainstorm ideas, and within forty minutes most students had a new "brand" name for their product. A soda bottle vase covered in colorful duct tape was renamed "Bottle of Cheer"; a small animal tent became "The Kitty Camper"; and an outdoor lamp made of plastic spoons became "Spoonlight." This activity demonstrated how relevant experiences enabled learning that was of high interest, had direct impact on students' investment in their own learning, and, above all, led to unique and important outcomes.

LEARNING FROM YOUTUBE AND POPULAR CULTURE: ANALYZING MEDIA

I suggested we watch a video clip of the *Shark Tank* program on YouTube and see if students had any additional thoughts or ideas before we set dates for presentations. (Many of my students regularly share information with me about YouTube videos they watch, as well as other uses they have for it, such as listening to popular music.) In the case of our upcycling project, YouTube offered opportunities for my students to discuss the important role of new Discourses (Gee 2008; Lankshear and Knobel 2011)—and helped me to welcome into our classroom the out-of-school-knowledges that they valued in their own lives and learning. I chose an episode I thought would be appropriate and interesting for my students titled "I want to draw a cat for you" (Knowledge is Power 2012). It was an interesting choice because I wanted the students to see how the central product was being marketed. The entrepreneur-contestant seeking the Sharks' financial support in this particular episode was a man who draws pictures of cats and sells them on his website.

After watching the 5-minute video clip together, I asked students to share any thoughts and insights about the contestant's presentation. One student pointed out that the *Shark Tank* theme music added suspense. Another commented, "You really have to know everything about your product because they [the "sharks"] ask smart questions." Several students commented on how the contestant told a little bit about himself, his inspiration for creating his product, and the way he engaged his audience by performing a rap song: "I want to draw a cat for you." This rap song described his product and included dance moves which "made you pay attention," according to my students. Their close analysis of media content, understanding the "rules," and sharing insightful commentary with others supports Gee's (2003) contention that we need to broaden our views of literacy to include skills that "have the potential to lead to active and critical learning" (p. 46) and that, when presented in an engaging way, students will happily take them up. Collectively we also decided on the following criteria for our own presentations: (1) appearance, (2) durability, and (3) usefulness.

A few days before their presentations, I asked for a student volunteer to give a practice presentation for students to make suggestions about anything we needed to think about before the big day. The *Shark Tank* theme music started and the volunteer walked up to the front of the class: "Hi my name is Alexandra, and my product is a Bottle of Cheer. It's upcycled from a soda bottle and I wrapped it in duct tape. You can stand it on a table and it won't fall over. I hope you invest in my product." I asked for suggestions about how she could improve her presentation, and the students reminded her about the YouTube video and how the contestant brought his personality into his product in an "entertaining" way. Alexandra wanted to practice at home and volunteered to present again the following morning. She began: "Hi my name is Alexandra, and my product is a Bottle of Cheer. It's upcycled from a plastic soda bottle. I wrapped it in colorful duct tape to make it look pretty, and I put in some flowers to make it look like a vase. You can put it on a table or in the kitchen; anywhere you want. It can make any room cheerful! I hope you like my product." The class applauded. Now it was time for questions from the audience: "Where did you buy the duct tape? Can you use different duct tape? Do you have to make it from a soda bottle?" *(Of course she could answer these questions—so could any one of us! My students could certainly come up with better questions. I had to intervene!)* Back to the YouTube video—this time with a different purpose: What type of questions do the Sharks ask? Afterwards, I posed the question, "What type of questions do Sharks ask?" "Smart questions", answered one student. Others commented, "Sharks wanted to know why he created the product"…"Who buys his drawings"…. "When he creates the drawings"….. "How did he become interested in drawing cats?" This second viewing with a specific "purpose" focused their analysis on the Shark investors' perspective. This opportunity was critical to understanding both (contestant-investor) perspectives.

PRESENTATION "SHARK TANK"

In the third and final week of our project, four to five students presented each day, averaging ten to fifteen minutes from introduction to question/answer session. Below is one student's introduction speech; most students followed this format, which is very similar to the *Shark Tank* television program:

> Hello. My name is Fotini. Today I am here to ask you to invest in my product, The Super Styler. The Super Styler is a vanity used for dress-up. It comes with two accessory containers. Inside the containers you can keep your favorite hair, makeup and jewelry accessories. There is also a hair brush. The Super Styler is durable. It is fun to use alone or with friends. It is colored pretty pink and orange. You can use the Super Styler to get ready for a fancy party or just playing with your friends. The vanity is made out of cardboard and wood. It has a mirror with stickers all around it. The accessory containers are made of plastic cups. They have pretty tape on them to make them look nice. My favorite part of the Super Styler is that it is made out of upcycled goods. I hope you enjoyed learning about my product: the Super Styler.

My students' presentations exceeded all my expectations about what was possible within our Thirdspace. Score sheets based on our previously developed criteria for each student presentation were distributed. After all students presented, I would enter scores for every student onto an Excel spreadsheet and tally the points to identify one winner for each of the six categories. Every student not only met the project requirements that we had outlined together but, in my opinion (and, I believe, theirs too!), exceeded them.

As a teacher in the state of New York, it is required that I plan lessons that address the Common Core State Standards. Therefore, even though I did not let the standards drive my instruction, I did take time after the project was completed to align our classroom work with these standards so that I could speak to the standards if asked. Taking the time to justify our work affirmed for me what I have always believed: that when you create the time and space to truly *know* your students and listen to their interests and ideas, you can develop learning opportunities that are important, impactful, and purposeful.

A week after the presentations, I gave a short presentation to the class. I thanked the student who initiated the idea and thanked all students for demonstrating their commitment to finding alternative solutions to an environmental problem. I awarded all students with a Certificate of Achievement for their outstanding designs and positive contributions.

Our *Shark Tank* presentations may have ended, but the impact remains for me and my class. Our Monday morning conversations often began with, "Did you watch *Shark Tank* on Friday night?" Conversation typically then moved to an analysis of the contestants and their negotiations of the "deals." Sometimes during math lessons, when a relevant context was presented (e.g., money, rounding numbers, values), we turned to YouTube and our business mentors from *Shark Tank* to teach us math. My students later expressed an interest in writing to *Shark Tank* investors, so I suggested creating a video clip explaining how the show inspired our thinking and creativity. I sent an email with the video clip to the Shark Tank network producers using a contact email address I found on the network website. Although we never received a response, the process of creating this "promotional" video was nonetheless valuable.

REFLECTIONS ON PROFESSIONAL LEARNING IN THIRDSPACE

My (Susi) own experiences concerning learning and teaching in the Thirdspace have helped me to understand the importance of professional learning that encourages teachers to provide opportunities within their classrooms for acknowledging and facilitating the development of individual interests and multiple literacies. In such ways, students can become more active, socially engaged citizens (Moje et al. 2004) as well as collaborators and self-directed learners (cf. Wohlwend 2010). For me, doing-it-ourselves approaches to professional learning necessarily entail learning from our students and, at the same time, supporting their learning as it unfolds. Indeed, developing and working within our Thirdspace allowed for learning and growth that no one-day workshop or outside consultant could have enabled and allowed us to develop a deep understanding of what it takes to troubleshoot an existing problem by means of creative innovation.

Similarly, in what follows, Kathy's Thirdspace classroom allowed for learning that otherwise may have been too difficult to achieve within the typical classroom. Evident in her Thirdspace work is the inclusion of students' families' voices, knowledge, and resources to improve literacy learning and proficiency opportunities for her English language learner students in particular and for all her students in general. In ways similar to my work, Kathy created a Thirdspace by creating a "space" for the imagined and theorized (funds of knowledge theory) to work with the reality of the classroom (literacy pedagogy) and developed a unique reality (Partners in Reading). Yet her work is also unique in that her Thirdspace developed out of her own uncertainty as to how best teach English language learners content and support their literacy learning in English.

KATHLEEN LISI-NEUMANN: SECOND-GRADE TEACHER

My (Kathy) story began when I started a new teaching assignment as a second-grade teacher in a linguistically diverse classroom. As an experienced teacher who has worked in kindergarten, third-grade, and fourth-grade classrooms, as well as having taught as an elementary enrichment teacher, I thought I was well prepared to take on this new challenge. A constructivist by choice, the learning environment in my new class was student centered and fostered respect for every student in our classroom, including the English as a second language and special education teachers with whom I co-taught as part of our daily literacy instruction. I strived to reach the highest standards by seeking professional learning opportunities that brought together critical thinking, curiosity, and reflection in my classroom teaching and practices.

In my Grade 2 classroom being described here, all members of the learning community were encouraged to learn at their own pace with the support of the other members. By inviting parents in as equal collaborators and welcoming their ideas, resources, funds of knowledge, and discourses, a Thirdspace was formed and became not only a "different or alternative space of knowledges and Discourses," but an integral and authentic place within which unique and pertinent learning experiences for the teachers, students, and their families were developed and fostered through an the iterative process of reflection, seeking information, and action (Moje et al. 2004: 41).

Our classroom community had English language-learners as well as English-speaking children who struggled with reading. As I share my story of professional learning and growth, I will explain how my realization that more needed to be done for my second-grade English language learners led my students and me on a Thirdspace journey that culminated with the development of a unique reading program (known as: We Are a Winning Team) filled with unexpected benefits for me, my students, and their families.

ENHANCING READING COMPREHENSION FOR ENGLISH LANGUAGE LEARNERS

As a native, monolingual speaker of English, I faced the daunting task of teaching children who were learning to speak, read, and write English while at the same time they were trying to learn school content. This is a reality that has become quite common for teachers in U.S. classrooms. As general education classrooms are diversifying linguistically (DeJong and Harper 2005; Villegas and Lucas 2011), English language learners often find themselves taught by teachers who lack knowledge of their learning needs and the teaching practices essential to addressing those needs (DeJong and Harper 2005; Lucas and Villegas 2011). In my classroom, approximately 30 percent of my students spoke home languages other than English. In light of such diversity, I urgently needed to rethink education "for all" in my classroom. Aware that research-based information regarding how best to teach linguistically diverse students was available (see the work of Lucas and Villegas 2011, 2013; Lucas, Villegas and Freedson-Gonzalez 2008), and spurred by the desire to help my students learn in my classroom, I began to research ways to support them better. I wanted to embrace my students' home languages, yet, at the same time, support their in-school learning and English language proficiency. Addressing this reality is central to the rationale behind the development of my Thirdspace learning environment.

OUR DEVELOPING READING PROGRAM

Fall parent-teacher conferences began in November (i.e., three months after the start of the school year) and, during a conversation with a parent of one of my English language learning students, I decided that the best way to meet the needs of their son was to elicit their help, because I realized that this child's knowledge—his resources and needs—would be best understood by those who knew him intimately. I invited them to come to school and do more than "take part" in class activities. By combining their knowledge (of their son and language) with my knowledge (of curriculum and pedagogy), we developed learning opportunities that worked. Parents as teaching partners in the school setting was a novel approach within our school and one that was not explored in the professional learning experiences I had previously encountered.

Taking an active role in their child's reading education on a regular basis and being involved in the teaching of reading meant that each student's parents became valued members of our classroom learning community. I viewed the parent as an instructional partner and provided the reading texts and supplemental materials necessary to help their child receive increased individualized reading instruction. I demonstrated and reviewed the instructional practices necessary for the parent to provide scaffolding, which strengthened the child's reading foundation. The student, parent and I would have monthly conferences to discuss reading progress, celebrate success and rectify any reading problems. Their child saw them as more than caretakers, and so did the other students.

It struck me that if this strategy worked for this English language learner, it should also work with the other English language learners as well as the native English speakers in my class who also needed more individual reading instruction than I could give them during the course of a day or even a week. It was at this point that I began formally re-evaluating the role of parents in the educational setting and created a family inclusive reading program, a program for parents to assist their children by providing additional reading support and instruction during the school day. To make this work, parents would need to "be part" of the instructional planning process as well as the implementation of the instruction. Each willing parent would play the role of teacher apprentice, a valued role in the learning community. This program offered parents of all of the students in my class the chance to play an invaluable role in their child's learning by providing meaningful support aimed at sustaining reading growth and developing language skills as they became proficient readers.

The reading program was titled *We are a Winning Team* and offered a socially and culturally equity-oriented reading approach that fostered a teacher-parent-student learning environment. It was a collective "Thirdspace, in which students began to reconceive who they are and what they might be able to accomplish" (Gutierrez 2008: 148) as readers. The idea was to construct a learning environment where the participants learned, grew and thrived in a culturally enriched, mutually inclusive setting, simultaneously ensuring that families of all language, ethnic and religious backgrounds had equal access to our classroom as well as to the reading instruction provided to their children. Creating this Thirdspace allowed all participants—teachers, parents and students—to play a meaningful and fulfilling role in our classroom reading process.

Instruction was individualized and planned during a conference between the parent, their child, and me. Parents were encouraged to provide additional reading materials from home such as favorite books or texts in their native language during sessions that lasted about 20–30 minutes. The students and parents would choose a book from our library or have one chosen from home. They would read together, talk about what they had read and jot down thoughts, feelings or questions as they read together. Then they would complete a brief written reflection sheet about their reading session and document what they had accomplished. These reflections provided important information discussed at our regularly scheduled conferences.

This space was conceived as a heterogeneous community of learners and as a way to help students grow as readers with the help of their parents under my guidance. In some cases, both the student and the parent struggled with reading English. On one occasion, as testament to her dedication to helping her child become a better reader, one parent brought her older high school child to class to read with her younger child and herself, because she felt that she needed family collaboration in order to provide the best support possible for her child.

Interestingly, along with the learning adaptations we put in place, the Third-space that was created with shared knowledge also sparked a redesign of our physical classroom. The physical space needed to include larger sitting areas and dual reading spots to accommodate the increase in classroom population. The hallway outside the classroom as well as hallway alcoves were readied as quiet reading nooks for students and their parents. More partner books of varying reading levels were added to our classroom library while pencils, paper and clipboards were organized for easy access for capturing thoughts while reading. Not all parents were able to commit to our school day reading schedule, so they were encouraged to take part in the reading program in the comfort of their home. The *We Are a Winning Team* reading program was designed to expand our classroom learning both figuratively and literally.

"WE ARE A WINNING TEAM" READING PROGRAM GAINS TRACTION

As the program expanded, I set up an after-school as well as an evening parent information session to explain and discuss the *We Are a Winning Team* guidelines and routines for the parent-student reading sessions such as when, where and how reading sessions would take place as well as describing the inclusion of conferences to discuss reading progress. I emphasized to those with limited English proficiency that reading with their children in their home language at school or home would support their children's literacy development. Cummins (2000) argues that students who are literate in their first language have an easier time learning a new language, so I was confident that this approach would be successful. With approximately 70 per cent of parent support, I surveyed parents' availability during the school day and created individual parent weekly reading schedules, based on their responses, to ensure continuity and commitment to the reading program. I focused on making every family feel welcome, and I stressed the need to support all readers, including English language learners, regardless of their current English language proficiency. Prior to the onset of this program, the parents of English language learning students spent very little time visiting or volunteering in our classroom, while English-speaking parents were always available to read to the class or to assist with class projects and activities. Finally, this imbalance began to change.

The student/parent weekly schedule was posted on our classroom bulletin board, and students would watch the clock, happily anticipating their parents' arrival. Every student/parent partnership was assigned a reading location for the week. Locations were based on student/parent preference and were available on a rotating basis depending on the amount of parent-child reading partners at a given time. The reading session was conducted independently of the class's lesson at the time of the visit. When the reading session was over, the student would return to the group and continue working with his or her classmates. On occasion, parents did remain in the classroom to assist with the ongoing class lesson or activity, making their entrance and exit as seamless and non-disruptive as possible.

BENEFITS OF THE READING PROGRAM

Gutierrez (2008: 153) suggests that a collective Thirdspace "[c]an be viewed as a particular kind of proximal development." That is, a space where "learning and development happen in the movement across various temporal, spatial, and historical dimensions of activity." The Thirdspace that *We Are a Winning Team* created did just that. It expanded the Thirdspace to include collaboration between the teacher and student/parent partnerships that were taking place simultaneously within that Thirdspace. Even though the partnerships were seemingly working independently of one another, they shared a mission of enriching reading instruction. In this sense, *We Are a Winning Team* enhanced and expanded the zone of proximal development (Vygotsky 1978) by providing engaging learning activities for parents and students during their reading sessions. The reading successes were uplifting to the students and their parent partners. As their reading improved, so did their motivation. Their enthusiasm was contagious and inspired me to work towards expanding and improving the reading program. This, in turn, created an optimal professional learning opportunity for me and for my students' parents, one that continually pushed us to work harder.

Creating this program also provided the opportunity to help my colleagues see the positive aspects of parent involvement in the classroom and deconstruct the sometimes negative connotations that surround the idea of parent involvement, such as the fear that parents will gossip about student abilities or criticize teaching practices. By creating school-wide transparency of our reading program through open discussion of the program to colleagues and invitations to administrators and teachers to visit our classroom, parents and their powerful role in the classroom were viewed as true partners and revalued as an educational asset to our classroom learning community.

A TURN-KEY OF PROFESSIONAL LEARNING

The *We Are a Winning Team* reading program was very successful. By the end of the school year, the students whose parents participated at home or in school were reading at or above grade level, based on district reading assessments. Students were sharing and recommending books to each other and were able to sustain silent reading for longer periods of time. Routine parent involvement was evident in our classroom, and parents expressed "feeling important" because of their involvement in their child's reading instruction. My grade-level colleagues were now interested in implementing the *We Are a Winning Team* reading program themselves.

The teachers who embraced the program re-designed various components to suit their own students and families' needs and schedules, thereby creating their own spaces for learning. By the end of the 2011 school year, "*We Are a Winning Team*" was recognized formally as a "best practice" in our school district.

This recognition helped me to realize that teachers outside our district also might benefit from our approach to professional learning that redefined, redesigned and re-valued the role of the parent community and how professional learning opportunities can be generated by converting at least part of our classroom ethos into a Thirdspace. During a collegial discussion with my colleagues Danielle Baczynski, a third-grade teacher, and Jaclyn Crowell, a first-grade teacher, about our reading program, I proposed turning our reading program into a mainstream idea by writing a book about it and to further our professional learning. As critical thinkers and by sharing our discourse of ideas, practice and theory behind *We Are a Winning Team*, together we documented our reading program experiences, which opened the door to another valued "space" for educators and subsequent students and families to learn and grow (see Baczynski, Crowell and Lisi-Neumann 2014).

THE PROGRAM TODAY

Today, the *We Are a Winning Team* reading program is going strong in Grades 1 to 3 in our school. It is heartwarming to walk down the corridor past these classrooms and see children curled into the laps of their parents, reading. Results or academic benefits can be measured in part by formal and informal reading assessments, but the true measure of the program's success can be seen on the students' faces when their parents arrive in the classroom and parents' proud looks when their child is demonstrating reading improvement. The teachers who participate in this program continue to see an increase in students' reading ability and level of reading engagement. The parent community has continued to be receptive to the program, and in many cases parents take part with more than one child who are in different grades.

Currently, I am teaching fifth grade and realized that parents' presence in their children's educational life was just as important in the older grades as it was in the primary grades, so I began to offer new ways for the parents to play a more active role in their "older elementary" student's reading life. This "new" form of parent-student participation in my Grade 5 classroom is as individual as the students and their parents. The students and I discuss and plan the ways in which their parents or caregivers can best support their learning needs. We conference together with their parents and devise instructional plans that are monitored and updated during the course of the unit that is being taught. Some parents still visit the classroom, but many prefer to work with their child at home. As such, Thirdspace work is fluid and interactive, never stagnant. I continually look for new ways to further the Thirdspace in my classroom and am inspired daily by my students to create professional learning opportunities that enhance and encompass the entire learning community.

OUR FINAL THOUGHTS

The lens through which we now view professional learning required a shift in thinking about where learning takes place, the roles of teachers and students and the cultural changes that promote and result from learning. Rogers and Freiberg (1994: 119) remind us that "[f]ully functioning professionals need a degree of independence to grow. Being constantly dependent on others to tell you how you're doing inhibits individual growth and creates a dependency that stifles an entire profession. Meaningful and lasting change occurs when we look inside ourselves for answers." For us that "look inside ourselves" led us to realize that we could achieve more for our students if we welcomed "more" into our classrooms—more voices, more knowledge, more discourses/Discourses—that were not typically welcomed in school settings. Through our humble navigation through professional learning, it was and still is within the Thirdspace of our classrooms where it becomes possible for students, parents, and ourselves as teachers to re-define what counts as knowledge and learning; to re-design learning that promotes collective intelligence and shared success; and to continually re-value the contributions each of us makes to our shared learning.

We remain idealistic and hopeful as we continue to learn and welcome others to do the same with their students and their families. We continue to strive (and urge others to do so) to authentically weave theory and practice together in "spaces" where education is not confined to the traditional role of student and teacher but inclusive of the experiences and knowledge of students, their families and the literacies they themselves contribute to the learning community. We continually re-evaluate our roles in our own ongoing professional learning choices and plans of action through continuous critical reflection of our practice, for it is honest, humble reflection that has been the driving force of our learning. No amount of pre-packaged one-day seminars or workshops could possibly enable the deep, impactful learning our cases highlight. For us, doing-it-ourselves with respect to our own professional growth has been rewarding—challenging at times, of course—but always deeply rewarding for us, our students and their families.

REFERENCES

Baczynski, D., Crowell, J. and Lisi-Neumann, K. (2014). *Engaging Parents as Literacy Partners*. New York: Scholastic.

Ball, D. and Cohen, D. (1999). Developing practice, developing practitioners: Toward a practice-based theory of professional Education. In L. Darling-Hammond and G. Sykes (eds), *Teaching as the Learning Profession: Handbook of Policy and Practice*. San Francisco, CA: Jossey-Bass.

Bostock, S. (2012). Thirdspace: A perspective on professional development. *Language Arts*. 89(4): 222–231.

Brooke, R., Coyle, D. and Walden, A. (2005). Finding a space for professional development: Creating thirdspace through after-school writing groups. *Language Arts*. 82(1): 367–377.

Casbon, C., Shagoury, R., and Smith, G. (2005). Rediscovering the call to teach: A new vision for professional development. *Language Arts*. 82(1): 359–366.

Coffey, H. (n.d.). Critical Literacy. *Learn NC*. Available at: http://www.learnnc.org/lp/pages/4437. Downloaded 29 August, 2015.

Cummins, J. (2000). BICS and CALP. In B. Street and N. Hornberger (eds), *Encyclopedia of Language and Education*. New York: Springer Science and Business Media LLC, 71–83.

Davidson, C. (2011). *Now You See It: How the Brain Science of Attention will Transform the Way We Live, Work, and Learn*. New York: Viking.

de Jong, E. and Harper, C. (2005). Preparing mainstream teachers for English-language learners: Is being a good teacher good enough? *Teacher Education Quarterly*. 32(2): 101–124.

Easton, L. (2008). From professional development to professional learning. *Phi Delta Kappan*. 89(10): 755.

Gee, J. (1990). *Social Linguistics and Literacies: Ideology in Discourses*. London: Falmer.

Gee, J. (2003). *What Video Games Have to Teach Us About Learning and Literacy*. New York: Palgrave.

Gee, J. (2008). *Social Linguistics and Literacies: Ideology in Discourses*, 3rd edn. London: Routledge/Falmer.

González, N., Moll, L. and Amanti, C. (eds) (2005). *Funds of Knowledge: Theorizing Practices in Households, Communities, and Classrooms*. New York: Routledge.

Grossman, P., Compton, C., Igra, D., Ronfeldt, M., Shahan, E. and Williamson, P. (2009). Teaching practice: A cross-professional perspective. *Teachers College Record*. 111(9): 2055–2100.

Guskey, T. (2002). Professional development and teacher change. *Teachers and Teaching: Theory and Practice*. 8(3): 381–391.

Gutierrez, K. (2008). Developing a sociocritical literacy in the thirdspace. *Reading Research Quarterly*. 43(1): 148–164.

Gutierrez, K., Baquedano-Lopez, P. and Turner, M. (1997). Putting language back into language arts: When the radical middle meets the thirdspace. *Language Arts*. 74(1): 368–378.

Hutchison, A. (2012). Literacy teachers' perceptions of professional development that increases integration of technology into literacy instruction. *Technology, Pedagogy and Education*. 21(1): 37–56.

Ingersoll, R., Merrill, L. and Stuckey, D. (2014). *Seven trends: The transformation of the teaching force* (CPRE Research Report# RR-80). Philadelphia, PA: Consortium for Policy Research in Education.

Knowledge Is Power. (2012). Shark Tank: I Want to Draw a Cat for You. Available at: https://youtu.be/Z3uXGGgOvR0. Downloaded 15 August, 2015.

Kopcha, T. (2010). A systems-based approach to technology integration using mentoring and communities of practice. *Educational Technology Research and Development.* 58(1): 175–190.

Lankshear, C. and Knobel, M. (2011). *New Literacies: Everyday Practices and Social Learning,* 3rd edn. Maidenhead and New York: Open University Press/McGraw-Hill.

Lucas, T., and Grinberg, J. (2008). Responding to the linguistic reality of mainstream classrooms: Preparing all teachers to teach English language learners. *Handbook of Research on Teacher Education: Enduring Questions in Changing Contexts.* 3(1): 606–636.

Lucas, T. and Villegas, A. (2011). A framework for preparing linguistically responsive teachers. In T. Lucas (ed), *Teacher Preparation for the Linguistically Diverse Classrooms.* New York: Routledge, 57–72.

Lucas, T., and Villegas, A. (2013). Preparing linguistically responsive teachers: Laying the foundation in preservice teacher education. *Theory Into Practice.* 52(2): 989–109.

Lucas, T., Villegas, A. and Freedson-Gonzalez, M. (2008). Linguistically responsive teacher education: Preparing classroom teachers to teach English Language Learners. *Journal of Teacher Education.* 59(4): 361–373.

McNeill, K. and Knight, A. (2013). Teachers' pedagogical content knowledge of scientific argumentation: The impact of professional development on K-12 teachers. *Science Education.* 97(6): 936–972.

Moje, E., Ciechanowski, K., Kramer, K., Ellis, L., Carrillo, R., and Collazo, T. (2004). Working toward thirdspace in content area literacy: An examination of everyday funds of knowledge and discourse. *Reading Research Quarterly.* 39(1): 38–70.

Moll, L. (1992). Bilingual classroom studies and community analysis: Some recent trends. *Educational Researcher.* 21(2): 20–24.

Moll, L. and Greenberg, J. (1992). Creating zones of possibilities: Combining social contexts for instruction. In L. Moll (ed), *Vygotsky and Education: Instructional Implications and Applications of Sociohistorical Psychology.* Cambridge, MA: Cambridge University Press, 319–348.

Moll, L., Amanti, C., Neff, D. and Gonzalez, N. (1992). Funds of knowledge for teaching: Using a qualitative approach to connect homes and classrooms. *Theory Into Practice.* 31(2): 132–141.

Plair, S. (2008). Revamping professional development for technology integration and fluency. *Clearing House.* 82(1): 70–74.

Polly, D. and Hannafin, M. (2010). Reexamining technology's role in learner-centered professional development. *Educational Technology Research and Development.* 58(1): 557–571.

Rogers, C. and Freiberg, K. (1994). *Freedom to Learn,* 3rd edn. Upper Saddle River, NJ: Simon and Schuster.

Rogoff, B. (1990). *Apprenticeship in Thinking: Cognitive Development in Social Context.* New York: Oxford University Press.

Rogoff, B., Paradise, R., Mejía, R. and Correa-Chávez, M. (2003). Firsthand learning through participation. *Annual Review of Psychology.* 54(1): 175–203.

Scull, T. and Kupersmidt, J. (2010). An evaluation of a media literacy program training workshop for late elementary school teachers. *Journal of Media Literacy Education.* 2(3): 199–208.

Soja, E. (1989). *Postmodern Geographies: The Reassertion of Space in Critical Social Theory.* New York: Verso.

Soja, E. (1996). *Thirdspace: Journeys to Los Angeles and other real-and-imagined places.* Cambridge, MA: Blackwell.

Stein, M. and Wang, M. (1988). Teacher development and school improvement: The process of teacher change. *Teaching and Teacher Education.* 4(2): 171–187.

Vasquez, V. (2004). *Negotiating Critical Literacies with Young Children.* Mahwah, NJ: Erlbaum.

Vygotsky, L. (1978). *Mind in Society: The Development of Higher Psychological Processes.* Cambridge, MA: Harvard University Press.

Wohlwend, K. (2010). A is for avatar: Young children in literacy 2.0 worlds and literacy 1.0 schools. *Language Arts.* 88(1): 144–151.

Wright, V. (2010). Professional development and the master technology teacher: The evolution of one partnership. *Education.* 131(1): 139–146.

CHAPTER FOUR

Professional Development from THE Inside Out: Redesigning Learning through Collaborative Action Research

HEATHER LOTHERINGTON, STEPHANIE FISHER,
JENNIFER JENSON AND LAURA MAE LINDO

WHAT IS THE PROBLEM?

That the complex clockwork of formal education has not kept up with the unfathomable rate of change in digital communication practices is old news. Modern schooling, rooted in 19th-century industrialization, is intended to run as a tidy assembly-line process where children are batched into classes and grades and processed in a monitored learning environment. Quality control is ensured by top-down regulatory structures. Learning in this paradigm is prescribed in the subject-specific curricular content established a century ago to benefit industrialism (Robinson 2006) and narrated to learners by teachers. The deposited knowledge is then measured quantitatively in examinations. Freire called this "the banking concept of education" (1998: 53).

Education in the province of Ontario is decidedly more flexible than the caricatured model profiled above. At the same time, the fundamentals of banking education are still firmly in place in the modus operandi of everyday teaching where a curriculum is to be "covered" and students prepared for provincially mandated standardized achievement tests. In this world of circumscribed and measurable learning, textual products are modeled: there is a "right way" to write a paragraph, letter, essay... and little place for play, creativity and innovation. Yet creativity and innovation are increasingly indexed as goals of 21st-century learning (Florida 2012; People for Education 2014; Robinson 2006; Sawyer 2006, 2011).

Learning and teaching *are* changing, despite nostalgia for passé educational models. Within the solid walls of schooling, innovation is taking place, and new ways of learning are picking at the seams of traditional education. For instance, in Ontario, recent moves by *Media Smarts* to interpolate the familiar curricular study of (mass) media literacy with (social media) digital literacy constitute a welcome upgrade. But formal education is a complex institution where constituent bodies "connect in non-linear and dynamic ways" (Radford 2006: 177). Change in one part of the networked system will be felt (eventually) in others, but the rate of change is neither constant nor predictable.

Teachers are faced with a conundrum. Learners in Ontario, as in many political jurisdictions around the world, are faced with mandatory standardized assessments at defined points in the grade school hierarchy. Such high-stakes tests form a significant bulwark against innovation, nesting, as Shohamy (2007) pointed out, a hidden curriculum. Inconveniently, school populations are anything but uniform, and their linguistic and cultural diversity creates problematic hurdles in measuring up to rigid passé expectations of homogenous, (majority-language) print-literate students working as independent, individual units (rather than as teams), a stance that ignores literacy as multimodal (Kress 2000, 2010; Kress and Van Leeuwen 2001), second language learning as sociocultural (Lantolf, Thorne and Poehler 2015); and communication as increasingly digitally mediated (Buckingham 2007; Crystal 2001; Lankshear and Knobel 2008; Thurlow, Lengel and Tomic 2004).

In Ontario, the Education Quality and Accountability Office (EQAO) rank orders not only students but also schools according to their students' level of accomplishment of approved learning on provincial tests. Ultimately, the teachers are held to account, deemed to be responsible for student learning and their performance on tests. How do they negotiate the calls to make learning more creative and innovative with professional self-preservation? There is no right way to innovate. Creative pieces are, by definition, not held to previous models. How do they figure out how to develop and institute collaborative, multimodal literacies while "covering" the monitored, jam-packed curriculum and preparing students for examinations so highly valued by their institutions?

Professors in teacher educator programs are publicly grilled as to why teacher candidates are not being adequately prepared for the new information economy. At universities, teacher candidates push back, demanding "training" that will enable them to get a job. Once hired, the teacher is absorbed into the prevailing culture of the school, and all too easily isolated in her or his classroom, boxed in, like the learners, by curricular demands, punitive assessment structures, and professional conformity demanding evidence of approved learning. Collaboration becomes chat over lunch.

That teachers want to optimally enable their learners goes without saying. But they are pinned into an uncomfortable corner: getting and keeping a job within formal institutional structures is at least partially reliant on their ability to perform according to past norms and expectations. Teachers then need to teach students swimming in a sea of communicative changes and using new learning tools for an unpredictable world. Where to start?

The problem, then, is this: "How does the teacher engage in dynamic, exploratory learning and teaching while at the same time, being held to account by rapidly obsolescing curricular requirements and measures?"

The challenges and pressures of teaching towards dynamic multimodal literacies within an educational framework designed on past models, principles and ideals are significant. Learning approaches and aims collide over assessment ideals in particular; for instance, examinations test individual mastery of established content and skills, but exploratory learning emphasizes creativity and collaboration. Examinations limit technological facilitation (e.g., using networked digital devices such as smartphones), but learning in the context of everyday practice is inextricably technologically mediated.

Where is the border between old and new ways of learning and teaching—between established content and innovative exploration? This is not solo work. We are all teaching and learning towards a nebulous and uncertain future in which the old basics have insufficient traction. How do we begin the arduous work of changing the complex educational infrastructure towards workable schooling in the 21st century? This is the story of how one school developed an in-house model of professional development that fundamentally changed how teachers taught and learners learned.

OLD AND NEW BASICS

First, how have the basics changed?

Education, once grounded in the 3Rs of reading, writing and arithmetic, must cope with a tectonic shift in dimensionality from physical space and tools (e.g., pencils) to virtual space and digital tools (e.g., smartphones). Contemporary literacies are enabled by powerful, portable mediating devices that not only connect us to, but, as Seel and Winn (2012) point out, immerse us in virtual environments. These new literacy environments allow us to connect globally; they enable social interaction across cultures and languages, modal complexity, and dynamic, collaborative text construction in addition to the flat-on-the-page alphabetic literacy driving print literacies (Lotherington and Jenson 2011). They affect not only access to knowledge and knowledge construction but also the concept of knowledge itself, which Kalantzis, Cope and Harvey (2003: 16) describe as "highly situated; rapidly changing; and more diverse than ever before." In this learning climate, fact-based banking education is on wobbly ground. So wobbly that Lankshear, Peters and Knobel (2002) query the extent to which education will continue to be concerned with knowledge transmission, the kinds of knowledge that will be important for school learning, and how schools will accommodate new directions in learning.

For over two decades, educators and educational theorists have called attention to the growing importance of digital technology-based competencies for a generation of children for whom majority-language print literacies constitute but a slice of the literate skills required for participation in a globalized, digitally mediated society (Buckingham 2003; Kalantzis and Cope 2000; Kellner 2004; Kress 2003; Lankshear and Knobel 2006; New London Group 1996). At the turn of the century, Carrington (2001: 98) warned:

> This is the literate landscape in which young children are immersed, and as educators we need to recognise and utilise the particular skills and practices that accompany these literacies into our curriculums and pedagogies. It is no longer appropriate or even educationally responsible to privilege print-based linear texts in our classrooms. Increasingly they are but one of a range of mediums in which children need fluency.

In 1939, Harold Benjamin, under the pseudonym J. Abner Peddiwell, wrote a spoof about the slowness of formal education to adapt to contemporary contexts (Peddiwell 1939). The story follows a post-Ice Age culture still teaching the historical truths of the extinct saber-tooth tiger. Educators in 1939, he implied, ran the risk of cultivating a saber-tooth curriculum by teaching literacy skills geared towards obsolescing media. The culture of literacy and the genres and conventions of communicating are evolving symbiotically with new technical devices flooding the public marketplace. These new and inarguably powerful technologies are both absorbed into and shaped by social communication practices. In short, we—as educators—need to identify, understand and teach the competencies needed for the communicative realities and needs of digitally mediated communication, such as knowing how to:

- approach and navigate multiple digital platforms;
- express content appropriately and to optimal expressive effect by choosing and combining different meaning-making modes;
- work in collaborative author partnerships, both online and off;
- learn by doing;
- hybridize and remix purposefully and ethically; and
- multitask (for more on this, see Lotherington and Ronda 2014).

Novel meaning-making possibilities afforded by evolving digital communications media and increasing social diversity were first brought to public attention vis-à-vis schooling by the New London Group (1996), encapsulated in the term "multiliteracies." Digital communications technologies invited the engagement of multiple modalities in the learning process by the incorporation of visual, audio, and tactile sensory engagement, in gestural and spatial communicative dimensions in combination with recognized written and oral language (Cope and Kalantzis 2000, 2009; Kress 2003; New London Group 1996). Researchers have been spurred to examine how multimodal forms of learning and knowing are shaped by the affordances of digital technologies which are, in turn, changing the ways in which we think of knowledge, curriculum and pedagogy (Hull and Nelson 2005; Jewitt 2006; Lotherington 2004, 2011; Mills 2010).

Teachers and teacher candidates are less confident as to what digital literacies comprise, often shrugging the idea off as "new technology" stuff. This is dangerously technologically deterministic. Whereas accessing the appropriate digital technologies for school use is clearly critical to changing educational practice, Granger and colleagues (2002) advised that simply purchasing digital equipment will not change practice or guarantee new learning. Educators have to learn how to use new tools towards new learning. What does that look like?

Lankshear and Knobel (2007: 21) offer a useful clarification of "new literacies":

> The more a literacy practice privileges participation over publishing, distributed expertise over centralized expertise, collective intelligence over individual possessive intelligence, collaboration over individuated authorship, dispersion over scarcity, sharing over ownership, experimentation over "normalization," innovation and evolution over stability and fixity, creative-innovative rule breaking over generic purity and policing, relationship over information broadcast, and so on, the more we should regard it as a "new" literacy.

What then are the learning basics in a climate of new literacies?

Kalantzis and Cope (2012) theorized the shift in communication from the 3Rs notion of literacy as reading and writing (plus numeracy as the third R) towards two "multis" in meaning making: "multicontextual," speaking to situated aspects of communication including social diversity; and "multimodal," speaking to semiotic diversity in communicating meaning. These new basics they track from their mid-90s work in multiliteracies (cf. New London Group 1996).

Another member of the New London Group, Gunther Kress (2003), stressed the importance of "designing" meaning using the affordances of new media, which call on a repertoire of grammars—of language, film, photography, and gesture, for example. Kress drew on the concept of "mode" in delineating the multimodal meaning-making potential accommodated in digital literacies, and provided an explanation grounded in social semiotics that is commonly referenced in discussions of multimodal literacies:

> *Mode* is a socially shaped and culturally given resource for making meaning. *Image, writing, layout, music, gesture, speech, moving image, soundtrack* are examples of modes used in representation and communication. (Kress 2009: 54; original emphases)

The idea of making meaning using varied semiotic resources is intuitively attractive, but coming to grips with "modality" for purposes of analysis is tricky. These examples of mode are not easily distinguished; they overlap, and they require cultural agreement for identification. This makes analysis of multimodality slippery.

Marcus (2009: 1933) took a design perspective on emerging media literacies, theorizing two (now mostly missing) pieces that are central to children's basic education today. They represent different kinds and qualities of thinking skills, and both represent fundamentals to build on with increasing sophistication attained as more media are added and practice increases familiarity—just like the alphabet eventually grows into reading and numbers eventually become arithmetic.

Kress points out that "communication is always and inevitably multimodal" (2005: 5). The potential for multimodality is greatly expanded with digital media, which are "mashable": they facilitate the combination and integration of data from different sources. Marcus suggests that using, creating and sharing ideas using digital media requires a digital lexicon. The pattern language basic to a digital lexicon is captured by a new symbol set: "the sensory alphabet" (Marcus 2009: 1934), which indexes "line, color, texture, movement, sound, rhythm, space, light, shape" (Marcus 2009: 1934). The sensory alphabet provides a helpful design focus on multimodal meaning making. However, the elemental linguistic component of alphabetic text is not accorded a place in this paradigm. Neither is language, nor the complexity of multiple languages facing culturally diverse classes today—an elemental "multi" according to Kalantzis and Cope (2012).

In updating the concept of "communicative competence" (Canale 1983; Canale and Swain 1980), which has guided second- and foreign-language teaching relatively uncritically for decades, Lotherington and Ronda (2014) proposed a revised framework of communicative competence 2.0, based on fundamental changes in the media of communication through which we communicate interactively and multimodally. Based on Elleström's (2010) intermediality paradigm, in which media are categorized as basic (defined by four modal properties: material, sensorial, spatio-temporal, semiotic), qualified, and technical, they proposed: "multimedia competency" (enfolding and enlarging on grammatical competence); "collaborative communication" (expanding on sociolinguistic competence); "agentive participation" (building from strategic competence); and "multitasking" (assuming discourse competence in complex relief). Communicative competence 2.0 described practical gear shifting: lifting alphabetic print from the page and recombining it with visual and auditory semiotic resources. The complex possibilities in multimodal text production invite immeasurably more creativity and innovation than fixed models of alphabetic print.

Learning—in innovative educational milieux engaged in learner-centred and discovery-oriented learning designs, such as project-based, game-based and "maker" approaches to learning—is being increasingly conceptualized not in opposition to play, but as a kind of play. Gerri Sinclair (2010), whose digital media portfolio includes academic as well as entrepreneurial and corporate leadership, conceptualized learners as knowledge makers, information as recombinant, and contemporary education as fundamentally requiring digital play. Her revision of the 3Rs basics encapsulated 4Rs for digital learning that are fundamentally ludic and collaborative, viz., "reuse" (backup), "revise" (adapt), "remix" (combine), and "redistribute" (share). Arguing that "the classical connection between 'learning' and 'playing' is long overdue" (de Castell and Jenson 2003: 658), de Castell (2011) made the case for "ludic epistemologies," asking what knowledge looks like when it is translated into the form of a game and learning into the form of play.

There are commonalities in these kaleidoscopic takes on new basics in literacy and learning: "collaboration" and "multimodality" figure centrally, for instance. Inherent in digital designs is the element of "creativity," which Florida (2012) pinpointed as the underlying motivating force of manifest social change, normally attributed to the integration of new technologies, access to a shared internet, and globalization. Sawyer (2011) noted that schools in the West and the East alike have a record of being inhospitable to creativity, associating it with unruliness, which is anathema to standardized convergent thinking. He reported teachers having limited ideas about creativity, associating it with the humanities and liberal arts and with gifted students. Creative thinking, however, relates to different fields of thought and to all children.

Sawyer contrasted controlled and obedient thinking with "the extreme creativity of children's play" (2011: 389), leading to divergent thinking. Robinson (2006) challenged us to rethink the principles on which we educate children, delineating intelligence as divergent, dynamic and distinct, qualities that are not encouraged in a climate of standardized and measured learning. de Castell and Jenson (2003: 663) comment:

> The cultural environment of schools today is, in many ways, antithetical to the immersiveness of play—it insists on timed activities (no room for "losing track" of time by being absorbed in reading a book or solving a mathematics problem); curriculum is designed

mostly to "survey" a subject area, with little opportunity to study one or two subjects in depth; and goals and immediate feedback (both punishment and rewards) are often held back from students in institutionally sanctioned power struggles between students and teachers.

This chapter describes how a research-focused learning community at Joyce Public School in northwest Toronto developed a situated, collaborative professional development model for the purposes of creating new pedagogies consistent with 21st-century realities—a model of professional development that took shape from the inside out.

THE STORY SO FAR: INCORPORATION OF DIGITAL TECHNOLOGIES AND PRACTICES IN PROFESSIONAL DEVELOPMENT

Henry Jenkins (2009) argued that schools need to prepare students for responsible citizenship in a digitally mediated, and rapidly globalizing society. Though some teachers are riding the exhilarating crest of new thinking, many, if not most, are uneasy, admitting to being ill prepared for the current generation of students. Familiar tried-and-true teacher-centered pedagogical practices that focused on well-trodden notions of print-based literacy, and indeed literature, are inadequate preparation for the exploratory, student-centered, constructivist learning facilitated by digital tools that encourage collaborative and creative thinking and enable innovative multimodal textual products.

Teacher competence is a concern at practice levels, as well as at policy levels globally. Teacher professional development that fundamentally incorporates new digital tools and pedagogies for multimodal learning is sorely needed in-service as well as pre-service. At the level of instructional practice, the integration of 21st-century skills, new digital technologies and learning has not been addressed in a systematic way in either teacher education or professional development, enabling the ongoing under-use of digital technologies in schools. In a survey of teacher readiness for the digital age undertaken at the turn of the 21st century, Moursund and Beilefeldt (1999) found that 71 per cent of teacher education programs did not offer adequate instruction into how information and communications technologies could support learning. Moreover, pre-service teachers rarely worked collaboratively with teachers or supervisors in developing digitally mediated instruction during field placement.

Research suggests that a decade and a half on from Moursund and Beilefeldt's report, it is still the case that few teacher education programs offer anything more than cursory and superficial education for and in digital tools and technology-enhanced learning (Hall 2006; Johnson and Maddux 2008; Lambert and Gong 2010; Thieman 2008; Whale 2006). Speaking to the American context, Lambert and Gong (2010: 55) pointed out: "the stand-alone educational technology course still serves as the primary means of pre-service teacher preparation in technology." These studies addressed the perceived ongoing disconnect between the needs and expectations of 21st-century learners, for whom digital technologies are increasingly ubiquitous, and the inadequate preparation of pre-service teachers to use digital technologies in meaningful ways. Moreover, where there is intensive, deliberate and sustained pre-service education on technology-enhanced learning, the focus is on using digital tools for instructional practice, not facilitating multimodal learning (Hall 2010; Lambert and Gong 2010; Thieman 2008).

That said, as Fragkouli and Hammond (2007) and Hammond and colleagues (2009) report, even educators who are well prepared by their pre-service education face significant barriers to integrating new technologies into their teaching (e.g., curricular constraints, lack of technical support, preparation time, and access to technologies). Speaking to the American context, a high percentage of school districts (81%) do not evaluate teachers' knowledge of digital technologies, and where such evaluations are in place, expectations are often vague and indistinct (Whale 2006). Furthermore, the majority of in-service, digital technology-oriented professional development programs are narrowly focused on honing instructional practice in particular subjects or introducing teachers to digital tools to use in their classrooms and do not provide teachers with a holistic vision of digitally mediated learning that stretches across the curriculum.

Despite a global push for education systems to adopt 21st-century learning models that support the development of digital competencies, the majority of teachers are unprepared to integrate digital tools into their classrooms in ways that are pedagogically effective or sustainable. Professional development opportunities are sometimes limited and often poorly designed and executed, further compounding the issue. One-day workshops that are more demonstrative instead of hands on, for example, cannot and do not provide ongoing support for teachers when they (arguably) need it the most—that is, when making practical and well-informed curricular connections. Teachers who are not tech savvy or feel unsupported when integrating digital tools can become overwhelmed and easily discouraged when something goes awry, and they are unsure of the value of what they are doing. Add to this a lack of supervision and assessment of teachers' implementation of technology-enhanced learning in the classroom and you have a recipe for spotty uptake, at best. Given the significant international attention and concern related to teachers' use of technology to prepare students for a digitally mediated future (Jenson, Taylor and Fisher 2010), it is imperative to develop and share models for professional development that support and scaffold teachers in their shift towards a 21st-century educational paradigm where the use of digital tools is synonymous with learning.

OUR STORY: PROFESSIONAL DEVELOPMENT FROM THE INSIDE OUT

Schools are finding flexibility, even those within staid government jurisdictions where political responses dictate learning outcomes. They are doing this by reinventing themselves, by rethinking the roles of teachers and learners, and experimenting with new ways of learning in an environment of security and trust. But this environment must be developed.

Our learning community at Joyce Public School was created to develop multimodal pedagogical designs that were culturally inclusive and digitally exploratory and playful. In so doing it became a teacher-researcher think tank: a sustained in-service professional development workshop espousing collaborative, dialogic learning, ludic design principles, and innovative pedagogical exploration. Our starting point was a half-decade before the slice of research we report on here, when the principal approved a small interventionist study over a shared frustration with the mismatch in old and new literacies, narrowly focused pedagogical expectations and multimodal social realities, monolingual pedagogical designs and multilingual classrooms (for details see Lotherington 2011).

Our learning community initially took shape in volunteer after-school meetings, which gathered momentum as we learned how to collaborate. From fumbling beginnings as we attempted to link theory and practice we worked towards more democratic sharing, breaking down established hierarchical expectations, which were inimical to collaborative learning (for details see Lotherington 2011). Developing a forum for dialogical learning took time and patience. Participating teachers expected to be told what to do and to have expected output specified; researchers wanted to infuse theory into classroom practice and to learn from it. After a teacher suggested we follow a regular meeting agenda of *learning, planning* and *sharing*, we started to speak each other's administrative language.

With research funding, we took up the principal's brave idea to make our collaborative planning a regular feature of her school and moved our fledgling learning community into the timetabled school day. With practice, we developed mechanisms for opening up, discussing, and tackling challenges and issues in classroom learning while at the same time creating spaces for exploration and experimentation. En route, we learned a great deal about how to plan, institute, troubleshoot and share focused, complex classroom interventions (Lotherington 2011; Lotherington, Paige and Spencer-Holland 2013). These interventions constituted the basis of our homegrown in-house professional development.

We began with tenets common to communities of practice (Wenger, McDermott and Snyder 2002): a shared interest, which was to update literacy pedagogy to be more inclusive of children's cultural and linguistic knowledge and digital media practices; a domain of knowledge, which, in our case, was elementary education, and specifically emergent and early literacy; and a professional community of informed, interested and involved teachers, graduate students and researchers. We met locally in the school during school hours at regular intervals and made plans that used available resources (supplemented by modest research funds), as opposed to resources demonstrated in off-campus professional workshops that might not be within the means of the school. Our knowledge was in many ways complementary: teachers were seasoned practitioners; researchers were steeped in theory; graduate students contributed insights from their vantage points as critical learners and administrators from a wide-angled managerial perspective. Learning was designed to be dialogic (Bakhtin 1975, 1981): mutually respected and shared. Our sessions studiously avoided top-down training; spaces for demonstrations developed organically and rhythmically in our shared domain as trust in our progress grew. There were, of course, inevitable hiccups.

The collaborative action research framework created a space for teachers during school time to think, work and act together to address the larger sociocultural issues affecting students and the school community through long-term interventionist multimodal projects in the classroom. These projects used a variety of digital tools and media such as digital-still and video cameras, voice recorders, photo and video editing, desktop publishing and presentation software, digital games and more. Each project facilitated a ludic learning experience that engaged digital play and included the languages of the children (and teachers) in each class by forging spaces for bilingual, multilingual and plurilingual inclusion in multimodal textual products (Lotherington 2011, 2013). Assessment required parental involvement, which handily included local languages. As our learning community developed into a feature of the regular school calendar, the thematic learning objective encompassed larger and larger groups of teachers, until several classes and grades were working towards the development of umbrella themes, such as *respect*, often across grades.

What sets this work apart from other research on teacher professional development is that it was framed and driven by a research agenda to create opportunities for students to showcase their learning multimodally. At Joyce Public School, the teachers did not learn how to use digital tools in a context that was divorced from the everyday lived realities they faced in their classrooms. Professional development did not focus on learning skills or even how to instruct differently using new technologies but rather on supporting students tackling annual, complex, community-based projects. The acquisition of digital literacies was incidental to the larger problem of curriculum development, knowledge formation and explication. The digital tools used were within reach of public schools in this province. Furthermore, digital tools and the texts they facilitated tapped children's social knowledge and expertise, often in unexpected ways. Once children were reassured their social knowledge of media was valuable in the school setting, they actively contributed ideas.

The use of technology-enhanced learning in the classroom was particularly pertinent for this school, where English is a second language for over two-thirds of the students. The focus on digitally mediated communication in these classrooms facilitated the creation of novel multimodal spaces for customized texts featuring the languages of each child's knowledge and needs (see Lotherington 2011, 2013) and, as such, functioned to a degree as a safeguard to ensure that no student was disadvantaged due to his or her unstable and developing understanding of English. The multimodal nature of projects opened myriad spaces for the inclusion of home languages, which strengthened ties between the school and community, naturalized the multilingual nature of the classroom, and aided the children in learning English, which was paired with other languages they understood, all of which further highlighted the importance of integrating facilitating technologies into classroom teaching practices (Jenson, Fisher and Lotherington 2010). Finally, because we were working in an area of Toronto populated by newly arrived immigrant families, the school became a location where students accessed digital tools that they may not have had at home, demonstrating that schools can be an equalizing force between "have" and "have not" students, but only if students are using them in everyday classroom practices (as proposed by Jenkins 2009).

A true strength of our grassroots professional development model was that skills acquisition (for both students and teachers) was not the focus. The projects in this study were consistently successful because they were intentionally designed to serve a greater purpose than simply getting digital tools into the classroom. Each classroom project was framed by a collaborative agenda, conceptualized to address curricular aims, multimodal literacies development, and community language knowledge, and this problem-solving agenda was a highly motivating rationale for exploring facilitating digital tools. Because they were driven by a passion to facilitate fundamental change to learning design through multimodal projects, the focus remained on fostering meaningful student learning and understanding of the core issues that each individual project was designed to address. As a result, teachers considered the applications of various tools in these projects more critically. In other words, the teachers at Joyce Public School were primarily concerned with the very thing that most professional development opportunities do not have the time or resources to adequately address: using digital mediation to facilitate students' learning. As teacher participant Brian explains:

I think people started to realize: let's define what we need to teach the kids or what we even would like to discover and then whatever technology we use that will be part of the process. So I think just switching those two ideas—choosing the process and defining what it is—was very important because people became more relaxed and the project became more meaningful. And they were able to space a timeline that wasn't based on learning a technology or teaching a technology to the kids. It had a mandate of this is what we wanted to learn, and we would along the way learn which technology would best serve that.

Couching professional development within classroom-based project creation also forced teachers to deal with the everyday challenges they inevitably faced as they continued to experiment with and integrate new digital tools into their practice. In the case of more experienced teachers, facing problems within the everyday classroom context was essential in shifting from outdated teaching philosophies. Researchers such as Sawyer (2006) have argued that 21st-century teaching and learning should be based on a constructivist model where the teacher is positioned as a facilitator, not the gatekeeper of knowledge. Under this model, students actively and collectively engage in knowledge-building activities, which are followed by reflection and discussion about what they are doing, and, importantly, how their understanding is changing.

Though typical professional development programs underline the shift from transmission to constructivist teaching in pedagogical practices for 21st-century learning, rarely do they sustainably support teachers who are trying to implement novel, constructivist pedagogies in their classrooms. This support was built into our situated professional development: the teachers in our study offered and received continuous, multidimensional critical and creative support from the members of the learning community.

Learning with digital technologies mitigates classroom power relations because digital competencies can privilege learners' knowledge. Knowledge and learning in this case are distributed, with the learner taking on more agency and authority than is normally expected (or allowed) in the public school classroom. The potential displacement of teachers from their traditional position of authority into a position where they are co-learner or facilitator is an important paradigm shift; it is also a challenging situation for inexperienced teachers who fear that they might lose control of the class. Because most teachers have been taught (and continue to learn) to position themselves as the ultimate authority in the classroom, it can be uncomfortable adjusting to having students self-direct their learning and learn with technologies that teachers are unsure of using themselves. In contrast, without ongoing support or encouragement to make this pedagogical change, teachers might not know how to take advantage of what new technologies can afford in terms of new horizons in learning and achievement.

AN EXAMPLE: *THE WINDOW WOMAN*

The Window Woman is an inspiring example of a boldly experimental class project. Special education teacher Rhea bravely put into action Sawyer's (2006: 41) advice to structure education "around disciplined improvisation, and … situated, collaborative knowledge-building activities." Rhea was troubled by students in her split-grade 4/5 special education class who she saw manifesting sexist and xenophobic views when discussing ongoing international conflicts, particularly in the Middle East. She decided to address these biases in a multimedia project, which she developed with educational assistant Brian and graduate education student Steph Fisher based on the chapter book *The Breadwinner* (Ellis 2001), which is a story about a young Afghani girl's bravery in overcoming political misogyny. Here is Rhea's description of the adventurous narrative twist they gave the story in the class project:

> *The Breadwinner* was an attempt to read a book about a girl in Afghanistan. The breadwinner [her father] was in jail when the Taliban came, and she's forced to become the breadwinner, to go out and work as a boy. There's a scene where she's in the market, there's a woman who looks out and sees her, and seems to know who she is. We don't know if it's a former teacher or some person from her past, or just some person. And we use that character to formulate another story, which was really interesting for us. We had a whole backstory, with a wedding in it. So basically we did an Oprah Winfrey show about this character's past. We made up this story—there's not much there so we made up who she was—what she does… and we created this story about her. It was quite the experience.

Brian explains how the technology they used fit in:

> We were reading a novel with the kids in terms of social justice. Then we began to think of having a project, and thought let's integrate the two. And, you know at first, we didn't know what technology we were going to use—maybe a drawing application on the computer using Comic Life—some kind of way to convey or retell of the story. But as we went on, the kids began to enjoy, really dive right into the story. They were excited about it. So from [this] excitement we were able to actually expand the project. So, regardless of the limited amount of time, and little limited knowledge that we may have had for any given technology, be it video or animation, we weren't concerned about that because the kids' excitement, they gravitated towards it, so naturally we wanted to learn the technology to teach them.

The students in Rhea's class read, wrote, directed, filmed and produced a fictional autobiographical movie called *The Window Woman*, based on a female character who enigmatically appears in *The Breadwinner*. The project is in the vein of Tom Stoppard's absurdist play, *Rosencrantz and Guildenstern Are Dead*, written about two bit-part characters in the Shakespearean play *Hamlet*, who are poorly developed in the original narrative. The children created a fictional backstory for the window woman to demonstrate their understanding not only of the narrative but also of the daily lives of women living in Afghanistan—a country far away from local geographic and social realities that was consistently reported on in the news.

To accomplish their curricular and technical goals, Rhea had to learn basic filming and video editing skills so she could teach and provide technical support to her students. She also learned how to facilitate students' understanding by relinquishing her control over the classroom and letting her students direct their own project. As an experienced teacher who was used to always having a plan and who was a self-proclaimed technophobe, this was in fact a steep adjustment. Often, she admitted to "freaking out" because she did not know how the project was going to turn out, at least in terms of having a final product that would showcase students' understandings.

Reorienting her teaching philosophy from a banking to a constructivist model is best demonstrated in the non-technological aspects of Rhea's project, in particular regarding the writing of the script. It would have been all too easy to simply dictate to students (all of whom were diagnosed with specific learning challenges) what to write in their scripts or even write the script herself. Instead she allowed students to work collaboratively, discuss their ideas and make decisions as a class, even though this comprised a longer process. As such, the script is truly a reflection of the students' understanding of how Afghan women live. Rhea passed the power and authority for writing choices to her students, and the resulting movie was a hit! The process left Rhea (and all learning community participants) utterly astounded by what her special education students could accomplish when she tasked them with producing a digital multimedia project and became a guide to their learning—not the director of the final product (see Figure 4.1).

Figure 4.1: Screen capture of the student film *The Window Woman.*

The point is this: when the driving purpose for technology-related professional development is exploratory learning rather than skill development, teachers are motivated to integrate new technologies into their classrooms in creative ways that nurture student understanding and learning. Rhea, for instance, did not try to design her project around a particular device or program because she knew how to use it; she identified an issue that she wanted to tackle, considered the technological support that would facilitate her goals, and then set out to learn to use the technological resources herself so she could support her students. The same can be said about Rhea's holistic approach to learning that was not focused on a specific grammatical skill or a static historical and geographical record but on the retelling of a human event in language/s and media that made contextual sense.

Internally motivated professional development towards new learning is demanding in the responsibility it asks of busy teachers, and it can be overwhelming for teachers who struggle to accomplish day-to-day tasks, let alone find time for radically new professional learning. Teachers must be well supported in making curricular connections when integrating new technologies into classroom practices, especially given inevitable challenges to established teaching philosophy. Our model for situated, collaborative, project-driven professional development was highly successful because ongoing support to teachers was woven into the school day.

REVISING EDUCATIONAL INFRASTRUCTURE TO INCLUDE IN-HOUSE PROFESSIONAL DEVELOPMENT

We offer, in conclusion, our response to the problem: "How does the teacher engage in dynamic, exploratory learning and teaching while being held accountable to rapidly obsolescing curricular requirements and measures?"

Developing a model of professional development was, in fact, a fortuitous by-product of our university-teacher action research project to develop pedagogies for multimodal literacies. The learning community developed organically as a framework for professional development towards innovative collaborative learning; it also contributed to building a culture of innovation in the school. Here, in a nutshell, is what we learned about building professional development from the inside out.

1. Learn together.

   a. The work we did was fundamentally collaborative from start to finish. We discovered that when working alone teachers often got lost or waylaid and became frustrated and discouraged, so they were required to work in teams. *Everyone at school learned from each other in varying pair, group, and class configurations.* Being part of a group provides a supportive, community environment for learning and carves out a safe space for teachers to share ideas, successes, problems, and anxieties, which the one-off professional development session cannot offer.

b. The establishment of regular democratic sharing sessions needs to be scaffolded: this is learned behaviour, not spontaneous combustion. Teachers were encouraged to pursue their particular interests and share their knowledge, which facilitated *distributed learning.* The teaching team who developed *The Window Woman,* for instance, paired Rhea, a teacher with 20 years of teaching experience who was not confident with digital technologies, with Brian, a young teacher who had been in the classroom for less than five years but who was very tech savvy.

2. Learn at home.

a. There must be a school vision for learning on multiple fronts as a regular feature of the school day. *This requires strong and trusting leadership* that provides the motivation and support for teachers to undertake difficult work and communicates its value and importance internally and externally. As Andrew, a Grade 5 teacher at Joyce Public School, put it: "if the administrator is not willing and able and enthusiastic, it will not happen."

b. Teachers learning together require detailed collaborative planning. To be valued, this *collaboration must be timetabled as regular sharing time during school hours.* Teachers at Joyce Public School used pooled prep time in addition to our funded workshops that paid for substitute teachers. We came together once a month for a morning (about 2.5 hours in total). Sometimes teachers had to come and go during workshops, but there was a concerted effort to share in collaborative discussion.

c. Learning at home means *using the affordances of the school and community.* The research grant we obtained funded small technical purchases, but researchers foregrounded the realities of doing multimedia projects in underfunded public schools and encouraged use of school-owned hardware (which was by no means new or cutting edge) and school board-licensed software. In this way, we could demonstrate to other public schools that they, too, could run similar projects. Furthermore, *using existing equipment helped to shift the focus from fancy hardware and software to the pedagogy behind its use*: how technological mediation was to be used, which is an extremely valuable lesson. Too often, superficial flash and dazzle effects are applied to technology-based projects that detract from what was actually learned by both students and teachers. Thus when it comes to highlighting the value of technology-driven multimodal learning projects, not having access to the latest equipment is not such a bad thing.

d. In our particular case, where we were working with children speaking multiple languages of different cultural origins, we *strategically welcomed parental and community members'* cultural and linguistic contributions in school-based learning. Parents who entered the school with trepidation because it meant trying to find the English words, feeling underprepared for education in this new country, were glad to contribute their linguistic knowledge. Whether community members had the exact Korean or Yoruba translation for children's work was not our concern; whether they were willing to contribute another way of saying or writing to children's work that led to greater awareness and learning was.

3. Remix the curriculum.

a. McLuhan (1965: 347), an early critic of separating subjects in school, remarked 50 years ago: "in education, the conventional division of the curriculum into subjects is already as outdated as the medieval trivium and quadrivium after the Renaissance." Project-based learning that harnesses learning across the curriculum is, thus, not a new idea. Our learning community co-learned and team-taught projects across subjects, grades, and ages that incorporated complex curricular aims and involved librarians and specialist teachers of music or French alongside grade generalists. Their carefully planned *across-the-curriculum (and into-the-community) projects* inspired investigative and distributed learning.

4. Failure is essential to learning.

a. Robinson (2006) points out that *failure is essential to creative production.* Exploratory learning cannot be neatly calculated. Part of our exploration was learning to revise notions of failure as not only non-fatal but as a vital element in learning. This thinking is antithetical to ideals of standardized learning and achievement where a measurable threshold level must be achieved to indicate satisfactory attainment or progress.

b. We lost a few teachers along the way who felt that they somehow "didn't get it." But this was not a pass-fail deal; most of the time progress was a matter of two steps ahead and one back. Just hanging in there, rebooting, and trying it all out again—as gamers do—was the way forward.

We needed room to experiment and tolerance for failure, given that not all experiments work, and certainly not at first. An essential skill we learned was to *cultivate resilience*.

5. Play to learn.

   a. A guiding principle of our project was a focus on learning as play. Being participants in a sustained, collaborative learning community geared to internal professional development was a learning adventure. Teachers were positioned as learners and as researchers, invited to question the status quo and to try out new pedagogies that employed digital communication tools and created novel textual products. As they gained confidence in what their learners could do, they stopped worrying whether the outcome of complex projects would be picture perfect or what they imagined them to be and stopped doubting themselves so much. *Teachers developed a sense of experimentation and gave their learners agency to play and to discover.* As they did, the spectre of provincial examinations lost volume. When the numbers were crunched, the children had dramatically improved on test scores. Far more importantly for our aims, the children voiced their enjoyment of and enthusiasm for class projects.

6. Be self-reliant.

   a. University partnerships have the means to address the lack of ongoing support and feedback for integrating technology into the classroom, which is a barrier to effective professional development. But what happens when the university-school partnership ends? While one-off grants can provide schools with the latest cutting-edge technologies, we did not do that. Seeding a self-sustaining professional learning community that continued beyond the university partnership was important, so project expenditures, including for graduate student assistance, were carefully thought out with *capacity building* in mind.

   b. Sometimes our learning community needed or wanted to learn things no one had expertise in, so *we drew on specialists*. A number of professionals as well as international visitors came to the school; we also invited specialists. People were generous and helpful, given our means and ends, and our learning community benefited from Ministry of Education consultants, film-makers, musicians, teachers in other schools, and international guests.

Our learning community redesigned school learning over time and below the political radar. We immersed ourselves in exploratory learning that was cumulative even though a perennially bumpy ride. But our response to the thorny question of teachers' need to learn and teach in new ways without being stalled by regressive structural assessments was also a moment in time when a school with an extraordinary principal invited curious researchers and inspired a group of teachers to come together to highly profitable ends.

Unfortunately, our original learning community was derailed after the principal retired and the initial grant finished. We had worked hand in glove with the principal to envision and develop our learning community. She had firmly believed in teachers owning their learning. When she retired, the incoming principal reinstated a climate of control and direct individual reporting, and the learning community was deeply affected. Many teachers left the school for other positions. But they took with them the know-how of implementing project-based learning, team teaching, community knowledge inclusion, and play-based designs and expressed their interest in developing learning communities in other schools for project-based collaborative learning.

Our model of in-house professional development remains a work in progress; we continue to attend to our principles: learn together, learn at home, remix the curriculum, build resilience to failure, play to learn, and be self-reliant. Will our model be transferable to other contexts? This we turn over to you.

REFERENCES

Bakhtin, M. (1981). Discourse in the novel. (C. Emerson and M. Holquist, Trans.). In M. Holquist (ed), *The Dialogic Imagination: Four Essays by M.M. Bakhtin*. Austin: University of Texas Press, 257–422. (Original work published 1975.)

Buckingham, D. (2003). *Media Education: Literacy, Learning and Contemporary Culture*. Cambridge: Polity Press.

Buckingham, D. (2007). Digital media literacies: Rethinking media education in the age of the Internet. *Research in Comparative and International Education*. 2(1), 43–55.

Canale, M. (1983). From communicative competence to communicative language pedagogy. In J. Richards and R. Schmitt (eds), *Language and Communication*. London: Longman, 2–27.

Canale, M. and Swain, M. (1980). Theoretical bases of communicative approaches to second language teaching and testing. *Applied Linguistics*. 1(1): 1–47.

Carrington, V. (2001). Emergent home literacies: A challenge for educators. *The Australian Journal of Language and Literacy*. 24(2): 88–100.

Cope, B. and Kalantzis, M. (2000). Multiliteracies: The beginnings of an idea. In B. Cope and M. Kalantzis (eds), *Multiliteracies: Literacy Learning and the Design of Social Futures*. Abingdon, UK: Routledge, 3–8.

Cope, B. and Kalantzis, M. (2009). Multiliteracies: New literacies, new learning. *Pedagogies: An International Journal*. 4(3): 164–195.

Crystal, D. (2001). *Language and the Internet.* Cambridge, UK: Cambridge University Press.

de Castell, S. (2011). Ludic epistemology: What game-based learning can teach curriculum studies. *Journal of the Canadian Association for Curriculum Studies.* 8(2): 19–27.

de Castell, S. and Jenson, J. (2003). Serious play. *Journal of Curriculum Studies.* 35(6): 649–665.

Ellis, D. (2001). *The Breadwinner.* Berkeley, CA: Groundwood Books.

Fisher, S., Jenson, J., Lindo, L.M. and Lotherington, H. (2011). Thinking through design: Indirect professional development. In M. Koehler and P. Mishra (eds), *Proceedings of Society for Information Technology and Teacher Education International Conference 2011.* Chesapeake, VA: AACE, 2439–2444.

Florida, R. (2012). *The Rise of the Creative Class, Revisited.* (Books 24x7 version). Online. Available at: http://common.books24x7.com.ezproxy.library.yorku.ca/toc.aspx?bookid=49938. Downloaded 2 March, 2015.

Fragkouli, E. and Hammond, M. (2007). Issues in developing programmes to support teachers of philology in using information and communications technologies in Greek schools: A case study. *Professional Development in Education.* 33(4): 463–477.

Freire, P. (1998). *Pedagogy of the Oppressed* (New revised 20th anniversary edn, M. Ramos, Trans.). New York: Continuum. (Original work published 1970).

Granger, C., Morbey, M., Lotherington, H., Owston, R. and Wideman, H. (2002). Factors contributing to teachers' successful implementation of IT. *Journal of Computer Assisted Learning.* 18(1): 480–488.

Hammond, M., Fragkouli, E., Suandi, I., Crosson, S., Ingram, J., Johnston Wilder, P., Johnston Wilder, S., Kingston, Y., Pope, M. and Wray, D. (2009). What happens as student teachers who made very good use of ICT during pre-service training enter their first year of teaching? *Teacher Development.* 13(2): 93–106.

Hull, G. and Nelson, M. (2005). Locating the semiotic power of multimodality. *Written Communication.* 22(2): 224–261.

Jenkins, H. (2009). *Confronting the Challenges of Participatory Culture: Media Education for the 21st Century.* Cambridge, MA: MIT Press.

Jenson, J., Fisher, S. and Lotherington, H. (2010, July). *Transcending the rigidity of bricks and mortar schooling: Ludic approaches to socially-responsive multimodal projects at elementary school.* Paper presented at Multimodality and Learning Environments: Rhetoric, Recognition, Play and Methods, Institute of Education, University of London, UK.

Jenson, J., Taylor, N. and Fisher, S. (2010). *Critical Review and Analysis of the Issue of "Skills, Technology and Learning."* Ontario Ministry of Education, Research Sector. Available: http://www.edu.gov.on.ca/eng/research/JensonReportEng.pdf. Downloaded 22 February, 2015.

Jewitt, C. (2006). *Technology, Literacy and Learning: A Multimodal Approach.* Abingdon, UK: Routledge.

Johnson, D. and Maddux, C. (2008). Introduction: Effectiveness of information technology in education. *Computers in the Schools.* 24(3): 1–6.

Kalantzis, M. and Cope, B. (2012). *Literacies.* Port Melbourne, VIC: Cambridge University Press.

Kalantzis, M., Cope, B. and Harvey, A. (2003). Assessing multiliteracies and the new basics. *Assessment in Education: Principles, Policy and Practice.* 10(1), 15–26.

Kellner, D. (2004). Technological revolution, multiple literacies and the re-visioning of education. *E-Learning.* 1(1): 9–37.

Kress, G. (2000). Multimodality. In B. Cope and M. Kalantzis (eds), *Multiliteracies: Literacy Learning and the Design of Social Futures.* Abingdon, UK: Routledge, 182–202.

Kress, G. (2003). *Literacy in the New Media Age*. London, UK: Routledge.

Kress, G. (2005). Gains and losses: New forms of texts, knowledge and learning. *Computers and Composition*. 22(1): 5–22.

Kress, G. (2009). What is a mode? In C. Jewitt (ed), *The Routledge Handbook of Multimodal Analysis*. Abingdon, UK: Routledge, 54–67.

Kress, G. (2010). *Multimodality: A Social Semiotic Approach to Contemporary Communication*. Abingdon, UK: Routledge.

Kress, G. and Van Leeuwen, T. (2001). *Multimodal Discourse*. London, UK: Arnold.

Lambert, J. and Cuper, P. (2008). Multimedia technologies and familiar spaces: 21st century teaching for 21st century learners. *Contemporary Issues in Technology and Teacher Education*. 8(3): 264–276.

Lambert, J. and Gong, Y. (2010). 21st century paradigms for pre-service teacher technology preparation. *Computers in the Schools*. 27(1): 54–70.

Lankshear, C. and Knobel, M. (2006). *New Literacies: Everyday Practices and Classroom Learning*. Maidenhead, UK: McGraw Hill/Open University Press.

Lankshear, C. and Knobel, M. (2007). Sampling "the new" in new literacies. In M. Knobel and C. Lankshear (eds), *A New Literacies Sampler*. New York: Peter Lang, 1–24.

Lankshear, C. and Knobel, M. (eds) (2008). *Digital Literacies: Concepts, Policies and Practices*. New York: Peter Lang.

Lankshear, C., Peters, M. and Knobel, M. (2002). Information, knowledge and learning. In M. Lea and K. Nicoll (eds), *Distributed Learning: Social and Cultural Approaches to Practice*. Abingdon, UK: Routledge Falmer, 16–37.

Lantolf, J., Thorne, S. and Poehner, M. (2015). Sociocultural theory and second language development. In B. VanPatten and J. Williams (eds), *Theories in Second Language Acquisition: An Introduction*. New York: Routledge, 207–226.

Lotherington, H. (2004). Emergent metaliteracies: What the Xbox has to offer the EQAO. *Linguistics and Education*. 14(3–4): 305–319.

Lotherington, H. (2011). *Pedagogy of Multiliteracies: Rewriting Goldilocks*. New York: Routledge.

Lotherington, H. and Jenson, J. (2011). Teaching multimodal and digital literacy in L2 settings: New literacies, new basics, new pedagogies. *Annual Review of Applied Linguistics*. 31(1): 226–246.

Lotherington, H. and Ronda, N. (2014). 2B or not 2B: From pencil to multimodal programming: New frontiers in communicative competencies. In J. Pettes Guikema and L. Williams (eds), *Digital Literacies in Foreign and Second Language Education*. San Marcos, TX: Calico Monograph Series, 9–28.

Lotherington, H., Paige, C. and Holland-Spencer, M. (2013). *Using a Professional Learning Community to Support Multimodal Literacies*. In the series: What Works? Research into Practice. Research monograph #46. Toronto: Literacy and Numeracy Secretariat. Available: http://www.edu.gov.on.ca/eng/literacynumeracy/inspire/research/WW_Professional_Learning.pdf Downloaded 6 January, 2015.

Marcus, S. (2009). New basics for new literacies. *Journal of the American Society for Information Science and Technology*. 60(9): 1933–1938.

McLuhan, M. (1965). *Understanding Media: The Extensions of Man*. New York: McGraw Hill.

Mills, K. (2010). "Filming in progress": New spaces for multimodal design. *Linguistics and Education*. 21(1): 14–28.

Moursund, D. and Bielefeldt, T. (1999). Will New Teachers Be Prepared to Teach in a Digital Age? *A national survey on information technology in teacher education*. Available: http://www.mff.org/publications/publications.taf?page=154 Downloaded 8 March 2014.

New London Group. (1996). A pedagogy of multiliteracies: Designing social futures. *Harvard Educational Review*. 66(1): 60–92.

Peddiwell, J. (2004). *The Saber-Tooth Curriculum*. (Classic edition). New York: McGraw Hill. (Original work published 1939).

People for Education. (2014). *Measuring What Matters: Beyond the 3 "R's."* Available: http://www. peopleforeducation.ca/measuring-what-matters/wp-content/uploads/2014/11/People for-Education-Measuring-What-Matters-Beyond-the-3-Rs1.pdf Downloaded February 10, 2015.

Radford, M. (2006). Researching classrooms: Complexity and chaos. *British Educational Research Journal*. 32(2): 177–190.

Robinson, K. (2006). *How Schools Kill Creativity*. TED Talks. Online. Available at: http://www.ted. com/talks/ken_robinson_says_schools_kill_creativity?language=en Downloaded 22 February, 2015.

Sawyer, R. (2006). Educating for innovation. *Thinking Skills and Creativity*. 1(1): 41–48.

Sawyer, R. (2011). *Explaining Creativity: The Science of Human Innovation*. New York: Oxford University Press.

Seel, M. and Winn, W. (2012). Research on media and learning: Distributed cognition and semiotics. In R. Tennyson, F. Schott, N. Seel and S. Dijkstra (eds), *Theory, Research, and Models of Instructional Design: International Perspective Vol. 1*. New York: Routledge, 293-326.

Sinclair, G. (2010, May). *Exploring Canada's Digital Future*. Featured "Big Thinking" Lecture at the Congress of the Humanities and Social Sciences, Concordia University, Montreal, PQ, Canada.

Shohamy, E. (2007). Language tests as language policy tools. *Assessment in Education*. 14(1): 117–130.

Thieman, G. (2008). Using technology as a tool for learning and developing 21st century skills: An examination of technology use by pre-service teachers with their K-12 students. *Contemporary Issues in Technology and Teacher Education*. 8(4): 342–366.

Thurlow, C., Lengel, L. and Tomic, A. (2004). *Computer Mediated Communication*. London: Sage.

Whale, D. (2006). Technology skills as a criterion in teacher evaluation. *Journal of Technology and Teacher Education*. 14(1): 61–74.

CHAPTER FIVE

Literacy Spaces, Digital Pathways AND Connected Learning: Teachers' Professional Development IN Times OF New Mobilities

OLA ERSTAD

INTRODUCTION

A core issue associated with implementing and using digital media in schools has been teachers' proficiency in using such media. From traditional courses like "IT driving licenses" in the 1990s to network and inservice orientations in the 2000s to online professional development webinars and Twitter groups in the 2010s, strategies for enhancing teachers' skills and processes in using digital media have been a key concern in many countries (Davis, Preston and Sahin 2009; Selwyn 2013; Barton and Lee 2013).

In one sense, teachers have been blamed for the lack of change in and innovation of educational practices using digital media. This lack of fluency in using digital media has been pointed to as one of the main reasons why digital media is not much integrated into classroom activities (cf. Law Pelgrum and Plomp 2008). Even though fluency in using digital media among teachers has increased in recent years, teachers often lack didactic strategies that take advantage of the potential in these media for pedagogic advancement in relation to students' learning. However, there is a danger of being too critical toward teachers over a lack of innovation when the system itself does not reward change, and not all aspects of digital media are necessarily positive for teaching and learning (Selwyn 2011). In short, digital technology is often portrayed as positive in its own right, with all its possibilities for information access and communication, while teaching practices are embedded in institutions facing issues in relation to existing bureaucratic and systemic framings that techno-logical developments are challenging in terms of teaching methods, administrative routines and the assessment system (Kozma 2003). What often is missing in such portrayals of teachers is an in-depth understanding of the professional identities of different teacher communities and the ongoing challenges teachers experience in their classrooms, in terms of pedagogical expectations imposed by curricula and school leadership, as well as challenges experienced by students and families.

One of the most important challenges for teachers today, due to the growth of digital media in our culture, is the gap between literacy practices inside and outside of schools (Hull and Schultz 2002; Erstad 2013). This gap has been documented for some time, and, contrary to many people's assumptions, in many ways it has grown even wider rather than smaller due to students using digital media in more complex and varied ways outside of school when compared to their uses inside school (Ito et al. 2013; Erstad 2013). At the same time, one might say that this same gap is lessening since information access is almost ubiquitous, and affordable communication possibilities can easily connect teachers and students with other teachers and students around the world, blurring traditional boundaries between what can and cannot be done in classrooms.

We are quite familiar with what constitutes in-school learning and liter-acy practices, partly from our own schooling experiences and partly through classroom-based research. These practices usually are defined in terms of using specific kinds of texts and materials (e.g., textbooks, notebooks), specific ways of understanding learning (e.g., often developmental in orientation), ways of stim-ulating reading and writing (e.g., daily journal writing, silent reading for plea-sure), and certain ways of assessing or evaluating learning (e.g., testing, portfolios). Out-of-school learning and literacy practices, or what some describe as "learning at not-school" (Sefton-Green 2013: 8), usually are more undefined and unclear. Alternatively, these contextual and situated understandings of literacy and learning have been described as differences between *formal*, taking place within the institu-tional settings of education like schools, *non-formal*, as organized activities outside of school, and *informal*, as self-initiated and not-organized activities outside of schools. Connecting or bridging different learning contexts and literacy practices in and out of school can be defined from two different perspectives. First, from the perspective of teachers, ways of connecting in and out of school are concerned with linking learning and literacy practices in classrooms to students' experiences and literacy practices outside schools, either in terms of texts they use in non-school settings or everyday experiences using digital media, and that are defined as rel-evant by the teacher. Second, from the perspective of students, such connections typically entail authentic experiences and making sense of these experiences and ways of learning across different settings, in what some describe as "new mobili-ties" (Leander et al. 2010).

As I show in this chapter, there is a need to move away from thinking about teacher professional development that focuses explicitly on digital media *per se*. Rather, the core challenge—and potential—lies in addressing central educational challenges in the 21st century in terms of seeing digital media as an important *embedded* part of everyday life, albeit linked to fundamental issues concerning how teaching and learning take place in schools today. As such, I focus on this challenge and how teachers handle the tensions and affordances between inside and outside of schools' meaning-making contexts and as created by digital media. Teachers today are increasingly concerned with ways of handling this challenge, and figuring out how teaching and learning in schools can connect usefully to activities students are involved in outside of schools. In my own research this is also the area which inservice teachers talk about as an "absence" in their teacher training and as something they often need to address through their own teaching experiences alone. In what follows, reference to my own research will be linked partly to how teachers conceptualize their own roles in these expanding learning environments (Erstad 2014) and to classroom practices that open up negotiations between teachers and students around crossing boundaries among different learning contexts.

LITERACY SPACES AND PATHWAYS

The need for a closer relationship between in- and out-of-school activities among young people has been identified as an educational issue in Dewey's work (1916) and in classical studies by Scribner and Cole (1973) and Heath (1983) but has not been foregrounded in the educational field during the last decades due to increased standardisation and testing in schools. Nonetheless, there has been a significant number of studies of informal literacies and learning in recent years (Hull and Schultz 2002; Coiro et al. 2008). This partly is due to the take up of digital technologies in all facets of everyday life and a general, increased emphasis on things such as lifelong learning and globalization. This body of research often is directed towards exploring what informal learning contexts and processes represent as sites for literacy practices and learning and can be read against the grain of formal, institutionalized sites for literacy learning.

Barton and Hamilton's study (1998) in Lancaster, U.K., is an example of a study that looks more closely at literacy practices in homes and communities, in terms of what they describe as "local literacies." While it might be possible to view this study in terms of social capital, that is, understanding an aggregated use of literacy as social interaction, it also suggests how approaches to learning literacy offer a way to assess the texture of a community. The ways in which people have access to and use texts in their daily lives as part of different situations, purposes and interactions with others provide them with opportunities to act on (and interact with) their environment in certain ways. This study is a good example of how a community approach to understanding literacy practices gives us a deeper sense of the meaning of "ecological literacy'" (Barton 2007).

Ecological literacy refers to ways of understanding ICT as part of people's everyday life comprising different literacy "timescales" (Lemke 2000). As such, it becomes important to focus on literacy *events*, as framed by certain activities and contexts and broader literacy practices across different contexts and over time in order to examine the ways in which "reading" and "writing" are performed (Barton et al. 2007; Sefton-Green 2013; Sefton-Green and Rowsell 2015). In 2012, Barton and Hamilton revisited the same community. The most striking change they noticed was in the communication practices within the community since digital communication tools and services, such as broadband coverage, mobile technologies and laptops, had become available and which had changed profoundly people's vernacular practices around literacy (Hamilton 2015: 100).

A major shift during the past ten years is found in user-generated content creation, that is, in the increased availability of new expressive ways for young people to make and share meaning and ideas. The cultural transformation that has made this possible is, of course, the technological developments comprising Web 2.0, which have created new possibilities for access to information and for creating, uploading, and sharing content in different modalities to a much larger extent than ever before (Drotner and Schrøder 2010). As such, these technologies, affordances and their use have created new cultural positions for media users in our societies.

Even though research on media literacies has raised key questions about what literacy is and about understanding how young people use and relate to digital media, this research is still largely embedded in immediate, situated perspectives and seems less concerned with following learners over time and across contexts. Studies of school, knowledge, learning, and curricula should instead be conceived as trajectories or pathways rather than as fixed and enduring bodies of knowledge (Dreier 2008; Edwards 2009; Ludvigsen et al. 2011). Literacy and learning are not static conditions inherent in a person, but, rather, change according to the context and situation each person moves through and over time as both the person and the environment change. Examining how these activities and practices are connected (Ito et al., 2013) and develop as learning pathways is important because it provides a deeper understanding of how literacy and learning are part of people's everyday lives (Erstad and Sefton-Green 2013).

Several scholars have explored how out-of-school literacies might have an impact on classroom practice (e.g., Bulfin and Koutsogiannis 2012; Erstad et al. 2009; Hull and Schultz 2002; Leander and Sheehy 2004; Wortham 2011). International research is picking up issues raised by Hull and Schultz (2002) in their exhaustive review of research studies that spanned in-school and out-of-school contexts. Well over a decade ago now, they called for closer research attention to be paid to the relationship between learning practices in and out of school: "research on literacy and out-of-school learning can help researchers to think anew about literacy teaching and learning" (Hull and Schultz 2001: 575). This research on contrasting and comparing in- and out-of-school literacy and learning practices has shaped a now well-established body of work conducted from within the New Literacy Studies orientation in countries like England and South Africa, as well as the U.S. Leander, for example, has been a key contributor to exploring the inter-connections and spatial dimensions of literacy (cf. Leander and Lovvorn 2006; Leander et al. 2010; Leander and Sheehy 2004). Other related research has con-tributed insights to broader conceptions of interconnections among in-school and out-of-school literacy practices in terms of "boundary crossing" (e.g., Akkermann and Bakker 2011) and "connected learning" (Ito et al. 2013). Scholarly attention to crossing borders or boundaries examines student activities across different settings or the ways in which references to other settings are included in activities in one specific setting like the classroom. Scholarly work on "connected learn-ing" is interested in biographical studies of how young people develop specific literacy practices over time using different digital technologies. However, despite this growing body of work focussed on issues of border crossings and ways of connecting in- and out-of-school activities within school settings, we still need more systematic approaches towards understanding or interpreting what all this means for learning in school and especially how teachers can be best supported in conceiving and planning for such connections as part of classroom activity.

TEACHER PROFESSIONAL DEVELOPMENT AND NEW LITERACY SPACES

Research shows that the teacher is a key person in making school literacy and learning practices relevant in any border-crossing activities (Edwards 2009). Scholars have for some time investigated how teachers can develop strategies for including students' experiences and knowledge in their classroom teach-ing (Cremin et al. 2012; Dworin 2006; Moje et al. 2004; Moll et al. 1992). For instance, Moll and colleagues (1992) have demonstrated the potential to be found in providing teachers with opportunities to become familiar with the practices that students engage in outside school so that teachers can use resources from these practices in their teaching (e.g., texts from home, ways of getting things done, etc.). Similarly, Hughes and Greenhough (2006) found that by encouraging students to bring to school different types of artifacts that meant something to them in their everyday lives, teachers managed to bridge the school-world and everyday-world in effective ways by genuinely acknowledging and recognizing students' own lived experiences and interests. In another study based in the U.S., Dworin (2006) showed how providing students with opportunities to write about their homes and community life in language lessons at school created an expanded educational practice in which students' lives outside school became relevant and important as resources for learning. This enabled English language learning students, in particular, to participate more fully in their classroom. Even if this strand of research is important for developing effective methods of including resources that are part of students' everyday lives in learning at school, other studies have shown that, when students are given the opportunity to participate in classrooms as accountable authors of their own learning processes by including experiences from outside of school, such activities will *not* automatically lead to meaningful learning (Kumpulainen and Lipponen 2010). As such, there is a pressing need to generate more knowledge about how teachers actually manage and use students' experiences and knowledge from their everyday lives as meaningful resources for learning within their classrooms.

Literacy—from a sociocultural orientation—has to do with certain ways of communicating in a particular discourse and which are recognized by the members of this discourse (Lankshear and Knobel 2006). In this field of research, some studies have documented "practice in schools where teachers and administrators are committed to working for social justice and equity, including the development of critical and multiple literacies that allow students to take action in their worlds and to design meaningful futures" (Comber et al. 2001: 452; see also Pandya and Ávila 2013).

Comber and colleagues argue that teachers and learning environments in school should not only provide students with opportunities to develop their own critical literacies through critical *reading* of already existing texts. Rather, teachers also should provide *students* with the opportunity to participate as composers or *writers*, developing their critical literacies through making things themselves and by taking their own communities as their point of departure. By creating learning environments that enable students to "combine production, design, and communication in a variety of modes, through a range of media," it becomes possible to bring students closer to members of communities that have direct significance to them (Comber et al. 2001: 453).

Such efforts by teachers also relate to their own sense of agency; that is, to what extent they have perceived possibilities for taking up critical literacies to define new spaces for learning (Lipponen and Kumpulainen 2011). Issues regarding teacher agency, however, are very much present in practices of and research into ways of using digital technologies in schools, since research suggests that even though access to technology has been increasing continuously over the last ten years, teachers in general have not changed their practices overly much with respect to using these technologies and have not demonstrated or defined a renewed sense of agency for themselves due to the potential of new technologies in classrooms (Krumsvik 2014).

DOCUMENTING TEACHER PROFESSIONAL LEARNING AND NEW MOBILITIES: SOME EXAMPLES

I use the term "new mobilities" from Leander and colleagues' (2011) work to indicate that the issues described above are not only to do with the need to empirically document activities inside and outside of school but rather are part of broader changes in people's lives and ways of learning in societies today. Within this context, "new mobilities" can be understood as a flow between different activities within everyday lives (Erstad 2012) and between offline and online activities (Nunes 2006). What is interesting is how these activities connect with each other as part of everyday life and how teachers might be in a position to take advantage of crossover activities as ways of engaging students' learning activities occurring face-to-face in the classroom or within a mix of offline and online settings.

In the report, *Teaching in the Connected Learning Classroom* (2014), produced under the aegis of the U.S.'s National Writing Project, Garcia and others present several examples from U.S. classrooms where teachers have designed classroom experiences in ever-changing contexts as ways of engaging students and have taken advantage of the various possibilities provided by digital technologies. For example, teacher Lacy Manship (2014) engaged her Grade 1 students in a collaborative documentary film project about their classroom's "underlife" (e.g., routines, non-curricular practices), while a high school teacher at a French American International School, Jason Sellers, involved his students in designing and writing interactive fiction games (Sellers 2014). Both these cases speak to the unique learning contexts to which these teachers adapted, including consideration of their students' cultural, social, geographical, and interest-driven backgrounds. Interestingly, all the case studies presented in Garcia and colleagues' edited collection offer disparate but consonant visions of connected learning in schools. Collectively, they challenge a one-way, teacher-to-student, approach to classroom pedagogy (Garcia 2014: 8). This resonates strongly with the cases I present below from my own investigation of teachers' professional development and digital technology use in a number of Norwegian schools.

In several projects I have led, concern with literacy practices inside and outside of schools has been central. Only in recent years, however, has the focus of my investigations been more on connections and boundary crossings between learning and literacy inside and outside of school. In this section I draw on data from several research projects I have led or been part of during the last ten years.

These studies include: "Local Literacies and Community Space" (2009–2013); "Student Research" (led by Erik Knain 2008–2012); "Two Schools on Prejudice" (2008–2009) and "Digital Storytelling and Student Agency" (2007–2008). Instead of presenting analyses from one data set, I examine data across several projects in order to show how teachers relate to in- and out-of-school through their practices in different ways. Methodologically all these projects are qualitative in design and mainly employ interviews and observation methods to collect data.

The examples below take the teacher in classroom settings as a frame of reference within a larger context of new mobilities, and the following discussion is divided into two sections: one focussing on teacher roles when initiating boundary crossing activities in the classroom and one focussing on project activities in schools where the teachers see learning potential in opening up digital literacy spaces for students.

Managing the Unpredictable

Teacher professional development in using ICT in classrooms is to a large degree dependent on teachers' self-conceptions and role identification in their classrooms. A traditional role conception as a teacher would easily just define the digital resources available as nothing more than a continuation of traditional teacher-led activities, often in terms of advanced writing requirements, using calculating machines in computations, or as presentation tools (e.g., PowerPoint). My interest is, rather, in how certain teachers see potential opportunities or affordances to do new things in classroom settings when implementing and using ICT. However, this also implies the development of new roles for and self-conceptions as teachers who move beyond traditional confines. As such, new roles and self-conceptions call for a willingness to redefine relationships with students when opening up new activity spaces. This implies being confident in managing the unpredictable, since unexpected contributions from students, such as reference to what was seen on television last night or details from holiday travel, etc., surface as part of student activities and the teacher cannot prepare activities and teaching plans the same way as a more "traditional" teacher might normally do. Two examples speak to this.

One example is taken from a study where the primary focus was on studying students and their in- and out-of-school activities, with a secondary focus on teacher and student interactions in classrooms (i.e., the "Local Literacies and Community Spaces" project). I spent about eight months sitting in classrooms observing classroom interactions and informally interviewed participating teachers. One teacher, Marit, taught social studies and mother tongue language. She had taught elsewhere before coming to this particular upper secondary school and had taken on administrative and teaching roles in her current school. In her own words, she was not very skilled in using ICT and did not use it a lot in her teaching. However, Marit knew that her students used digital technologies a lot and wanted to give them space wherein they could take advantage of this. In my observations of her teaching, it soon became clear that she tried to open up new learning and activity spaces for students in order to engage and involve them more in classroom activities. This was done in part by giving students themes to work on that related to their everyday life, such as "consumption" or "family relations," and having them use the internet to gather relevant information, write about their own personal experiences, and choose among different ways and tools for presenting their final work. Her commitment to opening up new spaces to students also was signalled in the way she initiated discussions and reflections with students about technology use itself, as in the following interaction within a larger conversation about literary genres:

Teacher: I would suggest that you are all postmodernists! Are you?
Several students at once: Yes.

Girl 1: My father says that it is negative that we spend so much time on Facebook, but at the same time that we are lucky that we have so many possibilities. However, it could have implications for our concentration.

Boy 1: I become distracted by the internet if I am tired.

Boy 2: I also get distracted when I am tired and when I get into Facebook I stay there.

Boy 1: I use more Skype. I think the communication possibilities are the most exciting. With two of my friends we log in at certain times in specific online spaces and discuss things, and sometimes meet new people.

Boy 3: The communication possibilities make you stay in touch. I have relatives in Pakistan and Saudi-Arabia that I can stay in touch with. But it is important to stay focused, so when I am [at] school, I am at school.

By describing these students as postmodernists and then asking them if they agree with her assessment, Marit seems to engage the students in thinking about technology in their lives and, at the same time, show interest in their out-of-school technology use. Technological developments in Norwegian society had been discussed in this class earlier in the same week. This practice of opening up spaces for and references to the lives of students outside the classroom was something Marit explained she had developed through personal experience. It is interesting to note, though, that her students seem to respond by referring to some of the possibilities provided by new technologies but at the same time take a moral stance heard mostly from adults concerning the negative aspects of using digital technologies. In conversations like these, activity is generated within Marit's classroom, and references to activities outside are made a part of this discussion. In this way, outside experiences with technology are "transformed" to suit expectations within the classroom and, in this case, students are critical and reflective in responding to their teacher.

A similar kind of border-crossing work was found in the case of another teacher, Tora, in a study of inquiry-based science learning in upper secondary grades. Tora was a very experienced teacher, like Marit, who had for several years been working as a science teacher. She joined the project because she had for some time been thinking about changing her teaching practice, both to renew her own interest in teaching and to engage students more fully in what they were learning and not simply reproducing what she was telling them. She had experience in using ICT in the classroom but did not consider herself to be an enthusiast or someone who saw significant potential in using digital resources. As part of this project, she was introduced to using an online collaborative platform called Knowledge Forum, developed by Scardamalia and Bereiter in Canada. The main purpose of this platform is to stimulate students' agency through writing activities and sharing ideas within this online space. Students write notes and post them within theme-based folders, visualized as concept maps, for others to further elaborate and comment on by means of new posts and links or by adding photos or videos. Writing activities are principally driven by the curiosity and ideas generated by students themselves.

At one point, I followed her class closely over a period of two weeks while they worked on a classroom project on global warming. The phases of this project comprised:

Phase 1: Watching a trigger film: *An Inconvenient Truth*. The students and teacher discuss the film and decide on certain research themes and questions that different groups of students want to work on during the project period.

Phase 2: Students discuss their research question and search for relevant information, using the internet in particular.

Phase 3: Students post notes to the Knowledge Forum and comment on the notes of other groups, creating a collective understanding of the project theme, "Global Warming."

Phase 4: Students connect with students at a school in Barcelona, Spain, who are working on the same theme. They ask questions and comment on posts from these other groups who are working on similar issues, all in English.

Phase 5: A video conference between the students in Norway and Spain.

As background information to students' points of departure, there were some reservations voiced among the students about participating in this project. One reason they gave was a concern that the project would take too much time and they would not have enough time left to cover the rest of the science curriculum for this grade level before their exams. Some students even complained to their parents about the project, who, in turn, contacted the headmaster at the school, with the consequence that the teacher was called to a meeting to explain and justify the project. The teacher defended her position and the reasons for this project and managed to convince the headmaster and the parents to agree to continue.

Ironically, but happily, when the project finished, the same students asked to have *more* projects of the same type, because they believed that they learned more and more effectively this way.

What Tora described in interviews was that she experienced her teacher role within this global warming project as akin to being a "chaos pilot." When opening up spaces for the students to use the internet to find relevant research data about global warming, to post notes and questions on the online platform, and to communicate with students in Barcelona, her role as teacher became more concerned with the often messy learning process of the students than with just the outcome of their work. In their reflection logs, written at the end of each project session, as well as in their postings online, Tora could track the progress of activities and developments in the students' reflections on their work. The classroom became more chaotic in the sense that students were physically moving around much more than usual, and there was increased noise as students were talking with each other more as they took on more responsibility for their own work and learning. Tora's own role became unclear since she now was more like someone who was guiding the students, like a pilot, in their work and making suggestions and giving feedback along the way. It seems that since she had a strong professional conception of herself as a teacher and knew the subject area very well, she had the confidence to open up these new literacy spaces, such as Knowledge Forum, for students to work on subject area content to let ICT be an important part of defining new directions in content work.

Both these examples are taken from school settings where teachers are addressing students' literacy and learning needs in different ways. Both teachers explained that they chose to open up the classroom environment in order to involve their students more fully in classroom activities. By doing so, they also made space for activities that are more unpredictable in terms of outcomes for students—compared to just following the curriculum—but that resulted in meaningful learning for students often not achieved when following set curriculum in lockstepped ways.

CREATING CONNECTED LEARNING SPACES

I now turn to two examples where teachers developed methodologies and approaches for letting students connect to the world outside their classroom. Of course, such methodologies and approaches vary across subject areas in terms of the extent to which students are encouraged to use digital technologies to connect to the outside world. This ranges from school subjects like media studies, where digitized connections to the wider world are made all the time, to mathematics, where such practices are not so prevalent.

The first example comes from a study located in two lower secondary schools (Erstad 2013). One school is located in the eastern part of central Oslo and the other in the western suburbs. Each has clear differences in terms of socio-economic status, with the western school having a higher socio-economic status than the eastern school. At each school, a group of students (about 20 in the east and about 40 in the west) took part in this two-week project. The school in the western suburbs comprised mostly students from families from high socio-economic backgrounds, with only one non-white student in the group (adopted from Chile). In the school in the eastern part of Oslo, students come from many different cultural backgrounds; about 65 per cent of them hail from minority-language-speaking families and from poorer socio-economic backgrounds. The teachers at the two schools were experienced in doing project work with students but had never collaborated across schools prior to the present project. Two teachers, Peter (in the western school) and Ole (in the eastern school), decided to complete a collaborative project between their two student groups, and their topic revolved around prejudices held by people living in east and west Oslo. A starting point for both classes was when Peter and Ole provided recent articles from national newspapers that reported people in eastern Oslo on average had a life expectancy of seven years less than those living in the west of the city. They asked students why this might be the case and used this as a guiding question for collaborative work between the two schools.

Different digital tools were used to collaborate and to create an online newspaper, one for each school, which reported on students on the other side of town, their community, and their school. Each of the two classes divided itself into an editorial board with smaller student groups responsible for different sections of the paper: culture, religion and ethics, sport, statistics about their communities, and interviews with inhabitants. They created and sent questions to each other using a collaborative online platform and via text chat. Halfway through the project, a group of students from each school travelled, without their teachers, to visit students at the other school using public transportation. None of these students had ever been in the area of the other school prior to this. To document this visit, each group made a video and used it in their online newspaper.

Data collected during this project captured students' learning about the lives of other students, as shown in the newspaper articles, and by their texts that examined and drew on their own life experiences in their own communities. In developing their newspapers, the two teachers enabled the students in each school to develop a sense of life-trajectories. This was exemplified in the ways in which the students combined different content they found on the internet with their own investigative work, where the latter included either written texts generated through collaborative writing or audio and video recordings. The editorial group at each school had the last word on how things should be presented in their online newspaper. The two teachers, Peter and Ole, acted as mentors and gave input as needed. They also kept a critical eye on the production of texts, because, as they told the students, "This has to be correct, because it can be read by anyone once it is posted on the websites of each school with links to each other." One event directly impacted both teachers, however. A group of students from the western school, all girls, had travelled across town to meet and interview students at the school in the east. Some boys at the school in the east lied to the girls from the west about access to drugs at the school and violence in the neighbourhood (blowing both out of proportion), and the girls accepted what they were told as true. When these girls wrote up their interview data in an article for the newspaper, both teachers intervened, asking if their account of rampant drugs and violence at the other school was really true and whether the girls had checked their information with other students at the school, which they had not done. When confronted with their lies, the boys, all with immigrant backgrounds, defended themselves, arguing that they were just expressing prejudices that the students from the west held about youth living in the east, especially about boys with immigrant backgrounds. Both teachers took this event as an issue for discussion in both student groups as an interesting example of prejudices they held about each other.

Observation fieldnotes from both groups showed an intense and creative process among the students as they worked with different materials and sent them between the two schools. Several issues came up as part of this process, and the teachers explicitly addressed them in their interactions with the students. In addition to the example discussed above, one of the Muslim girls at the school in the eastern part of Oslo explained why she was wearing a veil. This created a host of questions from students at the other school regarding what this meant in everyday terms, such as what she did during gymnastics lessons or whether or not she had friends with a Norwegian cultural heritage or what were her interests in music and films or what her parents thought about her growing up in Norway. In documenting this young woman's life story, the students remixed different materials they found on the internet about Islam, about world incidents connected to religious conflicts, and then connected them to this girl's personal narrative, which was ultimately presented in the online newspapers of both schools. As such, the students involved in this project were engaged on a personal level, drawing on experiences from outside the school yet reworking such experiences within their school contexts. In negotiating meaning making about differences and similarities between the two communities, students started reflecting on their own lives and on how they appeared to others and how the material conditions of their lives determined life opportunities; all of which was captured in the articles they wrote in the online newspapers. The use of personal stories set against found material facilitated this process of "placing" the self within larger narratives of growing up in Oslo. The teachers were very happy with how the project evolved and with how they had succeeded in generating thoughtful reflection in students about prejudices and the impact of living conditions on people and their life expectancy. As mentioned earlier, both Peter and Ole were experienced in using project work with students, but the collaboration between two schools that had very different student groups in relation to ethnic, cultural and socio-economic backgrounds was a new experience for them; one which opened up new possibilities of engaging students in living their lives and understanding others in different communities.

The second example that illustrates the possibilities afforded by connected learning spaces in schools is from a study of digital storytelling. Digital storytelling is a method where students make short (2–3 minutes) narratives of a personal nature based on a series of photos (their own and downloaded from the internet) combined with a voice-over track narrating the content. Data were collected at a lower secondary school in a city in Norway which actively used digital storytelling as a way to enhance student engagement. The project, initiated by a teacher within the support structures of a professional development project, was called "Young Today," where eighth-grade students (13- to 14-year-olds) in one class worked on a theme related to being young in the past and in the present (Erstad and Silseth 2008).

The teacher, Mary, identified digital storytelling as an engaging process for both low-performing and high-performing students. For her, digital storytelling was a progressive way to motivate traditionally low-performing students, in particular:

> [in using digital storytelling] we are able to stimulate the writing process of more students, when it does not center around these long compositions. If I can tell a student that he might write about something that he is preoccupied with in subject English, and we speak of approximately 150 to 200 words, then it is manageable.

Mary further explained that if a student struggles in writing a manuscript, the student can write down cues and, together with a tutor, try to formulate an oral story instead, which the student afterwards records as a voice-over to the images or clips included in their video. In short, some students in Mary's class were low performing in regard to traditional written assignments but nevertheless had the opportunity to express themselves in new ways by using technologies other than written text.

Mary emphasized open-ended assignments where students could be active and self-governing in their work on digital storytelling. For her, digital storytelling is more than just a tool for presenting subject matter; she believes it is an important tool for personal engagement in knowledge building. Mary gave several examples of how students have drawn personal elements into seemingly professional stories and crossed the boundaries between formal and informal social spheres. For instance, she talked about a student who created a historical story about World

War II, where the student came across a historical artifact from that particular period in the attic at home that became central to her digital story:

> It was a helmet, a German helmet that was in the attic, right. And then they had to talk about this at home, "Why is it lying around in our attic? What is the reason for this?" "It once belonged to a German soldier." And then they had this conversation at home, right. And these stories, which are mediated from one generation to another, and then the young people digitize it. ...

This is an example of one of the stories told by students that is situated outside the traditional division between formal and informal spaces of knowledge building. Used in this way, digital storytelling might be said to actively shift the epistemic orientation in school-based learning more towards the student than the curriculum.

These two examples illustrate some of the possibilities digital media in classroom settings create for opening up students—and the classroom—to the outside world. How this is developed and defined very much depends on the professional identity and confidence of the teacher. Not just in terms of using digital technology *per se*, but more in terms of how it is taken up in connecting learning and literacy across different literacy spaces. It also depends on the ways in which students themselves are able to navigate traditional and these new ways of engaging in learning activities within their classrooms, too.

TEACHER PROFESSIONAL DEVELOPMENT IN THE 21ST CENTURY

The examples described above all point to important aspects of teacher professional development in Norwegian schools today. The teachers mentioned are all experienced teachers who have been working in schools for some years but who nonetheless see a need to redevelop their strategies and professional roles to better engage their students. They approach this by becoming involved in university-school professional development projects or by exploring the educational potentials of new technologies. In doing so, they are taking risks in reconfiguring how they engage students with subject area content and in creating a common learning environment for exploration and personal engagement among students that deliberately draws on their lives inside and outside school. In this way, these teachers act on a strong, positive sense of students as learners and as people who do stuff with digital technologies in a range of formal and informal settings. This represents a construction of professional development that is always in process and not tied to one-off events where an expert comes in and tells teachers what to do, and, in my view, is much more in line with what is needed in current times.

Issues concerning teacher professional development are closely linked to questions about how we develop an education system that is able to face the challenges of the 21st century. A range of digital technologies is available in most classrooms in Norway, but most often they are simply used to support traditional teaching methods by means of standard word processing or presentation software. The teachers described in this chapter instead take the opportunity to explore new digital pathways for supporting student learning. In 21st-century economies and societies, the ability to respond flexibly to complex problems, to communicate effectively, to manage information, to work in teams, to use technology, and to produce new knowledge is crucial (Erstad 2013; Scardamalia and Bereiter 2006). Current economic and social trends have significant implications for teachers' development as professionals and their use of digital technologies in the classroom.

In her book, *Literacy for Sustainable Development in the Age of Information* (1999), Rassool argued that research perspectives on technology and literacy need to reconceptualise power structures within the information society and placed an emphasis on "communicative competence" in relation to democratic citizenship. Digital technologies create new possibilities for how people relate to one another, how knowledge is defined in negotiation between actors, and how it changes our conception of learning environments in which actors make meaning. Moreover, new practices are engendered by new social relations, new forms of collaboration and new social articulations. Personal empowerment, combining human and social aspects of learning, is related to the active use of different tools to meet particular social goals and purposes. This, in turn, is grounded in the prerequisite that actors have the competence and critical wherewithal to use these tools and attendant processes for learning. Literacy, seen in this way, necessarily implies processes of inclusion and exclusion. Some have the skills and know-how to use these processes for personal development, while others do not. Schooling is meant to counteract these cultural processes of exclusion.

What will the life of citizens be like in societies that are increasingly dependent on digital media and new mobilities in many aspects of social life? How should we, in our research and teacher professional development efforts, try to grasp what aspects of skills, know-how, and literacies are important for being a citizen and what knowledge is needed in order to participate fully in society, and what might the roles of teachers be in light of all this? The importance of educating the digital generation is not so much about being able to use digital media in and out of school as it is about creating a space for reflection, connected learning and building knowledge that will help all students participate as citizens in a digital culture. In this sense, we have to re-evaluate our sociocultural constructions of the school-aged learner in order to prevent new marginalizing mechanisms from developing. This also raises some basic questions about the role of teachers and their professional stance. In the next few years, it will be critical to debate and research these issues much more closely than they have been in the past and to move towards a better understanding of citizenship in terms of 21st-century digital fluency and what this, in turn, implies for the role of teachers and their professional know-how within these developments.

REFERENCES

Akkerman, S. and Bakker, A. (2011). Boundary crossing and boundary objects. *Review of Educational Research.* 81(2): 132–169.

Barton, D. (1994/2007). *Literacy. An Introduction to the Ecology of Written Language.* Oxford, England: Blackwell.

Barton, D. and Hamilton, M. (1998). *Local Literacies: Reading and Writing in One Community.* London, England: Routledge.

Barton, D., Ivanic, R., Appleby, Y., Hodge, R. and Tusting, K. (2007). *Literacy, Lives and Learning.* London: Routledge.

Barton, D. and Lee, C. (2013). *Language Online: Investigating Digital Texts and Practices.* London: Routledge.

Bulfin, S. and Koutsogiannis, D. (2012). New literacies as multiply placed practices: Expanding perspectives on young people's literacies across home and school. *Language and Education: An International Journal.* 26(4): 331–346.

Coiro, J., Knobel, M., Lankshear, C. and Leu, D. (eds) (2008). *Handbook of Research on New Literacies.* New York, NY: Lawrence Erlbaum.

Comber, B., Thomson, P. and Wells, M. (2001). Critical literacy finds a place: Writing and social action in low-income Australian grade 2/3 classroom. *The Elementary School Journal.* 101(4): 451–464.

Cremin, T., Mottram, M., Collins, F., Powell, S. and Drury, R. (2012). Building communities: Teachers researching literacy lives. *Improving Schools.* 15(2): 101–115.

Davis, N., Preston C., and Sahin I. (2009). ICT teacher training: Evidence for multinivel evaluation from a national initiative. *British Journal of Educational Technology.* (40)1: 135–148.

Dewey, J. (1916). *Education and Democracy.* New York: Macmillan.

Dreier, O. (2008). *Psychotherapy in Everyday Life.* Cambridge, England: Cambridge University Press.

Drotner, K. and Schrøder, K. (eds) (2010). *Digital Content Creation: Perceptions, Practices and Perspectives.* New York: Peter Lang.

Dworin, J. (2006). The Family Stories Project: Using funds of knowledge for writing. *The Reading Teacher.* 59(6), 510–520.

Edwards, R. (2009). Introduction: Life as a learning context? In R. Edwards, G. Biesta, and M. Thorpe (eds), *Rethinking Contexts for Learning and Teaching. Communities, Activities and Networks.* London, England: Routledge, 1–13.

Erstad, O. (2012). The learning lives of digital youth—beyond the formal and informal. *Oxford Review of Education.* 38(1): 25–43

Erstad, O. (2013). *Digital Learning Lives: Trajectories, Literacies, and Schooling.* New York: Peter Lang.

Erstad, O. (2014). The expanded classroom—Spatial relations in classroom practices using ICT. *Nordic Journal of Digital Literacy.* 1(1): 8–22.

Erstad, O., Gilje, O., Sefton-Green, J. and Vasbo, K. (2009). Exploring "learning lives": Community, identity, literacy and meaning. *Literacy*. 43(2): 100–106.

Erstad, O. and Sefton-Green, J. (eds) (2013). *Identity, Community, and Learning Lives in the Digital Age*. Cambridge, UK: Cambridge University Press.

Erstad, O., and Silseth, K. (2008). Agency in digital storytelling: Challenging the educational context. In K. Lundby (ed), *Digital Storytelling, Mediatized Stories: Self-representations in New Media*. New York: Peter Lang, 213–232.

Garcia, A. (ed) (2014). *Teaching in the Connected Learning Classroom*. Irvine, CA: Digital Media and Learning Research Hub.

Hamilton, M. (2015). The everyday and faraway: Revisiting local literacies. In J. Sefton-Green and J. Rowsell (eds), *Learning and Literacy Over Time*. London: Routledge, 98–115.

Heath, S. (1983). *Ways with Words: Language, Life and Work in Communities and Classrooms*. Cambridge, UK: Cambridge University Press.

Hughes, M., and Greenhough, P. (2006). Boxes, bags and videotape: Enhancing home–school communication through knowledge exchange activities. *Educational Review*. 58(4): 471–487.

Hull, G. and Katz, M-L. (2006). Crafting an agentive self: Case studies on digital storytelling. *Research in the Teaching of English*. 41(1): 43–81.

Hull, G. and Schultz, K. (eds) (2002). *School's Out: Bridging Out-of-School Literacies with Classroom Practices*. New York: Teachers College.

Ito, M., Gutiérrez, K., Livingstone, S., Penuel, Rhodes, J., Salen, K. Schor, J., Sefton-Green, J. and Watkins, S. (2013). *Connected Learning: An Agenda for Research and Design*. Irvine, CA: Digital Media and Learning Research Hub.

Kozma, R. (ed) (2003). *Technology, Innovation and Educational Change: A Global Perspective*. Eugene, OR: International Society for Technology in Education.

Krumsvik, R. (2014). *Klasseledelse i den Digitale Skolen* [Classroom Management in the Digital School]. Kristiansand, Denmark: Cappelen Damm Akademisk.

Kumpulainen, K. and Lipponen, L. (2010). Productive interaction as agentic participation in dialogic enquiry. In K. Littleton and C. Howe (eds), *Educational Dialogues: Understanding and Promoting Productive Interaction*. London: Routledge, 4863.

Lankshear, C. and Knobel, M. (2006). *New Literacies: Everyday Practices and Classroom Learning*. Berkshire, UK: Open University Press.

Law, N., Pelgrum, W. and Plomp, T. (eds) (2008). *Pedagogy and ICT Use in Schools Around the World*. Hong Kong, China: Springer.

Leander, K. and Lovvorn, J. (2006). Literacy networks: Following the circulation of texts, bodies, and objects in the schooling and online gaming of one youth. *Cognition and Instruction*. 24(3): 291–340.

Leander, K., Phillips, N. and Taylor, K. (2010). The changing social spaces of learning: Mapping new mobilities. *Review of Research in Education*. 34(1): 329–394.

Leander, K. and Sheehy, M. (eds) (2004). *Spatializing Literacy Research and Practice*. New York: Peter Lang.

Lemke, J. (2000). Across the scales of time: Artifacts, activities and meanings in ecosocial systems. *Mind, Culture and Activity*. 7(4): 273–290.

Lipponen, L. and Kumpulainen, K. (2011). Acting as accountable authors: Creating interactional spaces for agency work in teacher education. *Teaching and Teacher Education*. 27(5): 812–819.

Ludvigsen, S., Rasmussen, I., Krange, I., Moen, A. and Middleton, D. (2011). Intersecting trajectories of participation: Temporality and learning. In S. Ludvigsen, A. Lund, I. Rasmussen, and R. Säljö (eds), *Learning Across Sites: New Tools, Infrastructures and Practices.* Oxford, UK: Routledge, 105–121.

Manship, L. (2014). Wanna see the movie? In A. Garcia (ed), *Teaching in the Connected Learning Classroom.* Irvine, CA: Digital Media and Learning Research Hub, 28–32.

Moje, E., Ciechanowski, K., Kramer, K., Ellis, L., Carrillo, R. and Collazo, T. (2004). Working toward third space in content area literacy: An examination of everyday funds of knowledge and discourse. *Reading Research Quarterly.* 39(1): 38–70.

Moll, L., Amanti, C., Neff, D. and Gonzalez, N. (1992). Funds of knowledge for teaching: Using a qualitative approach to connect homes and classrooms. *Theory into Practice.* 31(2): 132–141.

Nunes, M. (2006). *Cyberspaces of Everyday Life.* Minneapolis, MN: University of Minnesota Press.

Pandya, J. and Ávila, J. (2013). *Moving Critical Literacies Forward: A New Look at Praxis Across Contexts.* New York: Routledge.

Scardamalia, M. and Bereiter, C. (2006). Knowledge building: Theory, pedagogy, and technology. In R. Sawyer (ed), *The Cambridge Handbook of the Learning Sciences.* Cambridge, MA: Cambridge University Press, 97–115.

Scribner, S. and Cole, M. (1973). Cognitive consequences of formal and informal education. *Science.* 182(1): 553–559.

Sellers, J. (2014). Interactive fiction game design: Text-based video games. In A. Garcia (ed), *Teaching in the Connected Learning Classroom.* Irvine, CA: Digital Media and Learning Research Hub, 56–60.

Sefton-Green, J. (2013). *Learning at Not-School.* Cambridge, MA: MIT Press.

Sefton-Green, J. and Rowsell, J. (2015). *Learning and Literacy Over Time.* London: Routledge.

Selwyn, N. (2011). *Schools and Schooling in the Digital Age: A Critical Analysis.* Abingdon, UK: Routledge.

Selwyn, N. (2013). *Education in a Digital World: Global Perspectives on Technology and Education.* Abingdon, UK: Routledge.

Wortham, S. (ed) (2011). *Youth Cultures, Language, and Literacy.* Thousand Oaks, CA: Sage.

CHAPTER SIX

A Digital Book Project WITH Primary Education Teachers IN Finland

REIJO KUPIAINEN, HANNA LEINONEN, MARITA MÄKINEN, AND ANGELA WISEMAN

INTRODUCTION

The growth of the internet in parallel with information and communication technologies and their potential use in the classroom has resulted in significant changes in curriculum and pedagogy in recent years. Particularly within the Finnish context, the National Core Curriculum plays a crucial role in determining the most valuable learning opportunities schools offer (cf. Alexander et al. 2008). That being said, the new National Core Curriculum for basic education has brought extra pressure on schools and on teachers and their professional development. The updated National Core Curriculum that will be implemented in Finnish schools in 2016 includes seven new transversal competence areas. The National Core Curriculum defines a competence area as a "body of knowledge, skills, values, attitudes, and will" (Finnish National Board of Education 2014: 20; authors' translation). "Competence" in this sense means "an ability to use knowledge and skills in ways required by a situation" (Finnish National Board of Education 2014: 20; authors' translation). Competence in this context is the holistic "know-how" of an individual brought into play when he or she uses skills and knowledge contextually.

The aim of these competence areas is to enhance students' readiness for challenges encountered in human development, work life, and citizenship, now and in the future. These transversal competence areas are not school subjects but are to be integrated across all school subjects and classes. Among these seven competence areas are two that are especially important from the perspective of literacy and digital technologies: (1) multiliteracy competence and (2) information and communication technology competence. Both are explicitly intertwined: "Information and communication technology (ICT) competence is an important civics itself and part of multiliteracy" (Finnish National Board of Education 2014: 23; authors' translation).

Multiliteracy (singular in the Finnish National Core Curriculum) is defined in the National Core Curriculum in the following way:

> Multiliteracy means skills for interpreting, producing and evaluating different texts; skills that help children understand multimodal cultural communication and build their own identity. Multiliteracy is based on a broad-based concept of a text. Text here means information expressed by verbal, pictorial, auditive, numeric and kinesthetic symbol systems. Texts can be interpreted and produced, for example, in written, verbal, printed, audiovisual or digital mode.
>
> Students need multiliteracy in order to interpret the world around them and perceive its cultural diversity. Multiliteracy means having the skills to access, combine, modify, produce, present and evaluate information in different modes, different environments and situations, and with different devices. Multiliteracy supports the development of critical thinking and learning skills [...] Students should be able to practice their skills, both in traditional and in multimodal media technologies, in different ways and by utilizing their learning environment. (Finnish National Board of Education 2014: 22, authors' translation)

Digital technologies within a multiliteracies framework in K–8 education have been implemented and studied for some time now, especially in Australia, Canada, the United Kingdom, and North America (e.g., Doherty 2002; Lotherington and Chow 2006; Kitson et al. 2007; Hill 2010; Hesterman 2011, 2013). The Finnish definition of multiliteracy includes two kinds of "multi" that also are consistent with international definitions (e.g., Kalantzis and Cope 2012): (1) social and cultural diversity and (2) multimodality, which means the set of different and combined modes of meaning-making material, such as written, visual, oral, spatial, tactile, and audio texts. This dual focus within academic research and scholarship provides a strong rationale for the union of multiliteracy and ICT competence within the National Core Curriculum.

TEACHERS' PROFESSIONAL DEVELOPMENT AND THE TPACK FRAMEWORK

Although Finnish teachers, from primary basic education to upper secondary schools, have strong academic qualifications and hold at least a Master's degree, they are not very well prepared for these new NCC competence areas. Existing research in Finland (see, for example, Taalas et al. 2008; Kankaanranta and Puhakka 2008; Survey of Schools 2013) confirms that teachers rarely use ICT in Finland for teaching. The students' digital media environment often is quite different from that inhabited by their teachers, for whom the textbook is still a crucial learning resource (Taalas et al. 2008; Kupiainen 2013).

The new National Core Curriculum and changes in classroom learning environments were a starting point for the project Mobile Learning and Digital Books in Primary Education (known as the "Digital Book Project"), funded by the Finnish National Board of Education. In the Digital Book Project, six primary schools in a mid-sized city in western Finland collaboratively designed a new learning environment for primary education based on digital technologies, especially iPads and Windows 8 tablets. One to two teachers and their respective classes from each of these six schools participated in this project. Schools were solicited via email, and school principals selected the participating teachers. The participating teachers did not have much experience with tablets or with the use of ICT in learning before this project. Altogether, the project included eleven Grade 1 and 2 teachers and their 7- to 8-year-old students as participants.

The Digital Book Project had three main goals: to (1) support teachers' implementation of digital technologies in their lessons, especially tablets, to enhance children's learning; (2) facilitate connections between children's own and the school's digital technology practices; and (3) develop effective pedagogy for the demands of multiliteracy and ICT competence brought into play by the new National Core Curriculum. The project started in autumn 2014 and ran until the end of 2015. This chapter describes the participating teachers' professional development during the first months of this project. Common to all teachers was that they were highly motivated to develop their professional knowledge in the context of digital literacies and to change the school culture that had been, prior to this, based heavily on textbooks.

Although Finland is a technologically rich country and the government has strongly supported the educational use of digital technologies, technological integration usually has been the result of different projects that have been supported by funding from outside the school (Niemi et al. 2012). However, project-based support for and investments in educational technologies and infrastructure do not automatically translate into better learning and pedagogy (Niemi et al. 2012). Digital technology is often externally incorporated in classroom work (e.g., located in computer labs or media resource rooms), and teachers may not possess technical or pedagogical understanding of how to use new technologies (Kupiainen 2013). Neither external nor short-term projects change the pedagogical culture in a school in ways where teachers can feel they are active professional agents in relation to technological integration in their classrooms.

The precondition for successful technology integration in a school's culture requires much more than the unquestioning acceptance of technology. This precondition is, as Neil Selwyn (2011: 28) argues, a need for restless consideration of "*what* education is, *why* education is provided and *how* education is carried out." As Koehler and Mishra (2009) argue in a similar vein, teaching is a complicated practice and requires different kinds of specialized knowledge, including techno-logical knowledge, but not technological knowledge alone. Teaching in this sense also requires teachers constantly "to shift and evolve their understanding" (Koehler and Mishra 2009: 61), especially in relation to knowledge areas concerned with school subject matter and student thinking and learning.

Despite the need for changing traditional pedagogical culture and learning practices in schools, business-as-usual thinking still seems to have a dominant role in many Finnish schools. School culture changes slowly and has stabile structures and institutional arrangements. Increasing the amount of technology within schools does not necessarily affect school culture unless this technology is connected to meaningful professional development and teacher knowledge development.

Successful teaching requires that teachers are able to integrate their knowl-edge of their content area, knowledge of pedagogy, and, ultimately, pedagogical content knowledge into their teaching (Shulman 1986). Knowledge of one's con-tent area refers to school subject matter. Pedagogical knowledge comprises knowl-edge of the processes and methods of effective teaching and learning. Pedagogical content knowledge, then, is "in a word, the ways of representing and formulating the subject [matter] that make it comprehensible to others" (Shulman 1986: 9). The latter is important because it includes transformation of subject matter in the way the teacher chooses a particular context or topic and aims at making it under-standable for students by means of carefully thought-through and implemented pedagogical strategies and methods. However, digital technology—like all educa-tional technology—sets in place a series of new qualifications for teachers' knowl-edge while at the same time remains far from being independent from content and pedagogical knowledge. Koehler and Mishra (2009) adopted and expanded Shulman's ideas about teacher knowledge and applied them to a more thoroughly "digitized" school context. For Koehler and Mishra, the intersection of content knowledge (CK), pedagogical knowledge (PK), and technological knowledge (TK)—collectively called "technological, pedagogical and content knowledge" (TPACK)—are important to successful teaching. The resulting TPACK frame-work for technology integration has been used to help educators around the world understand the relationships among technology, pedagogy, and content knowl-edge (cf. Watulak and Kinzer 2013). Teachers, we argue, need to develop profes-sional knowledge not only in each of these domains but also "in the manner in which these domains and contextual parameters interrelate" (Koehler and Mishra 2009: 66).

The TPACK framework oriented our Digital Book project in terms of how we approached participating teachers' professional development, but we expanded the framework by including the concept *professional capital* (Hargreaves and Fullan 2012). Although this study is ongoing, in this chapter we report on interesting early developments during the initial phase of this project.

DATA COLLECTION AND ANALYSIS

The data drawn on in this chapter comprise mainly meeting observations and semi-structured essays titled *Remembering the Future*. *Remembering the Future* essays have been used as an active and participatory method in the therapeutic practices of social work (e.g., Seikkula and Arnkil 2006), cognitive neuroscience (e.g., Schacter et al. 2008), studies of futurology (e.g., Hicks and Holden 2007), and studies of school development (e.g., Pyhältö et al. 2012; Pyhältö et al. 2014). These essays require participants to imagine a possible future and are discussed in more detail below.

The 11 participating teachers, along with their school principals, and project coordinators from the local eLearning Center, plus technical aides from the six participating schools were involved in regular meetings with the project team right from the beginning of the project. Project coordinators held two to four face-to-face meetings each term at each participating school and at the eLearning Centre itself. The first meetings are described in more detail below. Reijo Kupiainen, the study leader, attended five of these meetings, observed discussions, and recorded descriptive field notes during the meetings. The project coordinator—a key person from the eLearning Centre—also wrote memos about these meetings and shared the memos with the project participants and researchers. These notes and memos were included in the research data analyzed for this report.

The *Remembering the Future* essays asked the 11 participating teachers to imagine their future selves forward to autumn 2016 and describe their experience in the Digital Book Project from the perspectives of content, pedagogical, and technical knowledge. These essays were collected in order to have a concrete record of the teachers' interpretation of the predicted or imagined state of the Digital Book Project once it had run its course and the new National Core Curriculum was in widespread use. As a writing prompt, these teachers were asked to imagine a satisfying situation in which all major problems concerning new digital learning environments in their school have been solved and new technology has been integrated seamlessly into teaching and everyday schooling in relation to the National Core Curriculum. The aim of the essay was to bring teachers' own thoughts regarding their professional development and their range of imagined possible futures into our project analysis.

We wanted to focus on the participants' imagined future scenarios because the teachers had only a few months' experience with the project when we completed our initial phase of data collection. We wanted these essays to focus on future accomplishments without emphasizing the present problems that had emerged at the beginning of the project (e.g., technical issues, curriculum timetabling issues).

The instructions for completing the *Remembering the Future* essay were as follows:

Imagine yourself in September 2016. The new core curriculum is in use. You have participated in the Digital Book Project, and tablets have been taken up successfully for teaching in your classroom. In 2016, for you a tablet is an important and natural teaching device, along with other devices. You have experienced how the Digital Book Project has supported you in the introduction of the new core curriculum.

Teachers also were asked to imagine the challenges they confronted during the project, along with their experience with their professional development in technology, pedagogy, and content knowledge. The essays were collected at one of the Digital Book Project meetings in November 2014 from eight teachers, as well as from two additional teachers later in January 2015. One of the 11 teachers did not complete an essay for reasons beyond our control. The essay task included five demographic questions concerning the participants' gender, the grade they were currently teaching, teaching experience, use of digital tablets in their free time, and their in-service training in using ICT in their classes. In the study, we were interested in these experiences in terms of everyday schooling practices; how the teachers processed their content, pedagogical, and technical knowledge; challenges of the new curriculum, and the teachers' relationships with students and colleagues. In these essays, participating teachers had the opportunity to reflect on their own knowledge and experiences in terms of an imagined time scale. This, of course, does not measure objectively their professional development but provides narratives by which to usefully interpret teachers' lived experiences.

Finally, documents produced by the project coordinators as part of the development of the project were also collected and analyzed. These documents included summaries of discussion outcomes (see Table 6.2 later in this chapter, for example), a project blog, and meeting memos.

To begin, the teachers' written texts were thematically analyzed with attention to the content, pedagogical, and technical knowledge areas and categorized according to the challenges in different knowledge areas that teachers expressed in their essays. In this way, the analysis is theory based because it draws directly on Koehler and Mishra's TPACK framework and on Hargreaves and Fullan's concept of professional capital.

The research data consist of marks and signs of thoughts and experiences of the teachers, principals, and coordinators during the early phase of the project. At the same time, the written data are a part of social relations and structures. Blommaert and Jie write that "language appears in reality as performance, as actions performed by people in a social environment" (Blommaert and Jie 2010: 8). We studied the performances and social actions related to the schooling practices described by the school staff and project leaders. In particular, we analyzed our textual data in terms of teachers' meaning making in relation to challenging situations (i.e., via their essays) as well as ideal situations in schools (e.g., via records of their discussions; see Table 6.2).

THE DIGITAL BOOK PROJECT

The Digital Book Project began in six primary schools in autumn 2014, but the schools and teachers were enrolled earlier in the project during the 2014 spring term. The project was coordinated by the eLearning Center, a publicly funded center that offers support and in-service training for teachers in local-area schools. The eLearning Center arranged four meetings with project participants early in the spring of 2014 (see Table 6.1). Two of these meetings were for principals, and two meetings were for the 11 participating teachers, technical aides, and principals combined. Each meeting generally lasted approximately two hours and involved teachers, aides, and principals collaboratively planning the project for the forthcoming school year. Regular meetings continued in autumn 2014 and spring 2015.

Table 6.1: First project meetings

Meetings	Participants	Focus of a meeting
February 2014	Project coordinators, principals.	Introduction to the project, discussion of introductory topics with a focus on changing the pedagogical culture at the participating schools.
March 2014	Project coordinators, principals.	Sharing key ideas for the development of the project and for changing the school culture in terms of pedagogy and learning.
April 2014	Project coordinators, principals, technical aides, participating teachers.	Teachers started to discuss their own expectations and needs regarding teaching with the aid of digital technologies.
May 2014	Project coordinators, principals, technical aides, participating teachers.	Group work among four themes: (1) attitude and work, (2) evaluation and the National Core Curriculum, (3) technology and content, and (4) attitude and in-service training.
October 2014	Project coordinators, principals, technical aides, participating teachers.	ICT and multiliteracy goals from the perspective of the new National Core Curriculum (see Table 6.2 as well).

Discussions during the initial meetings and across the project were the basis of the project. The project was developed collaboratively by sharing the participants' ideas and experiences, engaging in short workshops during the various meetings, experimenting with different ways to achieve the goals of the National Core Curriculum, and so on. Although the eLearning Center coordinated the project, its staff did not set the project agendas. The whole project was co-constructed by all participants. This important collaboration is further elaborated on in a subsequent section of this chapter.

Despite the name, the Digital Book Project is not concerned with simply replacing print books with digital resources; it is attempting to change classroom practices and create new classroom curricula. Mobile technologies used in the project offer many possibilities; for example, apps, cameras, and audio recording software enable students to work on multimedia projects and walk away from the classroom with the world at their fingertips. As such, the project also aims at developing practical learning activities for students to use mobile devices within the context of the National Core Curriculum. Participating teachers were interested in the integration of mobile devices into a broader sequence of activities rather than in isolated use of devices or applications.

DISCUSSION

Multiliteracy is a new orientation within the National Core Curriculum. Research data suggest that, for participants, this new orientation was foregrounded in the Digital Book Project right from its inception. At the same time, it soon became apparent that truly understanding this new orientation requires sustained professional development for teachers in terms of their technological knowledge and their multiliteracy pedagogy knowledge.

Drawing on our analyses of the meeting field notes, documents produced by the project coordinators, and teachers' essays, we identified interesting themes regarding participating teachers and their professional development. Each theme is discussed in turn below.

Multiliteracy Pedagogy Knowledge

Although many participating teachers reported they had encountered technical problems with digital technologies in their schools at the beginning of the project, during their meeting-based discussions and with strong support from the eLearning Center, they nonetheless began to create new pedagogical knowledge and solutions to their problems in order to teach their Grade 1 and 2 students.

The *Remembering the Future* essays confirmed that these teachers did not have any special technological knowledge before this project. They had participated in basic inservice training, such as how to use interactive white boards in the classroom, but expressed a lack of technological knowledge in their essays (e.g., one of the teachers wrote, "I have been extremely on edge" about using technology in the classroom). It must be said that the project and the support of the eLearning Centre opened up new possibilities for teaching, learning, and pedagogy for the participating teachers, which are documented in Table 6.2. For example, within the subject area of mathematics, teachers had started to think in terms of pedagogical knowledge and strategies (i.e., classroom activities) within a multiliteracy framework; that is, the teachers could envision, for example, teaching by using drama, photographs, Quick Response (QR) codes, etc., in teaching students mathematical concepts and processes. This strongly suggests that, for these teachers, the worlds opened up by digital technologies were not simply technological but were *multimodal*. Technological and pedagogical knowledge were then combined as multiliteracy pedagogy knowledge; in other words, knowledge of using multimodal texts and technologies was applied to learning content and classroom contexts. Thus, in short order, multiliteracy pedagogy knowledge became an accessible resource for informing teaching and learning so that students are able to use *multimodal knowledge representations* (cf. Kalantzis and Cope 2012) to express their learning. For Kalantzis and Cope, mathematics is a kind of edge case for multiliteracies:

> But even there, mathematical notation is a form of writing. It requires grounding in the narrative of a problem, written explanations of reasoning, description of conclusion, and visuals that demonstrate in a parallel mode the mathematical reasoning used. It is not possible to infer from the correct answer, "C. The result is 42," that the student has fully understood the mathematics. We need a multimodal knowledge representation of their mathematics, not unlike those that mathematics practitioners such as engineers have to provide in real life (Kalantzis and Cope 2012: *Literacies for assessment across the discipline areas*, para 7).

Thus, the Digital Book Project demonstrates that incorporating multiple learning modes and materials (such as images, drama, games, or digital content) into classroom learning allows students to build their own knowledge in more meaningful ways and supports the integration of students' own experiences into their knowledge work and their engagement with knowledge production (Wiseman et al. 2015). Table 6.2 below summarizes some of this outcome.

Table 6.2: ICT and multiliteracies goals for students in Grades 1 and 2 (This table was adapted from a table produced by a project coordinator and based on teacher discussions.)

School subject	Goal (competences that students need to achieve from the point of view of the NCC)	Classroom activities (means to achieve the goals)	How to evaluate success (evaluation of achieving the goal)
Finnish Language and Literature	To teach "keyboarding skills" when writing with a computer. To steer a student to find information in different ways. To provide opportunities for the student to produce simple stories, narrations, and other texts in a multimodal environment.	Writing with the keyboard. Logic of information finding, source critique (with the support of the teacher). Image-writing, stop-motion animation, drama and recording it with video, recording stories.	Observation. Comparing knowledge that children have found from different sources, students sharing finding processes. Peer-based evaluation, process-based evaluation, continuous feedback.
Mathematics	To encourage students to present their own solutions and conclusions by concrete means, with drawings, verbal accounts and written text by utilizing ICT. Exploring coding. A student produces and interprets simple tables and bar charts.	By asking how students solved problems. Calculation stories. Drama. Photographs. QR codes. Geocaching and QR codes. Robot plays. Rush Hour [game]. Polls and diagrams from students' everyday life.	Observation. Apps for math, for example, online mathematic reference work, Math World [game].
Environmental and Natural Sciences	To guide a student to use ICT in information seeking and in recording and presenting observations.	Photography, video, QR codes, information seeking from different sources, apps (for example, space, physics, chemistry, atlas).	Self-evaluation, testing, evaluation of work samples and working.
Religion	To use ICT in a way that makes a student's thinking transparent.	Comics, concept maps, ready-made programs, and layouts.	

School subject	Goal (competences that students need to achieve from the point of view of the NCC)	Classroom activities (means to achieve the goals)	How to evaluate success (evaluation of achieving the goal)
Music	To give space for students' own musical ideas and improvisation and guide them to produce simple compositions and other things by using auditory, kinetic, and pictorial technologies, and other means of expression.	GarageBand on iPads. Fibble flute. MuseScore, Finale. Video recording. Digital music games. Recording. YouTube, Spotify. CC license.	The process is more important, not a work sample.
Visual Arts	To produce and interpret images by using ICT and digital networks.	Looking at art works from the internet. Taking photos. Digital drawing tools. Animation. QR codes.	Digital portfolios.
Crafts	ICT as a part of ideation and documentation.	Using videos in order to teach different work stages and techniques. Documentation of own work samples and work stages by photo or video camera and publishing on a blog.	Comments and peer evaluation on a blog.

Table 6.2 suggests that a multimodal shift—that is, moving beyond traditional pen-and-paper student work—happened in every school subject area taught by participating teachers and clearly is in line with the multiliteracy goal of the new National Core Curriculum.

Developing Professional Agency and Curriculum

According to the new National Core Curriculum, students' ability to interpret, produce, and evaluate multimodal information comprises important objectives for teaching and learning. This seemed to be well executed by teachers even before this new curriculum was published and implemented in schools, at least in terms of the teachers participating in the Digital Book Project. Participating teachers seemed to share the understanding that multiliteracies are not only concerned with integrating new technology and digital tools into curriculum but also entail reconceptualizing the curriculum itself. This means that multiliteracies are not only a means of teaching but also an inseparable part of rethinking why we teach, what we teach, and how we teach, all the while honoring the diversity of students at the school (cf. Boyd and Brock 2014: para 3). This collective understanding may well have come about due to the goals and collaborative nature of this project.

In Finland, teachers are self-sufficient professionals who are expected to organize their teaching independently and adopt new pedagogical strategies autonomously. Pyhältö, Pietarinen, and Soini (2011) explain how bringing new ideas into a school depends very much on the teachers' competence and knowledge. However, our own study outcomes strongly suggest that competence and knowledge in general are not enough. The National Core Curriculum requires specialized knowledge of multiliteracy theory and practice, which means that to teach well entails knowing a lot about digital technologies and how to use them. Therefore, the TPACK framework is applicable to what project teachers needed to develop and draw on as they worked on building multiliteracies into their classes. That being said, it also became apparent that the TPACK framework itself is not enough for explaining or supporting what these teachers needed. What is missing—as our data show—is attention to the importance of teachers' professional efficacy regarding themselves and their motivation to adopt new ideas within the context of everyday schooling. This includes connecting and engaging with their own professional communities.

Teachers with a strong sense of efficacy and who express the belief that they actually can make a difference typically are more open to new ideas and experiments (Pyhältö et al. 2011). Project teachers' *Remembering the Future* essays indicated that they all had strong self-efficacy and were ready to improve their own knowledge, as well as take responsibility for the professional development of their respective school communities in relation to multiliteracies and curriculum development. In their essays, the teachers wrote about their own competence in the following way:

- "I had to become familiar with educational apps and think about their feasibility from the perspective of core curriculum … My own way of working changed." (essay, teacher 1)
- "Within the project, I had to think carefully about essential and fundamental content from the perspective of learning." (essay, teacher 6)
- "The project challenged me to think about the content of the core curriculum from a new point of view." (essay, teacher 8)

These three teachers emphasized that the project, as it unfolds now and in the future, will no doubt challenge them to think *differently* about the learning process and to understand the National Core Curriculum from a new perspective. The emphasis in these samples—which are representative of all 10 essays—is on each teacher being able to shift for himself or herself. This suggests that right from the start of the project they were open to being active agents of their own development, especially when it came to their own classroom activities and pedagogical development. This sense of efficacy is important because it is a necessary precondition for change (Pyhältö et al. 2011).

Another implication from this project is that the National Core Curriculum has an important role to play in teachers' professional development. Because the new curriculum includes new key concepts, knowledge areas, themes, and topics, implementing it well requires teachers to *think* about learning and teaching in a new way. The data show that the teachers participating in the Digital Book Project collectively demonstrated active agency with a diverse and deep knowledge of the curriculum, even in the realm of digital technologies, and were able to apply their understanding of this new curriculum to different contexts:

- "There are a lot of practical learning activities for school subjects, and students' own information seeking is an important thing." (essay, teacher 3)
- "I have got enough readiness to answer the requirements of the [National Core] curriculum in terms of teaching ICT skills." (essay, teacher 4)
- "Learning is not only subject-based (all the time), but subjects integrate with each other. My pedagogical competence has been diversified." (essay, teacher 7)

Teachers emphasized the practical learning activities in which school subjects are not separate realms in the organization of time and space at the school but are more integrated and take the National Core Curriculum into account in everyday schooling. The Finnish National Core Curriculum is not a standardized script that must be followed to the letter by teachers. Instead, as before, teachers have full autonomy to plan class practices and learning materials. Therefore, implementing the National Core Curriculum in classroom activities is more like a local curriculum development process, where teachers' deep professional knowledge is still very much needed and may even be challenged. For example, project teachers wrote explicitly about curriculum implementation from the perspective of digital technologies and ICT in their *Remembering the Future* essays in the following way:

Tablet devices were a new thing [...] courage for new experiments has been developed. [...] I have also learned to endure failures [...and] been sometimes strongly out of my comfort zone. [...] My own way of working changed. The core content of the curriculum was implemented in more diverse ways by using electronic resources and using computers as a medium for learning, away from all-the-time use of textbooks. It has been good to discuss with myself why I am doing this with the students using a digital device while others [teachers] use a textbook. This is certainly a place for a growth! (essay, teacher 1)

In spite of their autonomy, Finnish teachers use textbooks quite frequently in class-room teaching. Textbooks have traditionally held strategic power over teachers, but the Digital Book Project actively tried to change this situation. The Grade 1 teacher quoted above felt this project would take her out of her comfort zone, particularly given that before this study she explained she did not understand anything about digital technologies. However, in her essay, she tells us that she reflected on why she started to use digital technologies instead of textbooks. She described her own "courage for new experiments" and articulated an interest in continuing to change her practice. Thus, even though the essay documents a yet-to-be imagined state, this teacher's text nonetheless exhibits self-discussion as a strong signal of reflective thinking about the connection between the curriculum and professional development within a new digital and multiliteracy learning environment. Even though she had some doubts about the widespread take-up of digital devices (i.e., "while others [teachers] use a textbook"), she seems to see that using digital devices within the context of the new National Core Curriculum could generate school success for her students: "Some students' enthusiasm for writing has grown due to the positive experiences after suffering pen writing" (essay, teacher 1).

From the perspective of the TPACK framework, the participating teachers seem to consider the content (curriculum), pedagogy, and technology simultaneously—at least on paper—and seem well disposed toward trying to find the best solutions to drawing on this framework in an integrated way as a means for teaching students. For example, another Grade 1 teacher imagined in her essay:

> Children progress at their own pace. Devices that we got from the Digital Book Project help in differentiation in both ways: top and down. Children are self-guided, and the teacher acts as a guide. Personal guiding and advancement have been focused with group work and collaborative learning. [...] There are lots of practical learning activities for school subjects and students' own information seeking is an important thing. [...] My own development shows I'm able to organize a flexible, versatile learning environment and provide necessary support. I count on students even more.

> The teacher does not need to manage more content of school subjects. Most important is that the skills of computer use are versatile, and students can be guided to use it. [...] Guiding critical thinking! (essay, teacher 3)

For this teacher, digital devices in school (technological knowledge) are integrated to fit a learning environment designed for diverse students and to guide them to work collaboratively. She also describes how she "counts on students even more" in terms of them taking on more responsibility for their own learning. All of this changes traditional classroom pedagogy and pedagogical knowledge. When she says that there is no need for more content knowledge, this teacher emphasizes her changing role: from "frontal" teaching—where the teacher usually is an owner of the knowledge—to facilitator, where students seek information and build their knowledge collaboratively.

Other teachers mentioned a change from the "continuous control of teacher" to "guiding," "the changing role of the students," and similar, as well. In their own predicted development, they saw a shift in their relationship to their students as especially important. In doing so, the teachers signaled they understood the teacher does not need to know everything. This served to locate students at the centre of the learning process in a supportive and flexible learning community.

The project was in an early stage when the *Remembering the Future* essays were collected and the teachers had only had a few months' experience with the project. However, they all seemed to resonate with Shulman's claims that teachers' professional development is deeply involved with their motivation to learn from their own and others' experiences and through active reflection on their actions (cf. Shulman and Shulman 2004). Interestingly, this same idea was seen in the data concerning participating principals.

PROFESSIONAL CAPITAL

The ideas suggested by participating principals and collected during their second project meeting (March 2014) are summarized in Table 6.3 and categorized into five themes: (1) technology and educational resources and their functionality, (2) cooperation between teachers and homes, (3) school culture, (4) support for the teachers, and (5) students' needs.

Table 6.3: Key ideas for the Digital Book Project according to participating principals

Technology and educational resources	Cooperation with teachers and homes	School culture	Support for the teachers	Students' needs
functional devices and network open learning resources interactive learning resources	cooperation sharing experiences information to homes meeting parents	unlearning continuous monitoring and reflection tolerating uncertainty failure enthusiasm for something new changing mindset safe atmosphere	training and competence peer support benchmarking	learning together open interaction individual learning equality differentiation special education

The column "Technology and educational resources" includes ideas about needed technological solutions in the classroom. "Cooperation with teachers and homes" includes schools' and teachers' needed connection to students' homes and parents. The Digital Book Project required strong cooperation with parents because they were not necessarily familiar with the digital technologies to be used in participating schools. Principals appeared to agree that without parents' support and trust, school culture changes will not be successful.

As mentioned earlier, the focus of the entire project was changing school culture. The column "School culture" in Table 6.3 above includes *unlearning* traditional schooling, changing mindsets in a safe atmosphere, and the like. This kind of change needs teacher support in the form of a commitment to enhancing their competence and in-service training, peer-based support, and benchmarking best pedagogical and technological solutions to problems associated with teaching or learning. The final column in Table 6.3, "Students' needs," refers to students' changing role in learning settings. This column, and as seen already in the teachers' *Remembering the Future* essays, provides a strong sense that project principals believe incorporating technology into the curriculum can be a more collaborative and differentiated way to teach and learn.

As shown in Table 6.3, the principals' collective perspective focused on a broad approach to culture change, where technological knowledge seems to be only one part of the project. Interestingly, these same themes were found across the teachers' *Remembering the Future* essays, too.

The teachers had a varied work history, spanning 2 to 30 years spent teaching, although only three had taught fewer than ten years. When answering our demographic questions, the teachers identified a dearth of inservice training in ICT in their experiences. For example, one teacher wrote that she did not have enough training "in order to teach students everything that I should" (demographic question response, teacher 4). She continued in her *Remembering the Future* essay: "I feel that I start from the beginning [when it comes to technological knowledge] in this project, or I have to learn a lot of new information first" (essay, teacher 4). Most teachers reported only sporadic inservice training days and mentioned training for using an interactive whiteboard and little else. Nonetheless, they were courageous in facing new possibilities and counted on the support of the eLearning Centre, which provided technological support as well as pedagogical support. When these teachers reflected on their existing and future technological knowledge, some mentioned the importance of peer support from colleagues. This signals the teachers' willingness to develop their own professional knowledge as they connect with their own professional community.

Their future-looking reflections centered most on pedagogical knowledge; however, they also included differentiation of student learning, broad information management, collaborative learning, their boldness to try something new, tolerating uncertainty, the importance of peer-based learning, investment in practical learning activities and individual learning, the importance of support from colleagues, and teachers as mentors to students in the classroom. In this collectively imagined future, these attributes seem to be a prerequisite for change.

The teachers' essays and the list of ideas generated by principals revealed that professional development can be viewed usefully from the perspective of what Hargreaves and Fullan (2012) call "professional capital." That is, teaching like "a pro," and having "a personal commitment to rigorous training, continuous learning, collegial feedback, respect for evidence, responsiveness to parents, striving for excellence, and going far beyond the requirements of any written contract" (Hargreaves and Fullan 2012: *Preface*, para 14). However, all this is possible only in an environment where colleagues, principals, other professionals at the schools, parents, and society can support the teacher—otherwise, teacher burnout or disaffection becomes the order of the day (cf. Cameron and Lovett 2014).

We contend that professional development in the age of digital technology cannot be understood solely within a framework of individual knowledge take-up, whether it be technological, content, or pedagogical knowledge. The collective process of developing professional capital, which is a systematic process and involves sustained professional collaboration, has important implications for the Digital Book Project and other projects like it. Significantly, the Digital Book Project drew attention to the importance of what we call "collective efficacy" (cf. Putney and Broughton, 2011) in developing school and pedagogical cultures. "Collective efficacy" within the context of this study took the form of developing ideas and learning activities collegially among participants. For Putney and Broughton (2011), collective efficacy requires the willingness of group members to work through difficult situations and relate to one another while working toward a common goal. From the point of view of professional capital then, collective efficacy is extremely important. It shapes school culture by enhancing cooperation among teachers and administrators and is responsible for the quality of trust among school faculty as well as among students and parents. The Digital Book Project is an example of this type of professional capital in action: Teachers are supported by each other, principals, and the eLearning Centre. Through this support, we argue that the teachers have opportunities to feel comfortable with sharing their knowledge with each other and with trying to solve pedagogical problems together. Our research data suggest that the principals, and teachers see that professional capital is necessary in the integration of digital technologies into teaching. This is shown in key ideas collected to date in the project (e.g., Table 6.3) as well as in the *Remembering the Future* essays, where teachers refer to collegial support, which indexes the staff of the eLearning Centre and other project participants:

- "Changing ideas with colleagues helped a lot, and experiments." (essay, teacher 2)
- "The staff of eLearning Centre came to the school and all the problems were solved [...]." (essay, teacher 3)
- "Fortunately, [the staff of the eLearning Centre] was able to come to the school, and their know-how was in our use in grass roots ways." (essay, teacher 6)
- "I learned to use devices both versatile and familiar, and I [...] help colleagues." (essay, teacher 7)

In addition, our current findings suggest teachers' professional development should be based on discretionary judgements (Hargreaves and Fullan 2012: 92). It is important to respect teachers' "professional discretion" (Hargreaves 1994: 260) in making informed choices and plans as they develop curriculum and make decisions in uncertain circumstances, especially within the context of digital technologies, which are always under conditions of change. The teachers who participated in the Digital Book Project wrote about the importance of "tolerating uncertainty" as they imagined pedagogical implementations in their classrooms. Principals also mentioned "tolerating uncertainty" as one of their key "ideas" for changing school cultures. Thus, we argue that professional capital is needed especially when the evidence for making decisions is not conclusive and when the evidence is not categorically clear in situations of uncertainty (cf. Hargreaves and Fullan 2012: 92). Professional capital accumulates through different experiences, practices, experiments, collaborations, and reflections and results in judgments and decisions made in circumstances where there are no fixed rules or manuals. Manuals can be used for technology to some degree, but not for pedagogy and content knowledge and their various combinations.

CONCLUSION

Because teachers today will be required to understand and utilise a wide range of communication media, such as websites, media, film, and databases, there is a need to understand how to support their professional learning. TPACK offers clues and approaches for teachers in the classroom (Mills 2006) who are looking for ways to transform their beliefs about teaching and rethink their practice. The new National Core Curriculum is an important development for connecting technology and media to the school curriculum. Teachers' approaches to implementing the National Core Curriculum in Finland provide possibilities for the creation of innovative and productive sites of meaning making in classroom contexts (cf. Mills 2010).

A key element of the new National Core Curriculum is multiliteracy, which is grounded in the goal that all students should be "active designers" of their social futures (Cope and Kalantzis 2000: 7). In order to achieve such a goal, teachers need the opportunity to actively design pedagogy and explore technologies within the domain of extending their own pedagogical and content knowledge beyond current boundaries. A pedagogy of multiliteracies—as writ large in the research literature beyond the National Core Curriculum—assumes teachers are more designers of learning environments and supporters of new relationships between students and their learning environments than people who "regurgitate the content of the textbook" (Kalantzis and Cope 2012: *Tomorrow's teachers*, para 1).

Research suggests that experiential modeling and exploratory practice allow teachers to find out about different meaning-making modes and online communication as they learn methods for integrating digital technologies into their classroom. A multiliteracies approach within the curriculum has the potential to transform the way that learning occurs. However, teachers have to become comfortable with the idea that students may have more digital technology affordances and digital design expertise than they do. The Digital Book Project suggests that teachers are gaining much through collaborating and sharing ideas with each other instead of relying on top-down, expert-driven professional development or working solitarily to try and get themselves "up to speed" with new digital technologies. This collaborative orientation toward pedagogical content knowledge and professional capital involves a significant shift away from traditional schooling in Finland. The teachers in this study demonstrated that the potential for change is positive when truly collaborative, professional development and support are put in place.

This ongoing study demonstrates the importance of understanding how to change the culture in schools as learning becomes more sensitive to technological advances. It is challenging for teachers to integrate new approaches when they themselves did not learn with digital technologies or multiliteracies in professional development courses and university-based teacher training. However, there is much evidence that changing the culture of a school from textbook-based to digital technology based is beneficial for the school's learning environment in general and necessary for producing 21st-century learners. In this study, teachers described their enthusiasm, motivation, and self-efficacy and collective efficacy for integrating technology in the classroom. This, in turn, reflects well on an approach to teachers' professional development that is grounded in collaborative decision making, knowledge sharing, and planning. If we are to take seriously claims regarding the importance of nurturing professional capital, then projects such as the Digital Book Project are useful models for how it can be done.

REFERENCES

Alexander, J. Walsh, P., Jarman, R. and McClune, B. (2008). From rhetoric to reality: Advancing literacy by cross curricular means. *The Curriculum Journal*. 19(1): 2–35.

Blommaert, J. and Jie, D. (2010). *Ethnographic Fieldwork: A Beginner's Guide* [Kindle iPad version]. Bristol, UK: Multilingual Matters.

Boyd, F. and Brock, C. (eds) (2014). *Social Diversity Within Multiliteracies: Complexity in Teaching and Learning*. London: Routledge.

Cameron, M. and Lovett, S. (2014). Sustaining the commitment and realizing the potential of highly promising teachers. *Teachers and Teaching, Theory and Practice*. 21(2): 150–163.

Cope, B. and Kalantzis, M. (eds) (2000). *Multiliteracies: Literacy Learning and the Design of Social Futures* [Kindle iPad version]. London, UK: Routledge.

Doherty, C. (2002). Extending horizons: Critical technological literacy for urban aboriginal students. *Journal of Adolescent & Adult Literacy*. 46(1): 50–59.

Finnish National Board of Education. (2014). *Perusopetuksen Opetussuunnitelman Perusteet 2014*. [Core Curriculum for Basic Education]. Available at: http://www.oph.fi/download/163777_perusope tuksen_opetussuunnitelman_perusteet_2014.pdf Downloaded 25 June, 2015.

Hargreaves, A. (1994). *Changing Teachers, Changing Times: Teachers' Work and Culture in the Postmodern Age*. London, UK: Cassell.

Hargreaves, A. and Fullan, M. (2012). *Professional Capital: Transforming Teaching in Every School* [Kindle iPad version]. New York; London: Teachers College Press.

Hesterman, S. (2011). Multiliteracies Star Warians: The force of popular culture and ICT in early learning. *Australian Journal of Language and Literacy*. 36(4): 86–95.

Hesterman, S. (2013). Early childhood designs for multiliteracies learning. *Australian Journal of Language and Literacy*. 36(3): 158–168.

Hicks, D. and Holden, C. (2007). Remembering the future: What do children think? *Environmental Education Research*. 13(4): 501–512.

Hill, S. (2010). The millenium generation: Teacher-researchers exploring new forms of literacy. *Journal of Early Childhood Literacy*. 10(3): 315–339.

Kalantzis, M. and Cope, B. (2012). *Literacies* [Kindle iPad version]. Cambridge, UK: Cambridge University Press.

Kankaanranta, M. and Puhakka, E. (2008). *Kohti innovatiivista tietotekniikan opetuskäyttöä, Kansainvälisen Sites 2006-tutkimuksen tuloksia*. [Towards an Innovative Use of ICT in Teaching. Results of International Sites Research]. Jyväskylä, Finland: University of Jyväskylä, Finnish Institute for Educational Research. Available: http://ktl.jyu.fi/img/portal/13816/SITESjulkaisu. pdf?cs=1228198530. Downloaded 9 January, 2015.

Kitson, L., Fletcher, M. and Kearney, J. (2007). Continuity and change in literacy practices: A move towards multiliteracies. *Journal of Classroom Interaction*. 41/42(2/1): 29–41.

Koehler, M. J. and Mishra, P. (2009). What is technological pedagogical content knowledge? *Contemporary Issues in Technology and Teacher Education*. 9(1): 60–70. Available: http://www.citejournal. org/vol9/iss1/general/article1.cfm Downloaded 9 January, 2015.

Kupiainen, R. (2013). *Media and Digital Literacies in Secondary School*. New York, NY: Peter Lang.

Lotherington, H. and Chow, S. (2006). Rewriting "Goldilocks" in the urban, multicultural elementary school. *Reading Teacher*. 60(3): 242–252.

Mills, K. A. (2006). Critical framing in a pedagogy of multiliteracies. In J. Rennie (ed) *Voices, Vibes, Visions: Hearing the Voices, Feeling the Vibes, Capturing the Visions.* Darwin, Australia: Australian Association for Teaching English and the Australian Literacy Educator's Association, 1–15.

Mills, K. A. (2010). A review of the "digital turn" in the new literacy studies. *Review of Educational Research.* 80(2): 246–271.

Niemi, H., Kynäslahti, H. and Vahtivuori-Hänninen, S. (2012). Towards ICT in everyday life in Finnish schools: Seeking conditions for good practices. *Learning, Media and Technology.* 38(1): 57–71.

Putney, L. G. and Broughton, S. H. (2011). Developing collective classroom efficacy: The teacher's role as community organizer. *Journal of Teacher Education.* 62(1): 93–105.

Pyhältö, K., Pietarinen, J. and Soini, T. (2014). Comprehensive school teachers' professional agency in large-scale educational change. *Journal of Educational Change.* 15(3): 303–325.

Pyhältö, K., Soini, T. and Pietarinen, J. (2012). Do comprehensive school teachers perceive themselves as active agents in school reforms? *Journal of Educational Change.* 13(1): 95–116.

Schacter, D., Addis, D. and Buckner, R. L. (2008). Episodic simulation of future events: Concept, data and applications. *Annals of the New York Academy of Sciences.* 1124(1): 39–60.

Seikkula, J. and Arnkil, T. (2006). *Dialogical Meetings in Social Networks.* London: Karnac Books.

Selwyn, N. (2011). *Education and Technology: Key Issues and Debates.* London: Continuum.

Shulman, L. (1986). Those who understand: Knowledge growth in teaching. *Educational Researcher.* 15(1): 1–22.

Shulman, L. and Shulman, J. (2004). How and what teachers learn: A shifting perspective, *Journal of Curriculum Studies.* 36(2): 257–271.

Survey of Schools: ICT in Education. Benchmarking Access, Use and Attitudes to Technology in Europe's Schools. (2013). *A study prepared for the European Commission DG Communications Networks, Content & Technology.* Available: https://ec.europa.eu/digital agenda/sites/digital-agenda/files/KK-31–13-401-EN-N.pdf Downloaded 5 February, 2015.

Taalas, P., Tarnanen, M., Kauppinen, M. and Pöyhönen, S. (2008). Media landscapes in school and in free time: Two parallel realities. *Digital Kompetanse.* 3(4): 240–256.

Watulak, S. and Kinzer, C. (2013). Beyond technology skills. Toward a framework for critical digital literacies in pro-service technology education. In J. Ávila and J. Pandya (eds), *Critical Digital Literacies as Social Praxis.* New York: Peter Lang, 127–153.

Wiseman, A., Kupiainen, R. and Mäkinen, M. (2015). Multimodal literacy and photography. Literacy practices that support and extend classroom learning. In T. Kaartinen (ed) *Monilukutaito kaikki kaikessa* [Multiliteracy Everything in One]. Tampere, Finland: University of Tampere Teacher Training School, 220–238.

CHAPTER SEVEN

Professional Development AND Digital Literacies IN Argentinean Classrooms: Rethinking "What Works" IN Massive Technology Programs

INÉS DUSSEL

What kind of professional development is taking place within the context of massive one-computer-per-child programs, when the use of digital technologies and the appropriation of digital literacies has become a common imperative? And, more broadly, what kind of knowledge do teachers mobilize when they use digital media when teaching in those contexts? I would like to approach these questions through a close analysis of two social science teachers' classroom practices. These teachers work in two Argentinean public secondary schools that are enrolled in a technology-intensive program called *Conectar Igualdad* (Connect Equality) that has distributed over five million laptops to students and teachers since 2010.

I met these two teachers through a research project that will be described below. As part of the implementation of the program, both had been trained specifically for participating in the *Conectar Igualdad* project in a process that included online courses, printed guidelines and materials, and on-site sessions covering both what is referred to as "instrumental knowledge" (e.g., Offimatics, software fluency) and content knowledge within the area of social science teaching. They also had taken several other profession-related courses, and one of the teachers was pursuing a two-year diploma in education and ICT (information and communications technology). Both teachers were enthusiastic about digital media and about their work as teachers. While they had not been "early adopters," by the time I met them through my research, they were nonetheless "energetic converts" that tried out new ideas and strategies in their daily practices. However, in my interviews with them and in my classroom observations, it became clear that the training they had received was failing to address some crucial dimensions of their technology use in their classrooms. These dimensions included the new "chronotopes" of digital classrooms, the tensions between disciplinary knowledge and media formats, and the challenges of working with audiovisual texts. Explained in more detail later, the notion of "chronotope" is taken from Bakhtin and is developed by Lemke (2004) to signify the arrangements of space and time that configure classrooms. Lemke explains it's "a way of making and seeing space in time. There is pacing, there are multiple timescales, expected durations" (2004: 5). This acknowledgement of pace, rhythm and duration is important for the analysis of digital classrooms, as it will be argued below. In short, the social contexts of teachers' practices and the many strands that constituted their classroom networks were left largely untouched by the several courses they had taken and the training they received while participating in this project.

The story I would like to discuss in this chapter, then, is not that of a successful professional development program. Instead, I would like to focus on the shortcomings and limits of information and communication technology teacher training programs and strategies that do not engage with the multiple networks of meanings and artifacts that configure teachers' practices and that conceive ICT as a single, autonomous corpus of knowledge that can, almost magically, change the way teachers teach. These shortcomings and limits are not exclusive of technology-intensive programs but are more evident in the shock-like training strategies that have to deal with a massive scale of delivery and, in the midst of competitive, electoral politics, are pressured to show almost immediate results for large public investments (see, for example, the construction of indicators for evaluating these programs in Cristiá et al. 2012). In these conditions, the search for "what works" effectively and efficiently might hinder the development of a strong professional judgment and decision-making space (Biesta 2007) that is needed for richer and more productive uses of digital technologies in the classrooms.

Using Actor-Network Theory (Latour 2005; Nespor 2012) and practice theory (Schatzki 2002), I intend to analyze the activities and interactions that took place in these teachers' classrooms, as well as their own narratives about them. The chapter is organized as follows. First I present the *Conectar Igualdad* program, understanding it not as an external and all-encompassing frame. Rather, I see it as a major player or "policy vector" (Strathern 2004) in these classrooms' networks. These included the teacher training strategies that were set in place, the particular knowledge about teaching and learning and about the use of digital media in classrooms it sought to distribute. Second, I discuss the research methodology and introduce the two social science teachers whose practices were studied. Third,

I present an analysis of two sets of activities with some detail: one of them is a history class that dealt with teaching topics concerning the recent past set in late 20th-century Argentinean history. The other one was a citizenship education class that addressed the legal and emotional aspects of discrimination. Both used the laptops distributed by the national program and a classroom data projector as the main resources for their teaching. Finally, I conclude with some remarks that come back to the relevance of professional development programs that take into account the contexts of practice that organize teachers' work.

"CONECTAR IGUALDAD" AS A POLICY VECTOR: DISTRIBUTING ICT ARTIFACTS AND KNOWLEDGE THROUGH A DIGITAL INCLUSION PROGRAM

Conectar Igualdad (Connect Equality) was launched in 2010 as an ambitious program to reduce the digital gap among students and improve public schooling. Focusing on secondary schools, it has already delivered 5 million netbooks to every student and teacher in public institutions and has expanded to teacher education institutions (tertiary level) and special needs schools (see Conectarigualdad.gob. ar for latest updates). Along with these netbooks, connectivity, electric wiring and plug-ins also were (to be) provided for over 15,000 secondary schools and teacher education institutions throughout the country.

The program involved the major distribution and dissemination of artefacts and knowledge throughout the educational system and set digital inclusion as the goal that should drive educational change. A word of caution should be given here, however. In presenting some of the central traits of this program, I would like to avoid the reification of "context" as an external frame that defines, as in a set of Chinese boxes, the inner cubes or boxes of classroom life. It is not a "preliminary 'setting the stage'" for the research project but a condition and a scale that has to be rethought throughout the research process (Sobe and Kowalczyk 2014: 6).

As will be shown in the next sections, the program is an important policy vector (Strathern 2004) that disseminates technological artefacts and knowledge through different educational scales, such as national, district, school, and classroom networks (Nespor 2004). A policy vector is a connector that allows knowledge (understood as a set of practices) to travel across different scales or levels. This "travel" (referred to as "impact" by other theoretical positions) needs particular entanglements and conditions that connect expert knowledge and social opinion (Strathern 2004: 28–29). In this chapter, I think of *Conectar Igualdad* as a policy vector that mobilizes some discourses and priorities from the national level in relation to teachers' practices. In my analysis, the scale is not to be considered as a separate layer—of graduated size—but as a certain arrangement of temporality and spatiality that is defined, among other characteristics, "by the way in which participants 'calibrate' school-based events to events elsewhere" (Nespor 2004: 312). The actions of connecting to and contextualizing within outer events are thus part of what defines a particular network, such as the classroom. That is why "[n]o description of teaching can be complete without a description of the spatial and temporal orders of the worlds to which it is calibrated by teachers and students" (Nespor 2004: 313).

One of the aspects that seems significant for understanding what is taking place in classrooms is the political rhetoric of rights and egalitarianism that underwrites the *Conectar Igualdad* program for digital inclusion. The presidential decree that created the program in 2010 framed it as part of recognizing education as a public good, as well as in terms of the personal and social right to a high-quality education (Dussel, Ferrante and Sefton-Green 2013). While there are some nods to transnational business speak ("enhance global competitiveness," "promote creativity"), the language of the program is fundamentally one of citizenship rights and of the State's responsibilities for citizens. The governments of the Southern Cone in America have enacted policies in recent years that have been called "pro-equity" (Brun 2011) and have heralded some "egalitarian experiments" in social policies, particularly in urbanism and in education, that make the region an interesting laboratory for radical politics at this time (see McGuirk 2014).

One interesting feature of *Conectar Igualdad* is that it includes a loud-and-clear pedagogical call to make public schools stronger and more appealing for young people, renewing pedagogies and bridging out-of-school and school cultures. Considering Selwyn's classification of ICT policies in education as either proposing to reconstruct schools or readjust them (Selwyn 2011), Argentina's program is inclined to the second trend: emphasis is placed on making schools perform better in terms of their contribution to public knowledge and social democracy. Furthermore, it endorses a critical stance towards new technologies. As the Argentinian Education Minister said in 2011:

> We don't believe a technological artifact will produce a magic trick in schools or in the classroom [...]. We are not overestimating the situation and saying, "netbooks are here, and the next day Argentinean education changes." Far from it! We make it clear every time we can. (Sileoni 2012: 74; author's translation)

This kind of rhetoric is different from what is prevalent in the U.K. and the U.S., where ICT programs are brought to schools predominantly by the business sector and are dominated by the goal of producing a competitive global workforce and a digitally literate global citizenship. In that respect, the Argentinean program stands out as an example of how local forces mobilize global vectors and artifacts in particular ways, and connect them to local strategies and fields. It has resisted the "what works," evidence-based approach to evaluating its results advocated by multilateral policy and funding agencies, but it also has struggled to produce a different evaluation framework that takes into account social inclusion of and appropriation strategies by low-income families and children, with unclear results so far (Benitez Larghi 2015).

Given the *Conectar Igualdad* program's strong appeal to transform pedagogy and schools, teacher training and curriculum policies necessarily are important components of the program (Dussel, Ferrante and Sefton-Green 2013). These strategies concerning training and policy are difficult to align in terms of deadlines and resources and always seem to take on a life of their own. Indeed, the "movement" of the program has been one of increasing centralization. In 2011, there were as many as five state agencies offering teacher training within the context of *Conectar Igualdad*, all of which had competing views on what and how to include in their courses. In 2015, the teacher training strategy was defined by a centralized agency, the National Program for Digital Inclusion (PNIDE), and includes massive online in-service certificate offering courses that collectively have around 310,000 teachers enrolled—out of a total of 850,000 teachers in service (Dussel, 2015). These certificate programs last one or two years, and some of them have as many as 50 short courses that include technological and content knowledge, discussions on digital culture, and pedagogical seminars on how to use digital media in classrooms. Their scope today is broader and has shifted from teaching basic digital skills to more complex pedagogical and content knowledge with ICT (SITEAL 2014).

In 2012, when I interviewed social science teachers and observed their classrooms, *Conectar Igualdad* was implementing a teacher-training program that consisted of regional and national meetings with school principals and inspectors to discuss strategies and steps in the adoption of new digital technology. These meetings were complemented by the development of online courses for teachers, based on teaching basic digital skills, and the dissemination of curriculum materials that established criteria for using digital platforms and software in the classroom and examples of lesson plans. According to a report from 2011, most secondary school teachers had received some kind of training in using digital technologies in their teaching, although some of this included self-directed courses based on prepackaged materials as well as tutor-run courses (Ministerio de Educación 2011a).

Overall, the teacher training documents and materials produced by the program promoted the centrality of teachers in educational change, but they provided only general advice, with a strong appeal to teachers' initiative and creativity—a common tenet of Argentinean teacher education policies in general (see Indarramendi 2015). For instance, the *Guidelines for Classroom Strategies* published by the Ministry of Education (and that were assumed to act as an orientation guide for school principals and teachers for the implementation of the *Conectar Igualdad* program) proposed as a set of general principles or standards of good practice:

> The teacher generates change and gradually incorporates the use of equipment according to her or his goals, training and classroom reality.
>
> The teacher will make progressive use of equipment when s/he feels more familiar with technology, and will increasingly use it in classroom practices. (Ministerio de Educación 2011b: 13, author's translation).

The guidelines tended to convey a somewhat simplistic trust in the affordances of digital technology to transform classroom pedagogy and lacked references to potential conflicts between new media use and classroom practices. For example, they stated that in order to make the most of the presence of digital technologies in the classroom, teachers could either use digital content (that is, use the internet as a set of educational resources), social media, multimedia materials, blogs or projects or collaborative assignments (Ministerio de Educación 2011b: 19). These options were unproblematized and envisioned only positive outcomes.

Even more significant is that, given the generality of the guidelines and their celebratory tone and the working conditions of most secondary school teachers who have many students and little time or resources to try out new strategies, the space that the policy documents leave for creative initiatives ends up being defined by the repertoires of practices that teachers already have or the ones they can gather from the "communities of practice" that are blooming on the internet, where the private sector is also replete with initiatives from telecom and software companies (Dussel in press). Thus, the freedom to create and develop teaching lessons with digital media is curtailed by working conditions and available pedagogical knowledge, dimensions that remain largely unaddressed in these policy documents and in the initial, recommended teacher development strategies. This will become clear in the cases discussed in the following sections. (As a side note, in more recent research on teacher education, it is apparent that new teacher development strategies that include pedagogical seminars and workshops that bring the different contexts of practice to the fore have been developed and implemented with some success. See Dussel 2015; Ros 2014).

METHODS

As previously noted, the social science teachers whose practices I observed were met in the midst of a research project that took place in 2012 in four public secondary schools in the province of Buenos Aires, Argentina. This project was developed with a group of colleagues (Patricia Ferrante, Delia González and Julieta

Montero) at the Universidad Pedagógica de la Provincia de Buenos Aires (see a description in Dussel et al. 2015). Because the study was conducted by this team, I use the plural voice in some parts of this chapter, considering that many of the comments and registers were collected or made by different members of the team as a collaborative endeavor.

Students were asked to report on two events: (1) The Ezeiza Massacre on 20th June, 1973, when a large but unknown number of activists was killed by a para-military group. This occurred at the time when Perón was returning to Argentina after an 18-year exile in Spain; and (2) The 1974 demonstration held on the first of May at the Plaza de Mayo, Buenos Aires' central square. This was the moment when the right/left division in the Peronist party became evident. The left-wing youth made a public break with the party by leaving the square. This second event will be significant later in my description of the teacher's teaching sequence.

The goal of the project was to analyze the ways in which classroom interactions and rules for evaluating what counts as school knowledge were being transformed with or by the introduction of digital media; if, that is, they were transformed at all. We were interested in looking at the changes in classroom organization, partic-ularly in terms of space and time, considering widespread discussions at the time about the end of common schooling as a historical technology that was to pro-duce a common culture through simultaneous instruction and a frontal pedagogy (Hamilton and Zufiaurre 2014). Would the presence of laptops break the frontal, facing-forward organization of the classroom? Would the "multiple screens" inter-rupt the flow of communication in a class that tends to radiate to and from the teacher? Would the centrality of disciplinary, subject-matter content be challenged by the use of social media and audiovisual texts that come from popular culture? These were some of the questions that oriented the start of our research project.

The schools that participated in the project were known to be good schools, with a strong leadership that promoted the introduction of digital media, and were referred to us by school inspectors and district authorities of the Province of Buenos Aires, the largest and most populated province of Argentina. The schools were located in a medium-sized city on the Atlantic coast. Their participation in our project was voluntary. The team observed two classrooms in each school and interviewed teachers before and after their observed teaching; we made as thick a description as possible, paying attention to the interactions between people and artifacts, the disposition of the bodies in the classroom and the arrangements of time and space. We also interviewed four students in each classroom and collected students' audiovisual productions that were part of their school assignments. As for analysis of the material, Actor Network Theory and practice theory nurtured a research sensibility that recognized the "complex, open, and multiply integrated mesh of practices and arrangements that composes the present-day site of the social" (Schatzki 2002: 25–39). For us, a practice is "a set of doings and sayings" that can "exhibit regularities" but also involve "irregular, unique, and constantly changing doings and sayings" (Schatzki 2002: 73–74). Teachers' practice, therefore, was to be approached not as the manifestation of a hidden logic, but, rather, as a changing, contingent arrangement of disparate actions and a calibration of different scales or levels within a particular network.

Of the classrooms observed in this project, I present two cases that seem relevant to underlining the available pedagogical knowledge and working conditions that configure the way in which these teachers make use of digital media in their social science classrooms. As mentioned before, these were enthusiastic teachers who received their initial teacher training in high-quality institutions and who had attended several in-service teacher training courses and completed a number of certificate programs. The first case follows a young 33-year-old, male History teacher who had graduated from a well-known public university. He did not receive any training in using ICTs while at his university but had taken several courses on the use of ICT since the launch of the *Conectar Igualdad* program. He particularly valued one course which centered on digital skills and delivered by the *Conectar Igualdad* program and another one delivered by the local school district on digital resources for teaching history. At the time of our study, he was completing a two-year-long certificate course offered by the National Institute for Teacher Education that included seminars on teaching history with digital media. He didn't like these latter courses much, however, due to their historiographic perspective. Referencing the notion of the "calibration" of classroom practices to outer events, for this teacher, the stronger connection to the outer world was his discipline, history, which organized his identity and his practice, and not so much the *Conectar Igualdad* program and its imperative for digital inclusion. He felt he would need more training on how to use specific software in his teaching, as he found he wasted his time when trying to learn from tutorials and searching online on his own. He mentioned he would have liked to have been taught how to use editing tools for audios and videos, for example. He considered he stood out among his colleagues as an intensive user of digital media because he produced PowerPoint presentations, videos, audios, and blogs for his students, and he communicated with students by email.

The second case is a female teacher, a 48-year-old graduate of the national Institute for Secondary School Teachers, which is probably the most prestigious institution for initial teacher training in Argentina, and it has a long tradition of high quality academic training. She holds a degree in social and legal sciences teaching and has taught citizenship education in several schools. She also had taken several courses focused on digital technologies, among them the basic digital skills course delivered by the *Conectar Igualdad* program, along with many other short courses provided by national and local school district authorities. She considered herself a moderate but curious technology user, and was helped by her teenage children at home who taught her about the affordances of various technologies and connected her to videos and software that they found interesting. For her, the most important feature of digital resources was their ability to attract the attention of teenagers; in one interview, she made frequent references to the need to avoid the generational gap by being up to date and current with what they (her students) watched and listened to. This issue of attention and attraction was her way of "calibrating" her classroom teaching to outer events, of connecting different scales in her classroom. However, it is important to underscore that, for her, the attention and attraction of teenagers was not a psychological trait but a scarce commodity in urban schools where students come to school hungry due to their poverty and need to be active and attentive in order to remain engaged.

The calibration for this teacher, then, occurred through a combination of a social inclusion discourse that connects to ICT policy and a pedagogical approach that values activity, participation, and engagement. Attraction could be achieved almost only with audiovisual texts; in her view, Microsoft Word was a "boring program" that made students' voices anonymous and homogeneous, which is why she preferred that they produced videos, conducted interviews, and expressed their opinions openly. "I cannot teach a lesson the traditional way because they do not pay attention," she said. Instead, she wanted to stimulate a permanently open dialogue that made them "think" (as though they did not do that regularly). She occasionally brought some readings to her classroom for her students to complete and discuss, but due to a lack of time she usually used PowerPoint presentations in her teaching and where she included relevant thoughts or sayings (i.e., from Hobbes or Machiavelli) that she wanted to share with her students. She also used pre-constructed Slideshare.com presentations that she found on the web and lots of short videos (mostly from popular television programs). Similarly, she invited her students to produce videos as school assignments, although she herself did not know how to edit digital videos. She seemed to feel confident with not knowing or knowing less than her students. She remained very active about bringing references, texts, and discussions to the table that kept the flow of the class heading in the direction she intended. Her criteria for evaluating students' video productions were the students' "dedication" and engagement with their media artifact and evidence of mastering disciplinary knowledge as displayed in each video. In relation to her students' knowledge, she reported her surprise at times when some teenagers did not know how to use some of the digital technologies' options; it seemed that she assumed they already knew everything and certainly more than she did. She found that young women were less skilled with a range of digital technologies than the young men in her classes and also more hesitant in their use of technology, but she did not design a particular strategy for dealing with these problems. She was more interested in teaching her students the specific content knowledge of her subject and also had great trust in the appeal of digital media to keep them attentive and attracted to the classroom activities.

The next two sections present an analysis of these teachers' use of digital resources in their social science lessons. The first account is a history class on the recent past and the second a citizenship education lesson on discrimination. I acknowledge that my analysis will be unfair to the complexities involved in their teaching, but I'm hopeful it will nonetheless show there is a dense network of relations, artifacts, and knowledge that constitute this teacher's and these students' practices. I also argue that professional development strategies have to address these complicated networks if they want to "work" within these specific contexts of practices in which teaching with digital technologies is taking place.

Teaching the Recent Past through Multimodal Production

The first teacher's history class was observed in 2012 in a public school located in a middle-class neighborhood of a coastal city in the province of Buenos Aires. The students were in their fifth and final year of secondary schooling. The class had to discuss the right/left division of Peronism, the ruling party in Argentina, during 1973–1974, which was the preface to the military dictatorship that began in 1976. This topic, while included in the curriculum, is highly controversial, as it continues to be the subject of a heated politics of memory within and beyond Argentina (Vezzetti 2007). The teacher asked the students to produce a journalistic text in an audio format as if they had been on-the-scene reporters of events that took place in 1973 and 1974. This teacher previously had used fictitious films about these events, 1970s television news clips, and excerpts from textbooks, to discuss some concepts and facts that he wanted his students to have access to while preparing their audio reports. In one interview, he commented on the fact that, when downloaded, some of these television clips were too pixelated and this made it difficult to distinguish what was being shown. The situation worsened when the data projector was not working and he had to pass these clips around on USBs so his students could watch them on their individual screens. For example, a television clip about the demonstration of May 1974, which was supposed to show how the left-wing youth left the Plaza de Mayo square and performed a physical and symbolic exit from the Peronist party, was of such poor quality that it was not possible to see that there were thousands of people leaving the square. He nonetheless chose to use it and was confident that his telling of the story would give the students enough information about the event to be able to read and interpret these poor-quality images.

It is remarkable that this teacher, trained as a historian in an extended five-year undergraduate program at his university, did not see that the technical weakness affected the content he intended to teach. How can we understand this lack of concern with the quality of visual materials? This question most likely is related to the widespread idea that images are not considered as a source that is equivalent to the teacher's oral lesson. But it might also be the effect of a certain pedagogical approach that dismisses data and facts as less important than concepts. At any rate, it seemed that, for this teacher, what images "tell" is not as valuable as the teacher's word, and they do not need to be treated as sources to be criticized and judged in their own right or as a language that requires some kind of analysis in order to be understood.

Going back to the teaching sequence I observed, the teacher proposed that students use the software Audacity (preinstalled on their *Conectar Igualdad* program laptops) to create their audio report. All students had their netbooks, if not in the classroom, then at least at home. He instructed them to do this as audio report homework in small groups and bring it to class so they could listen to each other's reports together and then produce a collaborative video using images set to the audio recordings the student groups had made. Prior to these instructions, he circulated a memory stick containing a folder of images from the period that he had collected already for students to copy, but he also encouraged students to do their own image searches and selections. The final video was supposed to be produced with Windows Movie Maker, which also came preinstalled on the program's netbooks.

During my observation of his classroom, the students' main activity was for small groups to create an audio report as their main task, then add digital images to their audio track to create a group video. Much of this work was to be done outside class time. The following day, the entire class then listened to or watched these audio only or audio + images videos (depending on how much had been completed since the last lesson). The chronotope—the configuration of time and space—of the classroom was relaxed and playful, with several peer-to-peer conversations going on at the same time. Each student group audio production was commented upon and critiqued orally by the students as they listened.

However, many of these teacher-planned activities remained more of a possibility than a concrete realization. When listening to the audio reports, most of the students laughed at or made fun of the voice tones or their peers' impersonation of a journalist. Students audibly reproduced the political chants that appeared in the audios, in a sort of reenactment of some of the depicted events. In short, there were several interruptions, caused by outbursts of laughter, ironic comments or expressions of surprise, and while this seems like a natural response for students this age, there were few substantive comments made about the historical content or the form of the audio reports. Besides listening to the reports, most of the class time was devoted to solving technical problems associated with students' final edits on their collated audio and image files.

The teacher, interviewed after this class, said he was satisfied with how things went: "Today the students paid attention to what their classmates had done. Friday mornings, they usually are sleepy, but today they paid attention. They were laughing at what was said. In their work, there were technical problems related to editing audio and video, but not problems of comprehension or understanding" (Interview, 2 November, 2012).

However, it could be argued that, if problems with understanding content knowledge did not appear, it might well be related to the shift from disciplinary knowledge to technical issues of editing multimodal texts in this particular lesson. There was not much explanation, neither on the part of the teacher nor on the part of students, of how they had produced those reports; and while this class is part of a longer sequence, it can be assumed, considering the teacher's responses in the previous and successive interviews, that there were no discussions about the production of the final artifact, the selection of texts and images, the language choices, or the historiographical perspective taken on the events reported. The class was playful, but there were no obvious cognitive challenges related to understanding an important and controversial period or reference made to these controversies or to the aesthetic or narrative choices made to represent events during this time period.

Another noteworthy trait of this class was the primacy of a journalistic discourse, which came as a substitute for academic discourse. It seems that in order to give voice to the students, the teacher privileged journalistic text over academic writing. This dominance of media formats and languages could be a topic to work on in teacher training so that other options such as assuming the position of a writer, an academic or reading more carefully and slowly might also appear as relevant work to be done in classrooms (cf. Lerner 2012). Yet this is often not included as a subject of the training sessions for this project. Moreover, it must be said that these new media pedagogies need to be understood within the "regime of opinion" that is prevalent in society (Boltanski and Thévenot 2006), where statements are validated on the basis of "Like/Not Like" options or on emotional and immediate endorsements (van Dijck 2013). This dominance of personal opinion—whether grounded in facts or analysis or not—has been related to what Bernstein called "horizontal discourse"; that is, a colloquial, local code that is intended to promote students' participation but whose privileging makes it difficult to move towards a "vertical discourse" that implies a higher level of abstraction and the use of disciplinary languages (Bernstein 1995: 414). This same privileging of the horizontal over the vertical will be seen in the next case, too.

The difficulty of moving beyond horizontal, local statements to more elaborate language and arguments might well be related to a particular context wherein academic requirements are not the main organizers of school life (Meo 2011). Many teachers are satisfied if their students participate in a lesson; their pedagogies celebrate engagement and enthusiasm and process over product, which is in line with a didactics that dismisses information as a sign of a traditional view of "learning by rote" (Le Roux 2004). In this pedagogical discourse and practice, there is a coupling of a pseudo-constructivist view of learners that casts them as needing to remain active in order to learn and a view that foregrounds the need to capture students' interest in a fragmented *in*attention economy (Stiegler 2009). The persistence of these pedagogic and didactic positions is generally invisible to most professional development strategies, especially to ones that trust that technologies will open up the way for creative teaching and significant learning. This also will be seen in the next case.

Citizenship Education as a Moral Lesson: Horizontal Pedagogies and Popular Culture

As previously noted, the second teacher analyzed here is a social and legal sciences teacher who works at a different secondary public school located in the same city as the previous teacher. Some of this teacher's traits are similar to ones described above; both teachers share a common concern over attracting the attention of students, although for this second teacher, fragmented attention is explained by her students' socioeconomic situation. They both appeal to multimodal pedagogies and invite teenagers to produce videos and written texts that take the form of journalistic or advertising artifacts. They both use television clips and other popular culture materials in their teaching as well.

This observed class lasted 120 minutes, and, to the teacher's credit, the students remained engaged most of the time. The topic of this class was discrimination and prejudice, and the teacher chose to present it through three short television clips: a parodic piece by an Argentinean comedian, Diego Capussotto, who personifies a pop singer—*Micky Vainilla*—who has Nazi sympathies (see Muraca 2010); a news report from Telesur (a Venezuelan channel) on cyberbullying on Facebook; and a report on discrimination among teenagers and produced by a political satire program, *Caiga Quien Caiga (Heads are Going to Roll)*, which has a nonchalant, casual tone that mocks almost everything. The three pieces were shown by means of a laptop and data projector, but before presenting them, the teacher distributed a USB drive containing the three video clips and a written questionnaire that had to be answered after watching the videos for students to copy to their own netbooks. The school does not have internet connectivity, so the only possibility of accessing needed materials was through a physical drive. The disposition of the data projector (kept in the school library until needed by a teacher), charging netbooks, and downloading files from the teachers' USB drive onto each netbook took almost half the lesson time. The classroom climate was relaxed, and while some students copied the files and charged their laptops, others chatted and took a look at pictures or videos on their own screens. Once the projection started, two of the videos could be seen, despite the poor sound and visual quality, but the third file was unreadable. This prompted a new wave of passing the USB drive around amongst the students because not everyone had copied the files to their hard drive the first time around, and the teacher needed to identify a laptop that would play this third video clip. Viewing the clips lasted 19 minutes in total. All in all, a significant amount of time (an hour, to be precise) was devoted to technical issues and troubleshooting.

Most of the students watched the projection and, as discussed in the previous case, made ironic or sarcastic comments and shared some laughs. The teacher presented each piece along with questions and prompts such as: "What does this clip have to do with our subject? Why are we using it? You have to relate it [to what we're studying] and think." Students responded as if guessing the content and seeming to direct their responses towards a curricular script ("it speaks about our rights") rather than discussing what actually was being shown. They asked some information-related questions that the teacher answered for them. Her own questions looked for some evidence of what they had learned from the videos and seemed to aim at eliciting empathy: Who is talking? What information does this convey? How does this relate to the previous video? Did you ever experience anything like this? How did you feel about it? Most of the students contributed short comments or observations, with some of them making fun of what was shown in the videos. This oral interchange among the teacher and her students in response to the videos was brief and soon made way for the written questionnaire and worksheet that was handed out earlier. Questions included identifying the type of discrimination that was shown in each clip (using a taxonomy or classification of discrimination types taught in a previous class), reflecting in small groups on their own ideas about discrimination and prejudice, producing a report (as a written document, a PowerPoint presentation, or a short webcam video) and sharing it with the rest of the group, reading some articles about the National Constitution on discrimination, and producing a slogan for a public service ad against discrimination.

The activities were rich in languages and in the critical thinking they demanded, but, as in the previous case, most remained in the realm of possibility and did not become concrete realizations. Students responded to the questionnaire in very short phrases that were plagued with orthographical and syntactic problems, and in many cases simply copied down information from the internet that they found with their smartphones. Even if copying "is not the simple, mechanical process of replication that it is often taken to be" but "entails a complex and ongoing alignment of observation of the model with action in the world" (Ingold and Hallam 2007: 5), when looked at more closely, these students showed only a very limited version of this "alignment with action," using examples from Spain without acknowledging the differences between conditions in Spain and the situation in Argentina. They explored few, if any, of the creative possibilities offered by the rich variety of digitally available texts and resources and by their almost immediate access to other contexts and experiences afforded by their smartphones.

Most of the activities could be completed by simply drawing on the students' or the teacher's earlier voiced opinions or on the projected videos, in line with the "regime of opinion" described earlier (Boltanski and Thévenot 2006). The only formal document mentioned in their questionnaire and worksheet was the National Constitution, but the paraphrasing of its articles in the students' own text productions was careless. The teacher did provide some categories concerning discrimination types and concepts to do with prejudice in their previous class, but these rarely appeared in the students' work. The moral of the videos they watched together was unequivocal: it is wrong and morally reprehensible to discriminate. Students reacted with laughter or ironic comments on this, but they did not challenge this moral openly or in their written texts.

Again, there were other possibilities. It can be said that there were several windows that could have opened to interesting paths for knowledge projects; however, due to the organization of time and the kind of learning activity designed by the teacher, none of these possibilities were followed up. One of these windows is related to "watching with others" (i.e., *voir ensemble*), a practice that makes room for talking collectively about what is seen and felt in and through images. According to some philosophers and historians, this is becoming less and less common (Mondzain 2003). Even through mocking, laughing, commenting or weeping, this watching together might open up some opportunities for youth to engage in conversations that are increasingly needed but even more increasingly sidelined in classrooms. Another window could have been to work with television clips and popular media culture in a way that enlarged the curriculum—for example, by analyzing the languages and genres of the clips she presented or discussing different interpretations of their content or message or scrutinizing their contexts of production.

However, the choices made by this teacher did not help develop any of these possibilities, and this might be the result of not knowing the promise and potential that these practices contain and a consequence of a certain type of knowledge that values engagement and oral participation over everything else. If laughter, empathy and distance emerged when watching the videos, these gestures and expressions were not reworked or reconstructed in any way in the classroom. Moreover, the three video clips appeared with an equal level of validity, as if there was no difference between an ironic piece of comedy and a news report that used testimonies or statistical data. All seemed to enjoy the same truth-claim of being sociological evidence of different types of discrimination. There was no work on language genres or on sources that made it clear that, in order to be understood, these materials required—at the very least—the critical academic practices of distancing and reflection. Somewhat unsurprisingly, the students' work showed little care with respect to content and form and made no distinction between the video texts, ending up with recommendations to produce, for example, an ironic slogan "with some comedy, so as to attract the public's attention," as one student noted.

It can be said that, due to many reasons—chief among them the teacher's choice of a horizontal pedagogy (Bernstein 1995) and his or her lack of awareness of opportunities to reflect on the audiovisual materials and their effects—the achievements that are visible in the students' productions and oral responses are weak, and the student-produced texts are limited both in their formal-expressive aspects and in their relationship to specific content knowledge. This does not mean that they could not be otherwise if reworked and reflected upon, and neither is the teacher to be blamed for this; what it seems is that, given the work conditions and the pedagogical assumptions that this teacher has, it is unlikely that more productive and intellectually challenging work could be produced by using digital media if there are not other professional development strategies that call this available knowledge into question and help teachers to find and explore the promises and possibilities of ICT that insofar remain largely invisible or unrealized.

Final Remarks

The analysis of the teaching practices of these teachers shows that they mobilized particular knowledge about teaching and learning in their use of digital media that went far beyond the basic digital skills and knowledge of platforms that were disseminated by *Conectar Igualdad* and that exceeded the aims of the policy. These examples reflect the relevance of the teachers' pedagogical knowledge for their own teaching approaches and strategies, a dimension that was barely touched on, at least in the initial phases of the program. This analysis also points to the ways in which these two teachers "calibrated" their own classroom practices to outer events and demands, be it those of an academic discipline or those of social inclusion of hitherto marginalized populations. As argued in the beginning of this chapter, the "micro" network of teaching practices is not an isolated and predefined circle but a shifting space that makes connections and translations in relation to different scales of policy, that, in turn, can be seen as "vectors" that mobilize knowledge and strategies in different ways. In the case of the history teacher, his teaching was governed by a notion of disciplinary knowledge that emphasized how particular historical events have to be told or shown to students; the inclusion of the recent past was a stronger force than the imperative of digital inclusion. The use of digital media, then, came to reinforce the production of a historical narrative that was already defined in the beginning, and the troubleshooting or the discussion of technical or narrative choices in producing audiovisual texts was not seen as an occasion for learning valuable knowledge. This position was not affected by his

ICT training, which defined digital skills as a package of technical knowledge separate from subject area or discipline knowledge. In the case of the citizenship education teacher, her practices were organized around capturing students' attention and their demonstration of engagement and participation; affective identifications and oral, spontaneous responses from students were more valuable than the appropriation of disciplinary knowledge. This teacher's connection to the *Conectar Igualdad* program was in terms of social inclusion and participation, but this did not result in an expansion of her students' citizenship knowledge and practice or their use of digital media.

More generally, if the "what works" approach to teacher training and professional development places emphasis on a set of principles and activities that should work for all teachers, these cases underline the importance of considering the specific contexts of practices, which are not necessarily original but always are singular and locally defined. An external reader might find these specificities more easily: the presence of heated political debates or sociological arguments, a playful climate, and a privileging of oral interventions. The lack of emphasis on academic content or on a rigorous use of languages (written, oral or visual; conversational or disciplinary) is also a remarkable trait found in the two classrooms studied. However, this very locality is made of lines that connect these scenes with others which might seem more familiar to foreign readers: cosmopolitan social media, expert discourses on what to teach and how to teach it, and concerns about students' new attention economy. As has been said earlier, the coupling of a pseudo-constructivist view of learners who have to remain active in order to learn, with the need to capture students' interest within a fragmented, larger attention economy that extends beyond school are important translators of Argentina's ICT policy for education and are relevant to what and how these teachers teach. "Contexts of practice," then, is not necessarily bounded to a physical territory or locale but is defined by the mesh of "practices and arrangements" that organize a particular social order as the classroom.

What does this say about professional development in the midst of technology-intensive programs such as *Conectar Igualdad*? The program's course on basic digital skills might be needed for some teachers in order for them to start using digital devices and artifacts in their teaching, but it is clearly not up to the challenges that teachers face when using digital media in the moment. On one hand, teachers continuously are mobilizing their available knowledge on how to deal with the changes in the chronotopes of their classrooms, in which technical issues often become more relevant than what is to be learned, and these issues may significantly hinder the pace and rhythm of lessons. On the other hand, the use of digital media, particularly in conjunction with social media and popular global media, brings to the fore different languages and genres that need to be interrogated by teachers and students alike. The two teachers presented in this chapter are using audiovisual materials as a way of attracting students' attention and for getting closer to their interests, defined—most of the time—in terms of their media consumption. But how these texts can be placed in line with other curricular activities, and most of all, how they can constitute good and productive venues for introducing in-depth conversations (understood as critical operations in any classroom) about what one sees, feels, and thinks in relation to these images and texts and about their language, their aesthetic and ethical choices, are questions that remain largely invisible in classrooms. Professional development programs should take up these challenges seriously and centrally in their designs and seek ways to open up spaces for teachers' reflection on and creativity with how to deal more productively with the tensions that digital media bring to the classrooms.

REFERENCES

Benítez Larghi, S. Fontecoba A.; Lemus M. (2014). Bibliografía comentada desde la perspectiva de la evaluación de los modelos Uno a Uno en Latinoamérica [An annotated bibliography from the perspective of the evaluation of 1:1 models in Latin America]. *Revista Versión, Estudios de Comunicación y Política.* 34(1): 162–169.

Bernstein, B. (1995). A response. In A Sadovnik (ed), *Knowledge and Pedagogy: The Sociology of Basil Bernstein.* Norwood, NJ: Ablex Publishing, 385–424.

Biesta, G. (2007). Why "what works" won't work: Evidence-based practice and the democratic deficit of educational research. *Educational Theory.* 57(1): 1–22.

Boltanski, L. and L. Thévenot (2006). *On Justification: Economies of Worth.* Princeton, NJ: Princeton University Press.

Brun, M. (2011). *Las Tecnologías de la Información y de las Comunicaciones en la Formación Inicial Docente de América Latina* [ICT in Pre-service Teacher Education in Latin America]. Serie Políticas Sociales. Santiago de Chile: CEPAL.

Cristiá, J., Ibarraran, P., Cueto, S., Santiago, A. and Severín, E. (2012). *Technology and Child Development: Evidence from the One Laptop per Child Program.* Washington, DC: IDB Working Paper Series 304.

Dussel, I. (2012). Más allá del mito de los "nativos digitales": Jóvenes, escuelas y saberes en la cultura digital [Beyond the myth of "digital natives": Youth, schools and knowledge in digital culture]. In M. Southwell (ed), *Entre Generaciones: Exploraciones sobre Educación, Cultura e Instituciones* [Between Generations: Explorations on Education, Culture, and Institutions]. Rosario: FLACSO/Homo Sapiens, 183–213.

Dussel, I. (2015). *Estudio de Profundización sobre la Incorporación de Tecnologías de la Información y la Comunicación (TIC) en la Formación Docente de los Países del Mercosur* [An In Depth Study of the Introduction of ICT into Teacher Education in Mercosur Countries]. Final Research Report. Buenos Aires: Programa de Apoyo al Sector Educativo del MERCOSUR.

Dussel, I. (in press). Governing teacher education through digital media: A comparative perspective on policy scales and translations. In H. Kothoff and E. Keftedis (eds), *Governance and Education: Global and Local Perspectives.* Oxford, UK: Symposium Books.

Dussel, I., Ferrante, P., Sefton-Green, J. (2013). Changing narratives of change: Unintended consequences of educational technology reform in Argentina. In N. Selwyn and K. Facer (eds), *The Politics of Education and Technology*. London: Palgrave-MacMillan, 127–145.

Dussel, I., Ferrante, P., González, D. and Montero, J. (2015). Transformaciones de los saberes y participación cultural a partir de la introducción de las netbooks en escuelas secundarias [Transformations of knowledge and cultural participation since the introduction of netbooks in secondary schools]. In A. Pereyra et al. (eds), *Prácticas Pedagógicas y Políticas Educativas. Investigaciones en el Territorio Bonaerense* [Pedagogical Practices and Educational Policies: Researching the Territory of Buenos Aires]. Gonet, Argentina: UNIPE Editorial Universitaria, 165–193.

Hamilton, D. and Zufiaurre, B. (2014). *Blackboards and Bootstraps: Revisioning Education and Schooling*. Rotterdam, Netherlands: Sense Publishers.

Indarramendi, C. (2015). *Entre Compensation et Promotion de l'Égalité: Analyse de la Gestion des Politiques d'ducation Ciblées en Argentine à Partir de l'Étude du Programme Intégral pour l'Égalité Educative (PIIE) 2003–2012*. [Between Compensation and Promoting Equality: An Analysis of the Management of Targeted Education Policies in Argentina based on the Study of the Integral Program for Educational Equality 2003–2012] Unpublished Doctoral Thesis, Université de Paris 8-Flacso, Argentina.

Ingold, T. and Hallam, E. (2007). Creativity and cultural improvisation: An introduction. In E. Hallam and T. Ingold (eds), *Creativity and Cultural Improvisation*. Oxford, UK: Berg Publishers, 1–24.

Latour, B. (2005) *Reassembling the Social*. Oxford, UK : Oxford University Press.

Le Roux, A. (eds) (2004). *Enseigner l'Histoire-Géographie par le Problème?* [Teaching History and Geography through Problems]. Paris: L'Harmattan.

Lemke, J. (2004). Learning across multiple places and their chronotopes. Paper presented at AERA 2004. San Diego, CA. Available: http://www.personal.umich.edu/~jaylemke/papers/aera_2004. htm. Downloaded 14 March, 2015.

Lerner, D. (2012). Entrevista [Interview]. In D. Goldín, F. Perelman and M. Kriscautzky (eds), *Las TIC en la Escuela: Nuevas Herramientas para Viejos y Nuevos Problemas* [ICT in Schools: New Tools for Old and New Problems]. México, DF: Océano, 23–88.

McGuirk, J. (2014). *Radical Cities: Across Latin America in Search of a New Architecture*. New York: Verso.

Meo, A. (2011). Zafar, so good: Middle-class students, school habitus and secondary schooling in the city of Buenos Aires (Argentina). *British Journal of Sociology of Education*. 32(3): 349–368.

Ministerio de Educación de la Nación Argentina (2011a). *Nuevas Voces, Nuevos Escenarios: Estudios Evaluativos sobre el Programa Conectar Igualdad* [New Voices, New Scenarios: Evaluative Studies on the Connect Equality Program]. Buenos Aires: DINIECE.

Ministerio de Educación de la República Argentina (2011b). *El Modelo 1 a 1: Notas Para Comenzar. Serie Estrategias en el Aula Para 1 a 1* [The 1:1 Model: Notes for Getting Started.] Buenos Aires: Ministerio de Educación.

Mondzain, M. (2003). *Voir Ensemble: Autour de Jean-Louis Desanti*. [Seeing Together: On Jean-Louis Desanti] Paris: Gallimard.

Muraca, M. (2010). ¡Yo sólo hago pop! Micky Vanilla y una crítica a la sociedad pos(?)menemista [I only do pop! Micky Vanilla and a critique of the post(?)menemist society]. In R. Carbone and M. Muraca (eds), *La Sonrisa de Mamá es Como la de Perón: Capusotto: Realidad Política y Cultura* [Mom's Smile is like Peron's: Capusotto: Political Reality and Culture]. Buenos Aires: Imago Mundi-UNGS, 15–22.

Nespor, J. (2004). Educational scale-making. *Pedagogy, Culture and Society*. 12(3): 309–326.

Nespor, J. (2012). Devices and educational changes. In T. Fenwick and R. Edwards (eds), *Researching Education through Actor-Network-Theory*. Oxford, UK: Wiley, 1–22.

Ros, C., Cimolai, S., González, D., Masnatta, M., Montero, J., Ochoa De La Fuente, L. and Segal, A. (2014). *Inclusión Digital y Prácticas de Enseñanza en el Marco del Programa Conectar Igualdad para la Formación Docente del Nivel Secundario* [Digital Inclusión and Teaching Practices within the Program Connect Equality for Pre-service Teacher Education for Secondary Schools]. Buenos Aires: Ministerio de Educación de la Nación.

Schatzki, T. (2002). *The Site of the Social: A Philosophical Account of the Continuation of Social Life and Change*. University Park, PA: Pennsylvania State University Press.

Selwyn, N. (2011). *Schools and Schooling in the Digital Age*. London: Routledge.

Sileoni, A. (2012). Inaugural words. In I. Dussel (ed), *TIC y Educación: Aprender y Enseñar en la Cultura Digital*. [ICT and Education: Learning and Teaching in Digital Culture]. Buenos Aires: Fundación Santillana, 73–77.

SITEAL (Sistema de Información de Tendencias Educatives en América Latina). (2014). *Informe sobre Tendencias Sociales y Educativas en América Latina 2014. Políticas TIC en los Sistemas Educativos de América Latina* [Report on Social and Educational Trends in Latin America 2014. ICT policies in educational systems in Latin America]. Buenos Aires: OEI-IIPE-UNESCO. Available at: http://www.siteal.iipe-oei.org/sites/default/files/siteal_informe_2014_politicas_tic.pdf Downloaded 20 October, 2015.

Sobe, N. and Kowalczyk, J. (2014). Exploding the cube: Revisioning "context" in the field of comparative education. *Current Issues in Comparative Education*. 16(1): 6–12.

Stiegler, B. (2009). The carnival of the new screen: From hegemony to isonomy. In P. Snickers and P. Vonderau (eds), *The YouTube Reader*. Stockholm: National Library of Sweden, 40–59.

Strathern, M. (2004). *Commons and Borderlands: Working Papers on Interdisciplinary, Accountability, and the Flow of Knowledge*. Abingdon, UK: Sean Kingston Publishing.

Van Dijck, J. (2013). *The Culture of Connectivity: A Critical History of Social Media*. Oxford, UK: Oxford University Press.

Vezzetti, H. (2007). Conflictos de la memoria en la Argentina: Un estudio histórico de la memoria social [Memory conflicts in Argentina: A historical study of social memory]. In A. Pérotin-Dumon (ed), *Historizar el Pasado Vivo en América Latina* [Historicize the Live Past in Latin America]. Available: http://etica.uahurtado.cl/historizarelpasadovivo/es_contenido.php Downloaded 12 September 2015.

CHAPTER EIGHT

Exploring Multidirectional Memory-Work AND the Digital AS A Phase Space FOR Teacher Professional Development

TERESA STRONG-WILSON, CLAUDIA MITCHELL, AND
MARCEA INGERSOLL

INTRODUCTION

Teachers are agents of memory; they mediate culture and knowledge through their interpretations of texts and development of teaching as a text. Arguably, schools are not simply at the receiving end of "memory institutions" such as libraries, museums, and national archives (Council of Canadian Academies 2015) but are memory-making institutions in their own right. Gadamer (2013) reminds us that we have a memory for some things and not for others. As agents of memory, teachers are formed by memories and shape others' memories (O'Reilly-Scanlon 2001; Strong-Wilson 2008). Indeed, they have been called the "chief storytellers" in the classroom (Rosen 1985). More, they are charged with helping students choose how to navigate competing stories and thus learn how to exercise their own agency. Although these stories may occupy one place (viz., the classroom), they arrive there by way of various locations: the histories of the students in the room, the teacher's own background, and others' voices, as represented in the texts and curriculum, or heard as loud whispers: elephants in the middle of the room. Mackey (1999) adopted the term "phase space" from novelist Phillip Pullman to describe all of the possibilities that are present yet remain unexplored in writing a narrative; these possibilities become as "ghosts" which linger around the main plot. A multidirectional approach to memory and teacher professional development, like that posited in this chapter, occupies a phase space but arguably so, too, has the digital in relation to teacher professional development. Mackey wrote about the phase space in 1999 in anticipation of the research that she would later do around the digital:

> In our contemporary era of major technological change, we can see stories shifting and altering their borders … yet the vocabulary for describing new hybrid forms of story that cross media boundaries and variously impinge on our daily lives is surprisingly limited. (Mackey 1999: 16)

This chapter sets out to explore the possibilities for teacher professional development of digital media, drawing on the vocabulary offered by the idea of multidirectional memory. Multidirectional memory is the name given by Michael Rothberg to "a model based on recognition of the productive interplay of disparate acts of remembrance" that combines "a revisionary gaze on the past with an optimistic sense of possibilities for the future" (2009: 309). This model departs from that tendency within memory studies and memory institutions (like schools) towards a competitive approach to remembrance, in which, post 1960s and the civil rights movement in the U.S., struggles occur between a dominant narrative (i.e., hegemony) and counter-narratives; but where emerging counter-narratives also implicitly compete with one another for "real estate space" and "air time." With ready access to the internet and the global exchange of information, this struggle has been only further accentuated.

In education, we have been driven by models that are outcome based, especially in the area of curriculum with its twin legacies of Taylorism and Tylerism (Luke, Woods and Weir 2013). Frederick Winslow Taylor was the architect of a scientific managerial approach to industry, while Ralph Tyler has been credited with distilling Taylorism into the four-part "Tyler Rationale," a homogenizing, top-down approach to curriculum development and classroom instruction. "Education reforms" such as No Child Left Behind and Race to the Top follow directly in line with such thinking and increasingly impact teacher education and professional development not only in the United States, where these policies originate, but also in Canada, as seen in the increasing pressure placed on schools and teachers to meet pre-determined outcomes (e.g., in Quebec, the Management Agreements that school boards need to negotiate with the Ministry of Education to promise to meet predetermined goals that align with Ministry funding priorities). To reiterate, as Pullman explains it, the phase space (which is a term that originally comes from physics) refers to all of the possible as well as the actual consequences inhering in a given moment. The storyteller, Pullman says, may wander about in the phase space ("possibilities") but remains focused on identifying the destination ("actual consequences"): "once you know where it is, you must make for it, and then go back and clear the path and make sure that every twist and turn is there because you want it to be" (Pullman 1997: 50–51 in Mackey 1999: 20). Currently, the predominant "gold standard" model (viz., destination) in teacher professional development tells a story that is evidence based, in which the strongest evidence of professional development effectiveness is the proof of student learning as ascertained by external measures: teacher learns X and as a result of applying X to instruction in the classroom, student test scores improve (Vescio et al. 2008). Effectiveness has in fact become a key term in descriptions of contemporary professional development frameworks, tied tightly to measures of impact on student learning or empirical identification of core features (Desimone 2009, 2011). However, what may be called a "clear-cut and even ruthless approach to storytelling," Mackey points out, has "its own substantial satisfactions," but left out is the "productive potential" of the phase space (1999: 20)—an exploration of *what ifs*, to which the fluid space of the digital can be especially receptive. We find Mackey's comment justly applies to current models of teacher professional development in which even recent modulations of the gold standard (e.g., adaptive and sustainable models of professional development embedded in local practices) do not stray far from the destination and goal of tracking student achievement in relation to teacher professional development and performance (Koellner and Jacobs 2015). A longer lens on teacher professional development, through examination of studies over a twenty-year period, reveals that fundamental to the field has been both the personal and the professional, even if questions have abounded about where one begins and the other ends (Clandinin 1985; Day and Sachs 2004; Goodson 1992; Goodson and Sikes 2001). In our work, we see the personal and professional not as binaries but as interdependent, with multidirectional memory-work in a digital phase space becoming a potentially powerful vehicle for teachers to explore deep and alternative pathways for personal/professional inquiry.

Since at least 2008, but earlier in our own teaching and research practices, we have been engaged in thinking through the implications for teaching and learning of memory-work and, particularly, forms of memory-work conducive to "productive remembering" (Mitchell et al. 2011; Strong-Wilson et al. 2013). Productive remembering, which draws on an eclectic range of memory methods that have been applied to diverse phenomena, argues for retrospection that is forward looking and that can result in social change by implicating and impacting the autobiographical stories of those involved. In other words, productive remembering begins from where teachers are, with their memories, life experiences, and their desires and aspirations and locating this memory-work within a broader landscape of others' memories along with a broader set of social concerns and where the focus is on galvanizing memories for the purpose of looking forward towards social change. Recently, we have been applying this work to thinking about and through digital tools. The present chapter reports on our ongoing work in a research project on social justice education with teachers and teacher-educators on multidirectional memory-work and the digital.

THEORETICAL FRAMEWORK: MULTIDIRECTIONAL MEMORY-WORK AND THE PHASE SPACE AS AN ALTERNATIVE FRAMEWORK FOR TEACHER PROFESSIONAL DEVELOPMENT

When memories of exclusion, oppression or simply of the past collide, what happens? Whose past, or whose version of the past, is heard? As memory scholars have been telling us, the past is not really the past. The past is remembered in the present and for a purpose that reflects a now rather than a then. As Hodgkin and Radstone (2003) have observed, the past is contested territory. This problem has manifested itself in various ways in contemporary society, from museum exhibits to naming museums to the creation of museums themselves (e.g., the hotly contested content of the recently inaugurated Canadian Museum of Human Rights, which opened in 2014 in Winnipeg, Manitoba) to government apologies and royal commissions (e.g., for residential schools in Canada found to have grossly abused children for decades) to the writing, publishing and endorsement of textbooks to curriculum development and teacher professional development. This contested territory, Rothberg (2009) notes, can be compared to the zero-sum game of the real-estate industry, in which parties vie for a share of the pie and, further, seek to acquire the greatest share. Holocaust memory long has been identified as a major preoccupation of memory studies, institutions and curricula, occupying scholarship, museums, commemorative sites, and teaching and learning (Radstone 2000). Rothberg proposes an alternative way of thinking about contemporary memory, which he calls multidirectional memory. Multidirectional memory entangles memories with one another without reducing one to the other, instead bringing together multiple traumatic pasts for a productive remembering in the present. In the Canadian context, for example, this could mean juxtaposing salient, previously overlooked or underemphasized episodes in our formation as a nation: residential schooling of Indigenous children with Japanese internment camps and the (mis)treatment of Chinese workers in the building of a transnational railway. While this entanglement sounds like some fantastic dream in education long associated with multiculturalism, Rothberg explains that multidirectionality depends on the non-erasure of distinctive histories, which, in being shared yet juxtaposed, retain their particularity, even as the shared space opens up a new space for re-thinking convergence and/or difference. Rothberg elaborates:

Fundamental to the conception of competitive memory is a notion of the public sphere as a pre-given, limited space in which already-established groups engage in a life-and-death struggle. In contrast, pursuing memory's multidirectionality encourages us to think of the public sphere as a malleable discursive space in which groups ... actually come into being through their dialogical interactions with others. (2009: 5)

The sharing of multidirectional memory is a form of memory-work, in the sense of memory becoming a working-through space for potential transformation (Rothberg 2009: 4)—in Mackey's terms, a phase space. Shared memory depends on communication of individual or collective memories and rests on a "division of mnemonic labor" (Margalit 2002, cited in Rothberg 2009: 15). Global media technologies have made this sharing more possible in "malleable discursive spaces," whereby "the lack of an Archimedean point of reference" can better ensure this division of labor (Rothberg 2009: 15). Archimedes was a Greek scientist who sought an ideal vantage point from which to see the earth itself: an impossible, indeed undesirable, ideal. What is more realistic is sharing and communication from different and varied subject locations, which digital affordances and the Internet make more possible.

Although Rothberg does not explicitly address it, the digital landscape is envisioned as central, even pivotal to, and certainly by its sheer presence, increasingly imbricated in multidirectional memory, beginning with this notion of shared memory as a network, which rests on memory-work being done at the same time, in different places that are connected or, rather, connectable. Multidirectional memory—and the attendant memory-work—refers to a space; a phase space: the possibility of imagining productive interaction and transformational thinking. It therefore also calls for a certain aesthetic. Even before he coined the term "multidirectional memory," Rothberg was interested in exploring aesthetic forms that could disrupt a predictable (and thus, implausible) narrative in which all's well that ends well in terms of its claim to represent trauma; for instance, he critiques a film like *Schindler's List* for its simplistic, heroic storyline (see Rothberg 2000). In his 2009 book, Rothberg devotes considerable attention to events occurring around the year 1961—a year in which the Eichmann trial took place in Israel and in France—and when the film *Chronicle of a Summer* appeared. The film's aesthetic brought into constellation Holocaust memory with emerging accounts of decolonization—the Algerian war/revolution and the independence of African nations. Produced by two sociologists, it was one of the first instances of cinema verité, using the video camera as a stimulant to provoke thinking about subjects supposedly remote but not far from the minds of those who were interviewed in the shadow of war and trauma (past and impending), using the prompt, "How do you live? Are you happy?" The interviews were conducted on the streets of Paris, and the main interviewer was a young woman,

Marceline, who was a Holocaust survivor. Rothberg examines how, through the filming, individuals whose histories seemed unconnected from one another are thrown together by way of an "ethnographic surrealism" (2009: 187) in which the participants come up against evidence of the past in the present and of incongruous threads that link their pasts to one another. One of the pivotal moments in the film happens when Marceline, in conversation over dinner, asks two African black men visiting from the Congo and brought there by the decolonizing movement in their own country, even as France was using aggressive tactics reminiscent of Nazism to try to control and subjugate Algeria, if they know why she has a number tattooed on the inside of her arm. This raising of the spectre of the Holocaust also occurs in the context of an uncomfortable moment of racism, in which Marceline says that she could never date a black man, even as African black men are seated as guests at the table. The contradictions, captured on film through this frank encounter, also become the subject of conversation and of working through different memories.

The film provides an example of multidirectional memory as "a process in which transfers take place between events that have come to seem separate from each other" (Rothberg 2009: 197). This new aesthetic or "form" (Rothberg 2009: 202) rests on a "malleable discursive space" (Rothberg 2009: 5) that can come into being through creative and critical ("self-reflexive"; Rothberg 2009: 202) juxtaposition of memories and histories. One of the main vehicles that can allow for this is the video camera. By way of the testimonial, details which haunt the personal and everyday details emerge into a space that is public and shared. This new aesthetic depends on "open" forms of address (Rothberg 2009: 215) which, through "circulation" (Rothberg 2009: 212), can create new publics by inviting in new audiences. What does this mean in relation to the digital? Our project intended to begin to explore these possibilities by drawing teachers together to work on their own memories even as they engaged shared memories (e.g., of the past—of relatives, families, communities, nations, etc.); this within a digital artifact that itself would become more "malleable" through being shared and circulated among the group as it was still being created and worked through.

The Digital and Professional Development

The explosion of digital technologies has changed the ways in which we can interact. While schools have been slow to embrace the digital tools that are ubiquitous outside classroom walls (Male and Burden 2014; Underwood 2014), there is evidence that Canadian teachers are actually more likely to seek digital knowledge than employees in other occupations. In a national study of Canadians, only 61 per cent of the overall labour force and 77 per cent of employed professionals had engaged in informal learning of computers; in contrast, at the time, 89% of teachers had sought informal opportunities to learn new technologies (Smaller et al. 2000). This individual desire on the part of teachers to engage the digital may be a necessary response to a delayed offering of formal opportunities to develop teachers' digital skills. A 2006 review of literature on professional development content and delivery modes for experienced Canadian teachers still contained no references to "digital" or information communication technologies (Broad and Evans 2006). Meanwhile, new forms of credentialing have emerged, with corporate organizations offering professional development recognition in the form of "digital badges" (Gamrat, Zimmerman, Dudek and Peck 2014). Gamification has infiltrated professional learning platforms where teachers register to participate in online professional development, learn about a digital age skill or tool, then earn a "digital learning badge" after demonstrating how they have successfully integrated the new technology into their instruction. Also referred to as microcredentials, the digital badges aim to incentivize teachers to undertake personalized professional development and support more personalized professional development. Simultaneously, though, they provide observable professional development data for employers. Such online professional development has been introduced more as a cost-saving measure in the face of budget cuts and increased accountability (Davis 2009).

Educators are seeking contextual, collaborative professional development activities that value experience, give them agency to make decisions about their learning, and are directly relevant to the issues of greatest concern. Teachers want to gain proficiency with technology, not just to earn badges but also to enact social change. Hargreaves (2003) notes that professional development should be lifelong, focus on engaged, sustainable professional relationships over time, and draw on the knowledge and experiences available within relational networks. Professional learning communities must be authentic, interdependent communities of teachers who invest in themselves, their colleagues, and their students—not simply another feature of labelling in a market fundamentalist economy. We know that personal interactions, participation in a community of learners, and creation and sharing of knowledge in small groups facilitate communication and learning (Tienken and Stonaker 2007). Deep, sustained engagement is possible when teachers come together because of a shared interest, such as in social justice. Ritchie's (2012) study of collaborative networks indicates that whether face-to-face in schools and communities or online via shared interest listservs or Facebook groups, collaborative networks play a key role in teachers' decisions to become critical educators and sustain a commitment to social justice. Such instances of democratic professionalism, driven by teachers in the field, take an activist approach to questions around teacher identity and educational quality (Ritchie 2012; Sachs 2001). Of particular relevance here, a report released by the Canadian Teachers Federation (2012), *Teaching the Way We Aspire to Teach: Now and in the Future*, is illuminating for what it says about teacher collaboration. The data collection method informing this report involved focus groups across the country, along with an online survey that drew on the responses of more than 4,000 teachers. The study found that collaborative relationships were very important to teachers:

> Teachers envisioned policies and processes that would enable the development of more opportunities for working together in ways that current school structures do not always allow or promote. Instead of being bound by traditional disciplines and grade levels, many expressed the desire to collaborate on cross-grade, interdisciplinary units, tasks, and projects that connected both teachers and students in new and diverse ways. Participants were enthusiastic in their support of challenging approaches to schooling that have supported traditional images of teachers working in isolation (2012: 9).

Guskey and Sparks (2004) suggest that three characteristics impact teacher learning: (1) the context in which the learning occurs, (2) the content of the professional learning activity, and (3) the processes used to impart the content. We can draw on these characteristics of professional development to frame multidirectional memory work as a tool for teacher professional development, which has the potential to influence student learning through intertwining the personal and professional with social justice elements of teacher lives and practices. For educators who seek dialogue, reflection, trust, collaboration, and ongoing learning over time, informal and contextual professional development guided by notions of social justice offer meaningful alternatives to district-mandated professional development days. Such learning, teacher led or teacher driven, involves teachers in exploring phase spaces.

METHODOLOGICAL FRAMEWORK AND DESCRIPTION OF THE PROCESS

Our multidirectional memory-work project drew on the idea of "digital retreats" (Mitchell and de Lange 2013) to bring teacher participants together to explore the uses of the digital in a workshop format. Located within the broader arena of participatory cultures (see Jenkins 2006), the idea of digital retreats acknowledges and nurtures the notion of participant collaboration, along with the idea of production and audience. As an example, Mitchell and de Lange talk about gathering teachers from two settings, one group in KwaZulu Natal and one group in the Eastern Cape of South Africa, to make cellphilms: movies "made with a cellphone and for a cellphone" (Dockney and Tomaselli 2009). While the teachers visited each other's provinces and schools, the most critical element of working with the digital was teachers working together and learning from each other (Mitchell et al. 2014).

Many went beyond the collective work of producing cellphilms related to common themes of poverty reduction and addressing HIV and AIDS to produce short cellphilms that documented aspects of their everyday lives, their families, their home villages and their classrooms (see also Schwab-Cartas and Mitchell 2015). These cellphilms, most three to five minutes in length, offered what seemed to be a set of individual reflexive moments framed within the social, as the teachers knew that they were going to be screening their own cellphilms for the whole group. This methodological way of working is located within what Schratz and Walker (1995) refer to as a "research as social change" approach, which connects the self with the social, situating the project within the kind of participatory forms of research that take account of dynamics of collaboration/collectivity (Achinstein 2002; Kapoor and Jordan 2009). Our project drew together work across several different areas of research in teacher education, including teacher action research and scholarship of practice (Cochran-Smith and Lytle 2009; Kemmis and McTaggart 2005; Loughran et al. 2004; Stenhouse 2012; Strong-Wilson et al. 2012), methods of memory-work (Haug et al. 1987), social autobiography and autoethnography (Hasebe-Ludt et al. 2009; Strong-Wilson 2008), participatory visual methodologies (Mitchell 2011) and self-study methodologies (Hamilton 1998; Kitchen and Russell 2012; Pithouse et al. 2009).

DESCRIPTION OF THE WORKSHOPS: WORKS IN PROCESS

In taking a "digital retreat" approach, the project supported teacher participants as they worked with and through memory in multidirectional ways, individually as well as in relation to one another, in workshops that we (Teresa, Claudia and Marcea) co-organized. The workshops focused on supporting participants as they drew on digital tools to explore memory as a phenomenon as well as a method. By phenomena, we mean various ways in which to conceptualize and approach the presence of the past in the present and future; examples we have used previously are memory as for the future; memory as feelings of belatedness; and memory as nostalgia (Strong-Wilson, Mitchell, Allnutt and Pithouse-Morgan 2013). By referring to memory as method, we were drawing attention to the multiple tools available for exploring productive forms of remembering, ranging from reading texts to writing them to analyzing or creating films to invoking objects as memory prompts to visual methods like taking photographs or returning to a photographic archive.

Twenty participants joined the project; we included ourselves in this count as co-participants. The group was composed largely of teachers: that is, teacher educators and graduate students (many of whom were practicing teachers) who had been teaching recently or who had returned to teaching after completing their

Master's degree. As a group, we ranged across being professors, post-doctoral fellows, doctoral or master's students, and/or teacher researchers, sharing interests in teaching, teacher education and social justice education. The group members were associated with five universities in the geographical area in or near to Montreal, Canada: McGill, Concordia, Bishops University, University of Ottawa, and Queens University. As a group of female participants, some new to research and others more experienced, we were working across a variety of research areas: from early childhood, elementary, secondary, or adult education to second-language education and fine arts education and artful forms of inquiry.

In taking a workshop and "digital retreat" approach, the project alternated between two-hour evening sessions and weekend day sessions, approximately two to three times per month over the winter and spring semesters. Workshops began in January 2015 and have been ongoing, with a summer hiatus; they will draw to a close in the fall of 2015 with a series of artifact sharing/screenings. A planned finale event, though, will have been preceded by "first draft" pre-screenings amongst ourselves; reading/viewing one another's artifacts through a multidirectional memory-work lens (Hampl 1999). This process, as we describe in this chapter, has occurred throughout and has been key to working through memory in multidirectional ways, by creating "malleable discursive spaces." We also have had the opportunity to share some of our draft artifacts in a Departmental Research Day event at McGill in May 2015. We have found useful Patricia Hampl's (1996) work on first-draft and second-draft remembering. Speaking of memoir writing, she observes: "I try to let pretty much anything happen in a first draft. A careful first draft is a failed first draft" (Hampl 1996: 206). A second draft calls for revisioning, "a new seeing of the materials of the first draft. Nothing merely cosmetic will do—no rouge buffing the opening sentence, no glossy adjective to lift a sagging line, nothing to attempt covering a patch of gray writing" (Hampl 1996: 210). By sharing our work with one another in an ongoing workshopping fashion, an environment supportive of thinking with and through multidirectional memory has been fostered, one more conducive to the creation of the "malleable discursive spaces" that Rothberg (2009) identifies as central to multidirectional memory.

The unfolding of the workshop/retreats is described below

Sessions One and Two: We began our memory-work by mapping our pasts and/or present lives, writing and/or drawing on paper and then sharing this with each other in response to the prompt "Write about or draw the place where you live presently or where you have lived (e.g., where you grew up)." Creating these maps comprised "first draft" sessions, although with our second prompt of "Write about or draw the other inhabitants. Who are the other present inhabitants or past ones?" We started to nudge these teachers towards a "second draft" and multidirectional thinking about their memories. The maps produced in response to the first prompt varied, from schematic outlines of the traces of early childhood memory to detailed renditions of early childhood landscapes and places to interpretive variations that played with line and representation to call to mind significant memories. As we have often found with this activity, this kind of map tends to generate intense, interior landscapes of especially childhood places, with participants commenting on how much they had forgotten—and remembered—either through the drawing or in the sharing of their map with others in small groups. We then invited participants to draw another map that attended more to others' memories and perceptions. Many supplemented their original maps, but in different ways. For instance, two participants had grown up in close proximity to a First Nations community; therefore, their maps reflected memories of relations between "settler" and Indigenous communities. Another drew the house and surroundings in which she had first taught, in an Inuit village, for four years, this as integral to her own "growing up." Others began to "people" their original map with other family members, trying to imagine how that same space looked from a different vantage point that they had not previously considered. One drew what an originally childhood landscape looked like across generations. Still others generated new maps: places to which they had re-located, reflecting on the traces of themselves and/or of others that persisted; for instance, the pencil sharpener left attached to a wall in the kitchen by the previous inhabitants of a newly bought house. The material for these early sessions was rich and engaging, taking place through small- and whole-group discussion within an evening two-hour session (Session One) and part of a follow-up weekend day session (Session Two).

Session Two: After our successive map drawings and sharing of these, we moved to discuss two readings—the introductory chapter to Rothberg's *Multidirectional Memory* and to Strong-Wilson, Mitchell, Allnutt and Pithouse-Morgan's *Productive Remembering and Social Agency*. Most of this discussion focused on wrestling with what was meant by multidirectional memory, and people's responses to this idea, as well as discussing tensions between the personal and the social, between what belongs to the individual and what is shared and becomes common. We also discussed how to move beyond competitive notions of memory, such as through intentional uses of memory-work, with emphasis placed on the memory-work involved. We then shifted to digital tools: what did people already know and use and what did they want to learn? Most participant responses focused on tools associated with digital storytelling, but it also was understood that people would not name what they did not yet know about. In so doing, we decided that we needed to introduce examples of digital work involving memory, beginning with projects that had already been created by participants within the group as part of their own earlier project or independent work. For this, we turned to the group itself, because individuals brought different levels of expertise with digital technologies, as well as varied experiences in working with the digital in previous contexts.

<u>Session Three:</u> We screened examples of digital work involving memory that had been created by group members in their previous research; these examples are described next. It seemed important to begin with what was already made rather than having participants feel as though they had to generate something new or "from scratch." Rothberg's multidirectional memory lends itself to pastiche—to bringing together what has already been made and that could be re-made, even re-mediated, by virtue of being shared. The idea of re-mediation is strongly associated with digital media, especially now in this time in between one dominant medium (the book and printed page) and another (the screen). Bolter and Grusin's notions (1999) of how one medium (e.g., the digital) borrows from a previous one (e.g., print) are especially useful. The screening of these examples proved highly generative, prompting extended discussion of the content as well as of the process by which the digital artifacts had been created. It also introduced the idea that participants already had been engaged in digital forms of memory-work without necessarily naming it as such. There were four examples screened in this session, which are briefly described next.

We watched a digital story that a doctoral student and teacher educator had created to accompany her Master's research on the Rwandan genocide (DeMartini 2012). She turned to video to help her work through difficult questions and emotions. The 10-minute film combines photographs and moving images from a particular place in Rwanda that was to be the site of a school but was instead turned into a commemoration site following the massacre in 1994 and where the initiative for commemoration came from the survivors of the genocide in that place. The video pauses over this site. The author combined images of green landscapes containing grave markers with the deserted rooms in an empty schoolhouse, artwork that depicts the genocide or places bearing traces of violent memory alongside soundtracks of silence, of Rwandan children playing (from a neighboring site and school), and of crickets, which is a sound heard while there. Some of the imagery came from her own videotaping of the scene (including its sounds and silences) and some from her archival research in Rwanda and Montreal. In her current teaching of pre-service teachers, she draws explicitly on a process of thinking through multidirectional forms of memory, first explored in her Master's, to generate examples and encourage her students to create their own digital projects.

Another example came from a Master's student in art education who interviewed her grandmother, a Holocaust survivor, also for her Master's degree. Her digital artifact was a performance piece, accompanied by a script based on her interviews with her grandmother. The video combined collaged (photoshopped) images taken from her visit to the town in Poland where her grandmother grew up, archival pictures, and images she took when witnessing the concentration camp sites, along with sounds (e.g., of trains; of goosestepping; from a Jewish wedding), and a video excerpt of her interview with her grandmother with her father as translator from Yiddish.

Yet another example came from a secondary school teacher who investigated the topic of depression and mental illness by interviewing a close relative, who is an artist. Again, the film was produced for a Master's class. The film used footage from the interviews, with scenes of her sister's everyday life over the course of several days, with these scenes dubbed over with audio of her sister's voice. This teacher commented how it was in putting together this video that she started to understand and realize the impact of depression on her sister's life, and she experienced a permutation of boundaries: "When you are making choices, you're thinking less about what they're saying and thinking ... [and instead] about the whole picture. It changes the way that you experience it whereas when you are just working with interviews. It was only in putting together the music and with the clips that I started to understand her story."

In a fourth example, a teacher educator showed a work in progress produced as part of her own ongoing autoethnographic inquiry as a researcher, which also served as a tool that she uses in teaching pre-service teachers to prompt reflection on how to cope with often overwhelming feelings of anxiety (highly relevant to teachers) and where digital representation was one of the tools she had been using to help her think through these feelings via a creative process. The video combined factual information (collected through research using internet sources) with excerpts from her own reflective journals, interspersed with images pulled from her own photographic archive as well as the internet. These images were key and meant to symbolize, through radiating, a complex constellation of meanings: preliminary understandings as well as ongoing questions.

Each of the four presentations was contextualized by each teacher explaining what she had learned from her project; the teachers' learning was further elicited through questions asked by the group, which also included practical queries, like: "how did you do that?", along with an understated "I want to do something" but with the understanding that these productions were about something that represented a significant learning experience. Participants were interested in the thinking behind the productions: the process of deliberation that was integral to the act of creating an artifact. "Why did you choose to use this (e.g., still images) rather than something else?", other teachers wanted to know. They were curious about what programs or software had been used and how they could learn to use them in turn. YouTube often was cited as a "do-it-yourself" approach indispensable to learning the fundamental elements by means of watching tutorials and how-tos. Participants were keen to hear the story of the story; the back-story (Mackey 2003) of how the teacher came to this subject in this particular way, using the digital, and drawing on these tools rather than others. They were drawn back repeatedly to the creative process—of how the visual aspects came together with the soundtrack; how "images and sound talk to each other" (Participant verbal communication; February 2015 Workshop); how the author used light and shadow to tell a story; the role of storyboarding in the creative process—and how that process communicated the intention of the author. The authors talked about what was not represented—for instance, in the Rwandan genocide digital story, the deliberate absence of bodies. The workshop participants particularly wanted to know whether or how the digital artifact told various stories: that of the creator, the one(s) whose story or stories were being narrated, and the creative tension among these. They asked how the viewers' own memories played a part in responses to the artifacts, leading to discussion of the emotional connections that such artifacts can elicit in students in classrooms. They wanted to know what to call the artifacts produced, as all shared commonalities but were distinct, serving different purposes and combining media differently. Particularly relevant to how such tools could contribute to broader issues of professional development, teacher participants wanted to know what realizations had come about through the process of so closely engaging with the subjects (topics, people) through producing a digital artifact.

Along the way, possible topics and issues for other participants' digital artifacts emerged. One participant, for example, became interested in producing a digital story using episodes (as time capsules) from teaching, exploring issues from the points of view and in the voices of student teachers. Another talked about using animation to show how the memory-maps shared in a previous workshop seemed to overlap with one another.

Subsequent Sessions: From this process, participants then orally generated ideas for digital artifacts and where the main criterion for choice of artifact was its importance as subject to the author/creator. This process has by far taken up the greatest space in the project, with the workshops continuing to circle back to participants' working through of their artifacts. People were invited to work alone, with one another in pairs, or in groups. Multidirectionality, while it could inhere in the artifact, could also (we decided) inhere in the spaces among the artifacts so as to allow the participants to create artifacts of genuine interest to them. By this we mean that multidirectionality could become more visible through sharing/ screening to the group and therefore in the spaces *between* multiple artifacts, as well as through a first-draft/second- (or multiple) draft process by which participants worked through their artifacts more in light of seeing and being moved by how others were working through memory. However, first, directly in response to viewing others' artifacts and in a spirit of curiosity, we found participants wanted to learn more about the digital tools themselves.

Several sessions then followed in which participants were provided with tutorials on digital storytelling and how to work (and play) with images, short movies and audio tracks, including how to import from social media sites like Facebook, Twitter and Instagram. Two of the teacher participants put together workshops and accompanying e-information about these processes to help people get started. Individuals were asked to bring some images and/or moving images to work with. A variety of digital tools were discussed and viewed, including: Voicethread,

Wevideo, and apps such as Augmented Reality—to explore distortion; Thing-link—from teaching blogging sites using push pins as points of memory on maps; and Moldiv—for creating and stitching picture collages.

These artifacts are still under construction. Many participants began by constructing drafts with materials readily to hand and where their focus has been on exploring the media. For example, one participant showed how, through multilayered video shots and editing, she could show the "same" space through three different yet simultaneous portals: her young daughter using a cell phone to move through time and space in the apartment as the child spoke to her grandmother, the mother videotaping the daughter, and the husband videotaping the mother taping the daughter. These techniques, we would argue, lend themselves to multidirectionality. Some productions have started to take on a multidirectional memory hue in more explicit ways. For instance, the teacher (and doctoral student) who taught in an Inuit community for four years juxtaposing photographs (stills) of the time she lived there with historical footage pulled from a national archive—black-and-white, grainy images—of the forced relocation of the Inuit community during the 1950s. Another teacher (and doctoral student) began instead with sound—the sounds of the red-winged blackbird to which she was deeply attached from growing up on a farmstead in Saskatchewan, and a Mennonite hymn, found on YouTube, that also contained echoes of her childhood. These she intends to weave into a complex narrative about growing up on land farmed by her family and settled by her ancestors yet belonging, originally, to the First Nations people, who still live there, conscious of their dispossession.

Leaving Things Open: As mentioned, we will have a finale screening in the fall of 2015. The project, though, already has been characterized by multiple screenings, which are actually drafting sessions. Some screenings are of the artifact in whole or in part, while some represent a talking through and visualizing of what will come. These shared "working through" sessions have been essential, resulting in deep changes in how artifacts are being conceptualized. Each time, as well, we also re-visit the broad questions: "What do these productions have to do with multidirectional memory work?", "How do they speak to story/history differently?" and "What difference can this memory-work and work with the digital make to teaching and learning in classrooms?"

CONCLUSIONS: MULTIDIRECTIONAL MEMORY AND THE DIGITAL FOR TEACHER-LED PROFESSIONAL DEVELOPMENT

Central to the workshop process has been an exploration of process within a collaborative context. This happened first on the level of memory-work—the mapping exercise and the production of first and second drafts of maps and the sharing of those memories imbricated in these maps—and where the sharing has played the key role of another phase in the drafting process, prompting reflection on and an intention to return to the map/memory-work and revise. What has been interesting to see unfold in this research is how the element of the digital has interacted with memory-work processes. The teacher participants began with a sense of curiosity about exploring a subject and with the desire to tell a story, most notably of living in juxtaposition with other people, other histories, whether within the confines of an apartment, an apartment building, a piece of land or territory, or a community. However, teachers also brought a keen interest in the digital, which became entangled in the process of investigating or working through a subject and finding an appropriate aesthetic platform for their explorations.

Teacher interest in the digital did not depend on knowledge of how to use digital tools. As in previous studies with teachers (e.g., Strong-Wilson et al. 2012), some teachers bring greater expertise in working with digital tools than do others, and there was certainly a sharing of expertise. We noticed that what brought this group together more was a focus and interest in learning about the capacity of digital tools to represent what they know and want to tell, in relation to what they don't yet know (yet want to tell), and where the digital signifies a continual moving wall, a phase space, the presence of what is possible yet unknown, even if that boundary or moving wall was subject to change. This was signaled in part by the fact that, apart from the initial memory-work itself, the most generative place for discussion in the project came through sharing artifacts in progress among those in the group. This sharing became integral to the workshop process.

It is tempting to want to make claims about multidirectionality and memory work even as we are engaged in an ongoing process of production and sharing and understanding its impact on teachers' professional development. As a group, we had opportunities to share Rothberg's writings on multidirectional memory and to view together a piece such as the digital story of the memorialization of the Rwandan genocide of 1994 alongside the digital story dealing with Holocaust survivors juxtaposed in the same session with videos perhaps even closer to home on mental health and depression. Here is where we see the relevance of multidirectionality as a "malleable" discursive space characterized by recursive reflection on one's own and others' productions, in relation to one another, which invariably leads to re-vision and re-mediation through a constant looping back into memory-work by reflecting forward on actual teaching and learning situations, whether in schools or in university classrooms. Perhaps what was most salient in our use of the digital retreat format was the appreciation of the personal situation of the person producing the piece (and about the piece) and less about what might seem like the grand narratives of social injustice. We do not take this to mean that there is no place for a more collective multidirectional memory, but, rather, that the juxtaposing of these stories is what appears to open up new spaces for a more nuanced understanding of multidirectionality and social injustices, one less bound by magnitudes of suffering and more about deepening an understanding of context and perspectives.

Given our interest in multidirectional memory work and the use of the digital in teacher-led professional development for teachers, there are several tentative conclusions that we can draw from this "in progress" work. First is the importance of intentionality along with the idea that in this work, you do not entirely know where you are going until you set out to do it. In this sense, the doing is in the doing. Hampl's notion of "first draft" production is a useful one in allowing for this "anything goes" as a starting point; this fits well with Mackey's linking of the phase space with digital work, which continues to represent the unknown because of its moving wall: there is always a new app, a new site, a new path to wander down and explore. The best exponent of this was one of the teachers who was the most digital savvy and who came to each workshop with laptop, iPad and cell phone, which she used simultaneously in relation with one another.

However, we also recognized the degree to which generating individual maps in the very first workshop was key when applied to participating teachers' digital work around memory. Participants started with their own experiences and individual memories, in a sense irrespective of the technology. This does not mean that the digital productions themselves are not important but only that the memory-work process, the planning process, and the laying bare of intentions are all critical, something that Pithouse-Morgan and colleagues (in press) found in a digital animation project with pre-service science teachers. At the same time, it has been fascinating to see how the teachers' queries into various forms of digital representation have informed their choice of subject and decisions about how to translate ideas and individual memories into a shared context via a digital artifact that they knew would be intended for a broader audience. With the multiple screenings of drafts, the possibility has been gradually emerging of a flexible space of shared memory that is multidirectional, whereby the artifacts themselves draw on multiple memories and, through being shared, enhance and galvanize individual projects while also contributing to a deepened understanding of the interconnectedness of memories.

Although we cannot claim at this point that the professional development initiative we are describing is fully teacher led, we see the potential for this work to be teacher driven. As such we see the potential for digital technology to continue to expand the possibilities for teachers to engage in what one rural teacher in South Africa refers to as doing "my own work" (see Mitchell et al. 2009). In that study, Tembinkosi, a young teacher who participated in a curated album documentary project, created a photo album that offered an account of his sister's death as a result of complications associated with streptomeningitis, HIV and AIDS. His reflections are captured in the video documentary, *Our Photos, Our Videos, Ourselves* (Mak 2004). By "breaking the silence" in his own family, Tembinkosi realized that he could use his position as a teacher in a rural community to help to break the silence around HIV and AIDS. What is relevant to our current project is this sense of agency—of "doing my own work"—and working with memory and having an audience of teachers. As with many artistic endeavours where the artist may stay with a particular theme (e.g., abandonment, identity, mobility), it is likely that teachers in their own professional development work, including that carried out through digital forms of memory-work, might follow some recurring themes in their work. The digital productions can often become part of a larger project that could go in different directions, including with students. We would suggest that, as has been our experience in this research project, these possibilities can multiply in significant ways when teachers enter "phase spaces" of what could happen or be seen differently, in collaborative settings like the multidirectional digital workshop retreats. Multidirectionality is constituted as a "malleable" space for working through memory and where the digital enhances those "phase space" possibilities through exploration and sharing of drafts of in-progress digital artifacts, suggesting its potential for alternative, digital forms of professional development learning.

As we noted at the beginning of this chapter, teachers are already agents of memory in relation to schools and learners. Notwithstanding complex issues related to ethics, as we explore elsewhere (Strong-Wilson, Mitchell, Morrison, Radford and Pithouse-Morgan 2015), we see how the idea of a digital archive (to be developed elsewhere) could contribute to a long-term strategy for professional development and where, in light of our work around multidirectional memory, this archive would comprise a malleable discursive space. What does that mean, concretely? It would mean that the creation of artifacts (viz., archive as collection of artifacts) would not be the main goal; instead, the *memory-work* would be, and where there would be opportunity for professional growth through sharing of digital drafting processes in collegial spaces.

REFERENCES

Achinstein, B. (2002). Conflict amid community: The micropolitics of teacher collaboration. *Teachers College Record.* 104(3): 412–455.

Bolter, J. and Grusin. R. (1999). *Remediation: Understanding New Media.* Cambridge, MA: MIT Press.

Broad, K. and Evans, M. (2006). *A Review of Literature on Professional Development Content and Delivery Modes for Experienced Teachers.* Toronto: Ontario Ministry of Education.

Canadian Teachers' Federation. (2012). *Teaching the Way We Aspire to Teach: Now and in the Future.* Available: http://www.ctffce.ca/Newsroom/news.aspx?NewsID=1983984761andlang=EN Downloaded 9 March, 2015.

Clandinin, D. (1985). Personal practical knowledge: A study of teachers' classroom images. *Curriculum Inquiry.* 15(4): 361–385.

Council of Canadian Academies. (2015). *Leading in the Digital World: Opportunities for Canada's Memory Institutions.* Ottawa, ON: The Expert Panel on Memory Institutions and the Digital Revolution, Council of Canadian Academies.

Cochran-Smith, M. and Lytle, S. (2009). *Inquiry as Stance: Practitioner Research for the Next Generation.* New York: Teachers College Press.

Davis, M. (2009). Online professional development weighed as cost-saving tactic. *Education Week,* March 13. Available at: http://www.edweek.org/dd/articles/2009/03/13/04ddprofdev.h02.html Downloaded 3 March, 2015.

Day, C. and Sachs, J. (eds) (2004). *International Handbook on the Continuing Professional Development of Teachers.* Maidenhead, UK: Open University Press.

DeMartini, A. (2012). *Learning to Think with the Incomprehensible: Human Remains, the Murambi Memorial and the Intimacy of Personal Memorial Practices.* (Order No. MS00013, York University, Canada). ProQuest Dissertations and Theses, 129. Available: romhttp://search.proquest.com/docview/1509922972?accountid=12339. Downloaded 11 October, 2015.

Desimone, L. (2009). Improving impact studies of teachers' professional development: Toward better conceptualizations and measures. *Educational Researcher.* 38(3): 181–199.

Desimone, L. (2011). A primer on effective professional development. *Phi Delta Kappan.* 92(6): 68–71.

Dockney, J. and Tomaselli, K. (2009). Fit for the small(er) screen: Films, mobile TV and the new individual television experience. *Journal of African Cinema.* 1(1): 126–132.

Gadamer, H-G. (2013). *Truth and Method.* (Translation revised by Joel Weinsheimer and Donald G. Marshall). London: Bloomsbury Publishing.

Gamrat, C., Zimmerman, H. Dudek, J. and Peck, K. (2014). Personalized workplace learning: An exploratory study on digital badging within a teacher professional development program. *British Journal of Educational Technology.* 45(6): 1136–1148.

Goodson, I. (1992). *Studying Teachers' Lives.* New York: Teachers' College Press.

Goodson, I. and Sikes, P. (2001). *Life History Research in Educational Settings: Learning from Lives.* Buckingham, UK: Open University Press.

Guskey, T. and Sparks, D. (2004). Linking professional development to improvements in student learning. In E. Guyton and J. Dangel (eds), *Research Linking Teacher Preparation and Student Performance: Teacher Education Yearbook XII.* Lanham, MD: Rowman & Littlefield, 11–21.

Hamilton, M. (ed) (1998). *Reconceptualizing Teaching Practice: Self-Study in Teacher Education.* London: Falmer Press.

Hampl, P. (1996). Memory and imagination. In J.McConkey (ed), *The Anatomy of Memory: An Anthology.* New York and Oxford: Oxford University Press, 201–211.

Hampl, P. (1999). *I Could Tell You Stories: Sojourns in the Land of Memory.* New York: W.W. Norton & Company.

Hargreaves, A. (2003). *Teaching in the Knowledge Society: Education in the Age of Insecurity.* New York: Teachers College Press.

Hasebe-Ludt, E., Chambers, C. and Leggo, C. (2009). *Life Writing and Literary Métissage as an Ethos for our Times.* New York: Peter Lang.

Haug, F., Andresen, S., Bunz-Elfferding, A., Hauser, K., Lang, U., Laudan, M., Ludemann, M. and Meir, U. (1987). *Female Sexualization: A Collective Work of Memory.* London: Verso.

Hodgkin, K. and Radstone, S. (eds) (2003). *Contested Pasts: The Politics of Memory.* New York, NY: Routledge.

Jenkins, H. (2006). *Fans, Bloggers, and Gamers: Exploring Participatory Culture.* New York: NYU Press.

Kapoor, D. and Jordan, S. (eds) (2009). *Education, Participatory Action, Research, and Social Change: International Perspectives.* New York: Palgrave Macmillan.

Kemmis, S. and McTaggart, R. (2005). Communicative action and the public sphere. In N. Denzin and Y. Lincoln (eds), *The Sage Handbook for Qualitative Research.* London: Sage, 559–604.

Kitchen, J. and Russell, T. (eds) (2012). *Canadian Perspectives on the Self-study of Teacher Education Practices.* Ottawa, ON: Canadian Association for Teacher Education.

Koellner, K. and Jacobs, J. (2015). Distinguishing models of professional development: The case of an adaptive model's impact on teachers' knowledge, instruction, and student achievement. *Journal of Teacher Education.* 66(1): 51–67.

Loughran, J., Hamilton, M., LaBoskey, V. and Russell, T. (eds) (2004). *International Handbook of Self-study of Teaching and Teacher Education Practices.* Dordrecht, The Netherlands: Kluwer Academic.

Luke, A., Woods, A. and Weir, K. (2013). Curriculum design, equity and the technical form of the curriculum. In A. Luke, A. Woods and K. Weir (eds), *Curriculum, Syllabus Design and Equity.* New York: Routledge, 6–39.

Mackey, M. (1999). Playing in the phase space: Contemporary forms of fictional pleasure. *Signal.* 88(1): 16–33.

Mackey, M. (2003). At play on the borders of the diegetic: Story boundaries and narrative interpretation. *Journal of Literacy Research.* 35(1): 591–632.

Male, T. and Burden, K. (2014). Access denied? Twenty–first–century technology in schools. *Technology, Pedagogy and Education.* 23(4): 423–437.

Mitchell, C. (2011). *Doing Visual Research.* London and New York: Sage.

Mitchell, C. and de Lange, N. (2013). What can a teacher do with a cellphone? Using participatory visual research to speak back in addressing HIV and AIDS. *South African Journal of Education.* 33(4): 1–13.

Mitchell, C., de Lange, N. and Moletsane, R. (2011). Before the camera rolls: Drawing storyboards to address gendered poverty. In L. Theron, C. Mitchell, A. Smith and J. Stuart (eds), *Picturing Research: Drawing(s) as Visual Methodology.* Rotterdam, Netherlands: Sense, 219–231.

Mitchell, C., de Lange, N., and Moletsane, R. (2014). Me and my cellphone: Constructing change from the inside through cellphilms and participatory video in a rural community. *Area.* First published online 14 December, 2014. Doi:10.1111/Area.12142.

Mitchell, C., Strong-Wilson, T., Pithouse, K. and Allnutt, S. (eds) (2011). *Memory and Pedagogy.* New York: Routledge.

Mitchell, C., Weber, S. and Pithouse, K. (2009). Facing the public: Using photography for self study and social action. In D. Tidwell, M. Heston and L. Fitzgerald (eds), *Research Methods for the Self-study of Practice.* New York: Springer, 119–134.

O'Reilly-Scanlon, K. (2001) *She's Still on My Mind: Teachers' Memories, Memory-work and Self-study.* Unpublished doctoral dissertation, McGill University.

Pithouse, K., Mitchell, C. and Moletsane, R. (eds) (2009). *Making Connections: Self–study and Social Action.* New York: Peter Lang.

Pithouse-Morgan, K. Van Laren, L., Mitchell, C., Mudaly, R. and Singh, S. (in press). Digital animation for going public on curriculum integration of HIV & AIDS in higher education. *South African Journal of Higher Education.*

Radstone, S. (2000). Introduction. In S. Radstone (ed), *Memory and Methodology.* Oxford, UK: Berg, 1–22.

Ritchie, S. (2012). Incubating and sustaining how teacher networks enable and support social justice education. *Journal of Teacher Education*. 63(2): 120–131.

Rosen, H. (1985). *Stories and Meanings*. Sheffield, UK: National Association for the Teaching of English.

Rothberg, M. (2000). *Traumatic Realism: The Demands of Holocaust Representation*. Minneapolis, MN: University of Minnesota Press.

Rothberg, M. (2009). *Multidirectional Memory: Remembering the Holocaust in the Age of Decolonization*. Stanford, CA: Stanford University Press.

Sachs, J. (2001). Teacher professional identity: Competing discourses, competing outcomes. *Journal of Education Policy*. 16(2): 149–161.

Schratz, M. and Walker, R. (1995). *Research as Social Change: New Opportunities for Qualitative Research*. London: Routledge.

Schwab–Cartas, J. and Mitchell, C. (2015). A tale of two sites: Cellphones, participatory video and indigeneity in community–based research. *McGill Journal of Education*. 49(3): 603–620.

Smaller, H., Clark, R., Hart, D., Livingstone, D. and Noormohammed, Z. (2000). *Teacher Learning, Informal and Formal: Results of a Canadian Teachers' Federation Survey*. NALL Working Paper 14, Toronto. Available: http://nall.oise.utoronto.ca/res/14teacherlearning.htm Downloaded 9 March, 2015.

Stenhouse, L. (2012). Research as a basis for teaching. In J. Elliott and N. Norris (eds), *Curriculum, Pedagogy and Educational Research: The Work of Lawrence Stenhouse*. London and New York: Routledge, 122–136.

Strong-Wilson, T. (2008). *Bringing Memory Forward: Teachers, Remembrance, Social Justice*. New York: Peter Lang.

Strong-Wilson, T., Mitchell, C., Allnutt, S. and Pithouse, K. (eds) (2013). *Productive Remembering and Social Agency*. Rotterdam, The Netherlands: Sense Publishers.

Strong-Wilson, T., Mitchell, C., Morrison, C., Radford, L. and Pithouse-Morgan, K. (2015). "Reflecting forward" on the digital in multidirectional memory-work between Canada and South Africa. *McGill Journal of Education*. 49(3): 675–695.

Strong-Wilson, T., Thomas, B., Cole, A. L, Rouse, D., Tsoulos, D. and with teacher authors (Bonnie Mitchell, Kelly Ryan, Manuela Pasinato, Marie-Claude Tétrault, & Penny Bonneville). (2012). *Envisioning New Technologies in Teacher Practice: Moving Forward, Circling Back Using a Teacher Action Research Approach*. New York: Peter Lang.

Tienken, C.H. and Stonaker, L. (2007). When every day is professional development day. *Journal of Staff Development*. 28(2): 24–29.

Underwood, J. (2014). Digital technologies: An effective educational change agent? In C. Karagiannidis, P. Politis and I. Karasavvidis (eds), *Research on e–Learning and ICT in Education*. New York: Springer, 3–14.

Vescio, V., Ross, D., and Adams A. (2008). A review of research on the impact of professional learning communities on teaching practice and student learning. *Teaching and Teacher Education*. 24(1): 80–91.

CHAPTER NINE

Expanding Notions OF Professional Development IN Adult Basic Education

ERIK JACOBSON

Adult education long has taken advantage of ongoing developments in technology. Over the course of the 20th century, adults gained access to educational resources via mail, radio, television and, most recently, computer. This was not only true for adult education understood more broadly but also for education provided to adults learning to read and to English language learners studying to become fluent in English. Increasingly, technology itself has become the object of study in adult basic education, and teachers are helping students develop their facility in using digital devices alongside learning literacy and numeracy. In fact, the most recent Programme for the International Assessment of Adult Competencies includes a new construct—*Problem-Solving in Technology-Rich Environments*—which is described as "using digital technology, communication tools and networks to acquire and evaluate information, communicate with others, and perform practical tasks" (Programme for the International Assessment of Adult Competencies 2009: 8). The fact that a fair amount of adult educators are not confident in their own knowledge and use of technology has made technology-related professional development a priority for the field.

"Adult basic education" is sometimes used as a catch-all term, grouping a number of distinct educational efforts together. It typically refers to adult literacy programs and classes that prepare adults to pass high school equivalency exams, but it often includes English as a second language classes, as well. In this way the "Basic" can mistakenly imply that learners are starting nearly from scratch—a conception that many in the field have been working hard to counter. Work taken up from a sociocultural perspective rejects a deficit model of adult learners and, instead, considers the diversity of learners' experiences with literacy and literacy practices (Perry and Homan 2015). With respect to technology, this means moving beyond essentialized notions of what adults can't do and towards identifying the knowledge learners already possess and the practices in which they are already engaged. This shift in focus includes working with adult learners to develop lessons and curriculum based on what they actually *want* to learn about technology rather than on what their teachers assume they need. Of course, the same is true for professional development opportunities; they should build on teachers' particular experiences, and activities should be tailored to address what individual teachers have identified as important for their students and their teaching situations.

In what follows, I outline an approach to professional development that focuses on the agency of teachers as learners. In doing so, I draw on semi-structured interviews I conducted (via a variety of modalities such as telephone, email, video conferencing) with eight adult literacy educators who have years of professional development experience. I also draw on the reflections of adult basic education teachers who have been involved in several professional development projects I have helped initiate. I believe the collective professional wisdom these teachers shared with me is helpful in grounding discussions of professional development theory in the lived reality of students and teachers.

ISSUES WITH TECHNOLOGY-RELATED PROFESSIONAL DEVELOPMENT IN ADULT BASIC EDUCATION

Although there is a pressing need for teachers in adult basic education programs to be able to use technology in productive and creative ways, there are a large number of issues that complicate the professional development situation. Three of them are described below:

1. Diverse Student Population

As noted above, adult basic education is a large conceptual and practice-based umbrella term. It includes adults looking to finish their high school education (or obtain an equivalent certification) and others who are just learning to read. It also includes immigrants learning to speak English who may have limited literacy in their native language and those with professional degrees in their home countries who are looking to move beyond mal-employment in positions that do not fully utilize their knowledge, expertise and previous workplace experiences (Fogg and Harrington 2013). This means that, within the U.S., there is no uniform curriculum or framework that cuts across all of these types of adult student learning needs (although the recent U.S. government-supported *Career and College Readiness Standards* are a move in that direction).

In addition to this diversity in program needs, there is diversity with respect to each student population, especially with regards to digital technology. For example, while internet access has increased dramatically across the U.S., inequities remain in learners' access to and use of digital resources. There also are variations in the amount and type of experiences learners have had with technology prior to them taking basic education classes. This can range from having no experience at all to being adept at using a smart cellphone through to being able to write code for software programs. Additionally, adult learners' current literacy or English language fluency may make working with some online content or digital programs difficult for them. Teachers cannot simply hop online and readily download lesson materials or assign online activities that will be accessible to or useful for all of their students (Jacobson 2012).

2. Diverse Teacher Population

Teachers and tutors working in adult basic education also demonstrate important variations in their work backgrounds and educational experiences (Bell, Ziegler and McCallum 2004; Snow and Strucker 1999). Some teachers are certified to teach, either explicitly for adults or for Kindergarten to Grade 12 students. Other teachers are not certified at all and may not have formally studied approaches to education. Many of these tutors go through a training period lasting between 12 and 20 hours, but some get fewer hours. Opportunities for follow-up training vary (Belzer 2006a), so teachers working within a single school or program may not share a sense of how best to support learners in developing their language, literacy and other skills and processes.

As with students, among teachers and tutors there also is a range of facility in working with technology. Berger (2005) identified what appears to be some consistent patterns. Some teachers and tutors are early adopters, trying out new resources when they become available. Others are more technology averse and have little interest in developing their own skills with devices and software. Some see little connection between teaching someone to read and using digital technologies. Additionally, some teachers identify themselves as necessarily behind the times because of their age, embracing the identity of "digital immigrants" who cannot keep up with "digital natives." Although this immigrant/native dichotomy is misleading in the ways it essentializes digital technology users (Jacobson 2012), it certainly resonates with many people, and identities such as "technology resistant" or "technology embracing" (and everything in between) may shape teachers' and tutors' goals and choices when it comes to their own professional development.

3. Limited Resources

Compared to budgets for K-12 education, adult basic education programs in the U.S. have never been that large. Indeed, in recent times they have been shrinking at both the federal and the state level (Foster 2012). This means there are built in limitations to what states and municipalities have available to spend on digital technology and training. Some states that do have specific funds allocated for developing the use of technology in adult basic education, such as California and Minnesota, have large territories to cover. In states with little or no funding for training around technology, training is taken up by smaller agencies and volunteer organizations. Most programs have limited resources for reimbursing teachers or tutors for professional development. Efforts that do receive funding tend to prioritize reaching as many people as possible rather than the intensity or depth of any particular project or initiative. This means placing a heavy reliance upon one-shot workshops (typically held at conferences or other in-person meetings; Smith and Gillespie 2007; Webster-Wright 2009). To date, online efforts at the state level tend to include a focus on discussion lists, webinars, study circles, and pre-crafted modules for teachers and tutors to work through. Most of these activities are of short duration and may be offered in an *ad hoc* fashion rather than as part of an articulated series of activities.

CONCEPTUALIZING PROFESSIONAL DEVELOPMENT

As it is often used, the term "professional development" is somewhat vague and unsettling. One reason for this is that *develop* is a transitive verb—we develop some *thing*. For example, in the sentence—"I am going to develop this photograph"—the subject ("I") is acting upon ("developing") the direct object ("this photograph"). Of course, the object being acted upon can also be an aspect of the subject completing the action, as in this sentence: "I am taking a class to develop my own Haitian Kreyol fluency." In this case, I am taking action to increase, or develop, my ability to speak Haitian Kreyol. In discussions of professional development; it often is unclear which of these two situations is intended or implied. Is the teacher or tutor being developed by somebody else or are they developing aspects of themselves? In other words, is the teacher the object or the subject of professional development?

Freire (1970) places this question at the heart of his project of liberatory education. He argues that students who have been oppressed by systemic inequality are dehumanized into an object status and that literacy—and education more broadly—can help them realize their status as the *subjects* of their own lives. Rather than being educated *by* somebody else, they grow and learn in dialogue with others. As part of his analysis, Freire (1985) critiques what he calls the "banking system" of education in which teachers are expected to place pre-established, fixed bits of knowledge into students' minds and instead argues for education that enables learners to create new knowledge and to transform their own understanding of the world with the goal of actually changing the world in positive ways for as many people as possible. Not only should we reject a banking model of education for adult basic education students, we should do the same for adult basic education teachers. Professional development activities thus should focus on creating professional learning opportunities (Smith 2010; Webster-Wright 2009) in which teachers can dialogue with others to understand the world and their professional activity in it. Rather than being the object of development efforts, teachers can define, construct, resource and sustain a learning trajectory for themselves.

The sense of the teacher as the object of professional development rather than its subject is also clear in some descriptions of state- or institutionally directed efforts. For example, the New York State Education Department notes: "it is essential to ensure that teachers are provided with ongoing, high quality professional development to sustain and enhance their practice" (New York State Professional Development Standards 2015:1). Here, professional development is *provided* in a banking-type process. It is *something* given by the system and its representatives to the teacher. The consultants and other experts given this charge often suggest that they "do professional development," which is somewhat reminiscent of how people describe being paid to work on somebody else's hair or nails. Additionally, within current accountability regimes, both providers and teachers are tracked for how many hours of professional development have taken place. Often, teachers have to accumulate a certain amount of professional development *hours* to meet the requirements for continued employment. Teachers who attend a conference, workshop or webinar get credit for seat time, regardless of whether they feel like their understanding of the topic presented has been advanced or whether they have actually learned anything. The same is true for state-run and other adult basic education programs. The programs are credited for the cumulative hours of seat time their teachers and tutors have accrued.

In many ways, this system of professional development is not particularly helpful. It does little to analyze what is happening in workshops and conferences, and it perpetuates banking models of education that serve to reduce teacher agency. Instead of conceptualizing professional development as a thing given from (or done by) one person to another, we should speak of providing *professional development opportunities*. These are activities in which teachers can realize learning gains that expand and extend their professional wisdom and help them support their students' learning. These opportunities should help teachers articulate their evolving pedagogy, focus on a topic or issue they want to examine, identify initial resources for productive exploration of the issue and provide spaces for dialogue about their ideas as they develop. Although these opportunities can be conceptualized in different ways, three approaches are discussed below: self-directed learning, collaborative projects, and facilitated exploration. Each is consistent with a pedagogical model that emphasizes the need to respect the agency of the learner and to recognize the social basis of knowledge generation.

SELF-DIRECTED LEARNING

Although professional development for adult educators is often operationalized as workshops and webinars, research about the usefulness of one-shot "development" activities indicates they have a limited impact on teacher practice (Joyce and Showers 2002; Smith 2010). Indeed, teachers themselves often attend inservice training or professional development sessions with low expectations. In part, this can be attributed to teachers' pre-assessment of the quality of the workshops or to past workshop experiences, but it also reflects preferences many adults have for learning on their own as opposed to being in a formal educational setting. For example, in her study of adults' approaches to learning how to use technology, Strawn (2008: 16) reports that, except for the 31–39 years age group, all other learners (i.e., 19–24, 25–30, 40+ years) preferred learning from family and friends over going to a class. Additionally, respondents also preferred learning by trial and error over going to a class. In fact, classes for technology were valued so low by respondents that learning from an expert ranked at the bottom for all age groups, which calls into question the very notion of institutionally based professional development around digital technology.

This preference for learning via experimentation and from members of a personal network also can be seen in the experiences of those who have strong track records of working with technology and professional development in adult basic education. One example of this is David Rosen, who is active in adult basic education as a columnist in journals, as a blogger (davidjrosen.wordpress.com), and a consultant. Each year he leads multiple technology-related workshops at conferences, and he also facilitates webinars. When asked about his own learning and professional development, he describes "a focused process that grows from either or both of two opposite purposes" (email interview, 2/21/15). These purposes are:

1) To meet an education goal or objective. I have a task that needs to get done and am looking for a piece of software that is described as being able to do that.

2) To understand what new digital tools are available, in the way I suppose that farmers go to agricultural fairs, and knitters go to knitting fairs to see what the materials and tools are that other practitioners in their chosen pursuit use to solve problems in their work or lives.

He goes on to explain how that process works: "I am not against courses, and have taken a lot of them, and enjoyed them, but I don't think they address these technology-related purposes very well. For me, it's more efficient to pursue these purposes as a self-directed learner."

Here Rosen is drawing on a concept, "self-directed learning," that has long been an influential idea in adult education (Tough 1971; Knowles 1988). One reason for its continued resonance is the way in which it calls into question the privileging of the student-teacher relationship as the locus of learning. For example, Brookfield and Holst (2011: 37–38) suggest that self-directed learning "means control over the definitions, processes, and evaluations of learning rests with those who are struggling to learn, not with external authorities or formal institutions." Although the term can take on different nuances, they explain that:

> One of the most consistent elements in the majority of definitions of self-direction is the importance of the learner's exercising control over all educational decisions. What should be the goals of a learning effort, what resources should be used, what methods will work best for the learner, and by what criteria the success of any learning effort should be judged are all decisions that are said to rest in the learner's hands. (p. 38)

Since teachers also are adult learners, a focus on self-directed learning helps put decisions about professional development in their own hands.

Marian Thacher, currently a senior researcher with the California Adult Literacy Professional Development Project (calpro-online.org), has for many years been an influential figure in adult basic education teaching circles within the U.S. for her understanding of how technology can be used to enhance educational opportunities for both students and teachers. Like Rosen, she has identified some limitations to learning about technology in formal educational settings. She recounts, "I did take some face-to-face trainings, such as on Excel, and online courses. I was never very happy with them, though, and usually didn't complete [them] if they were more than an hour. One size doesn't fit all and it didn't fit me" (email interview, 2/19/15). Consistent with the adults in Strawn's study mentioned earlier, Thacher does not look to learn from formal instruction by experts. Instead, she describes a much more informal process:

> As with everything, I learned what I needed to learn to do what I wanted to do. For instance, I can make a Google form that feeds into a spreadsheet, and I've collected a lot of information this way. There were challenges with the spreadsheet, and I found someone to show me how to add worksheets to a Google spreadsheet. There are probably lots of other things I could do that I don't know how to do, but I won't care until the problem is staring me in the face.

Consistent with Rosen's experiences, Thacher points to learning how to do something to deal with a specific problem rather than as part of a decontextualized walkthrough of a particular piece of hardware or software.

Although Thacher is highlighting how her professional development is taking place on her own terms, it is important to note that this is not an isolating activity; she explicitly draws on the insights and experiences of others in order to address the issues with which she is wrestling. Indeed, she explained how an essential element of the process was the fact that "I sought out other people who were interested in the same things and knew more than me, both in person and online." In this way, self-directed does not mean autonomous. The locus of control remains with the person engaged in the learning project, but the social nature of information and knowledge development is not elided in her practice, either.

Jen Vanek, a consultant to the Minnesota Literacy Council and one of the developers of the Northstar assessment of computer and online knowledge and practice (digitalliteracyassessment.org), suggests that this kind of learning on the part of teachers requires both a curiosity about technology and a willingness to take risks (personal communication, 2/19/15). There are certainly plenty of times that adults engaged in self-directed learning can run into problems, and they need problem-solving skills to handle setbacks. Part of this comes down to disposition. A teacher in a project I coordinated in New Jersey noted this about working on her own:

> It took longer to find info on the internet (it is not the old way of sequential learning as in learning from a book) but you may have to search for the info and jump around following abstract links that may or may not lead to the information you need. Sometimes I did not get a full resolution and you are not sure if it is your misunderstanding or if it the limitation of the tool/program you are using.

Thacher takes an optimistic view of this process. She suggests, "I came to understand that the frustrating things, although at times due to user error, were usually a reflection of the state of the technology at that time, i.e., it was still clunky. The next year, it would either be better or be replaced by something else" (personal communication, 2/19/15). For some, the real possibility of frustration can place a damper on their willingness to explore technology. Rosen reports:

> During a focus group I conducted as part of a research fellowship in 1995 on how adult educators and students were using the World Wide Web, a teacher in California asked, "Can you assure me that the time I spend learning technology will be as useful or satisfying as the time I spend practicing my musical instrument?" As a part-time musician I had to answer "no."

When professional development is understood to be an on-going project of a self-directed learner rather than a discrete collection of information presented in a controlled fashion, there are no guarantees of success. We have all taken up learning projects that crashed and burned far short of the goals we set for ourselves, and I believe that sharing these struggles with students helps teachers and others to create a more honest and constructive learning environment. As an example, I can report on a personal project of my own that was not nearly as satisfying as making music.

For a number of years I have been involved with WE LEARN (welearn-women.org), an organization that is focused on women's literacy. At one conference I attempted to create opportunities for those not in attendance to interact with those who were, and I was working with no budget. I did not have a model to follow, so I started by investigating several options. I finally decided to create a public Google document that would serve as an interactive writing space. Prior to the conference I shared the URL to the document via several adult literacy discussion groups and networks and invited people to monitor and contribute to the Google doc once the conference got started. At the conference I set up a computer dedicated to the Google doc and projected it against the wall so that attendees could see what others were writing. After a few initial contributions, things slowed and then stopped on the doc. After a fair amount of time spent learning how to make all the pieces fit together, I think there were less than a dozen people that participated in contributing to the Google doc, despite my best efforts to draw in a much larger crowd. I certainly did not accomplish my goal of creating an interactive space, and it felt like a waste of time. However, as it turned out, I learned a lot about how Google documents function, and they have become an important part of my own teaching toolbox. In the moment it may have been more satisfying to have spent the time playing music, but in the long run I consider this an important part of my own professional development regardless of how it played out during one particular conference.

In taking up and discussing their own self-directed learning projects, teachers can serve as models of lifelong learning. For example, Susan Gaer's website (susangaer.com) constantly evolves as she experiments with social networking resources on an individual basis (e.g., Flickr, Twitter, Delicious, Diigo, etc.) and develops curriculum that addresses students' goals. Another example is Dave's ESL Café (eslcafe.com), a site that was set up in the mid-1990s and has continued to grow over the years. The English language learning field really benefitted from people who early on set up their tents online, since they provided both information and resources and examples of the curiosity and risk taking that Jen Vanek (above) noted as required for self-directed learning about and with technology. In these and other examples, professional development takes place in the world as we are navigating it rather than as part of a fixed, pre-packaged curriculum.

Although Rosen's response above notes the efficiency of self-directed learning, Brookfield and Holst (2011) call to attention the ways in which this approach to education also is consistent with the goals of emancipatory pedagogies. Control of educational processes and resources is always associated with exercises of power, whether it is with respect to students in the classroom or their teachers' learning. Thus, rather than focusing on how a system can *provide* professional development to a teacher, we need to re-affirm that "[e]ducators must be at the centre of their own learning if changes in practice are going to happen" (Moriarty 2011: 28). Teachers need to decide for themselves what kinds of changes they would like to make in their approach, philosophy, or strategies. In this way, recognizing the primacy of self-directed learning in professional development is not simply a question of technique; it is an issue of who has the power to determine the nature of a teacher's professional development.

COLLABORATIVE PROJECTS

As noted above, valuing self-directed learning projects does not mean devaluing work done with others. Indeed, research on professional development indicates that teachers really benefit from working in groups on activities that matter to them. In comparison to one-off workshops, studies indicate that teachers who engage in collaborative, project-based professional development reflect more on and are more likely to change their practice (cf. Smith, Bingman, Hofer and Medina 2002). Teachers need the chance to try things out for themselves, but they also benefit from being part of a learning community (Senge 1990) that encourages self-assessment and reflection, provides additional resources and perspectives, and allows teachers to rethink their approaches (Belzer 2006b). In what Wenger (1998) refers to as a community of practice, cooperating participants share a common goal and a commitment to intentionally learning together. Intentionally formed communities of practice attempt to harness shared knowledge and resources while still enabling organic growth of the project.

One noteworthy example of collaborative learning as part of professional development is the Adult Literacy Education Wiki (of which I was a co-founder). The ALE Wiki was started as a place for those in the field to share resources and ideas about adult literacy education in general (i.e., contributions were not confined to teaching with technology), and, in particular, to extend conversations taking place at adult literacy education conferences. That is, the founders (see Jacobson 2012 for more on this wiki's development) explicitly recognized the limited nature of one-shot workshops and wanted to move towards the kinds of ongoing collaborations argued for above. At the time it was launched (i.e., 2004), there were very few wikis dealing with education and no large ones focusing on adult education. This meant that when the ALE Wiki began, those involved needed to learn both the coding involved in creating a wiki and the routines and practices that would encourage others to join and contribute actively.

The first few years after its founding were the wiki's most active period (Jacobson 2008). The person who set up the initial wiki site, David Rosen, created a discussion list for contributors to share questions, answers, ideas and insights. Those initial participants discussed how to code, how to organize information, how to select resources to highlight, and how to manage the growing size of the wiki. Core group members also demonstrated how to participate in the wiki when they were at conferences and other meetings and provided people with the necessary guidance to make contributions in real time. These facilitators were careful not to present themselves as experts on wikis and, instead, invited participants to join them in the wiki as a communal learning and resource project. As a grassroots effort, nobody was getting paid to contribute to or oversee this wiki, and as a collaborative effort, nobody had authority to make unilateral decisions about the nature of the wiki. One member noted at the time, "I believe endeavors such as this ALE Wiki capture the spirit of democratic participation and innovation" (in Jacobson 2008: 333).

Ten years later the site remains live, but activity and participation have dwindled. Based on comments from people in the field, it has proved to be a helpful resource, but the collaborative effort never moved beyond a limited number of core contributors. That being said, an analysis of the wiki's activities (Jacobson 2009) suggests that participation in the project was productive for many of the members and certainly contributed to their own professional development. Several members started other wikis, one member of the core group found wiki-related work, and another noted that talking about his wiki experience during a job interview helped secure a job offer. More generally, contributors suggested that helping build the wiki increased their knowledge of adult literacy, their skills with technology, and their sense of how to build and maintain online communities. Contributing never became simply a task, and participants were certainly left with a sense of having learned together.

The development of the ALE Wiki involved teachers and other adult basic education professionals working together, but collaborative learning for professional development can also take place between teachers and students. For example, Eubanks (2012) provides an account of the efforts of a group of students and teachers housed at the YWCA of Troy-Cohoes, New York. Drawing on several traditions that prioritized collaborative work (such as popular education, participatory action research, participatory design), the students and teachers worked together to identify technological resources that were beneficial as well as the ways in which technology was a part of the oppression they were experiencing. Eubanks (2012: 24) refers to this approach as "popular technology," and she explains, "[p]opular technology assumes that all people have a rich array of experiences with technology, shaped by their social location, and that these experiences provide a valuable resource for thinking collectively and critically about the relationship among technology, politics, citizenship, and social justice." This approach explicitly rejects a deficit model of education in which adult learners, especially adult basic education students, are lacking fundamental aspects of technology knowledge. Although it may be the case that a particular learner does not have much experience working with computers themselves or does not have a facility with a range of apps, this does not mean they do not have important insights into the way their lives are shaped by information technology. For example, Eubanks shares learners' critiques of how reporting systems built into the welfare system work to limit their flexibility and reduce their sense of agency. The learners noted that social service agencies are able to track the purchases they make with their Electronic Benefit Transfer (EBT) cards, and they are questioned on their spending choices by their case managers (Eubanks 2012: 90). Clients also must typically sign a form that allows their data to be shared with other databases, even ones not directly connected to the assistance office with which they are dealing. A refusal to allow these data to be shared can be grounds for withholding support. Although dealing with the privacy implications of the use of technology to monitor social service clients is unlikely to be on international surveys of adults' abilities to problem solve in technology-rich environments, it is unfortunately a reality for many adult learners.

For that reason, we need to think not only about the devices we and others hold in our hands, we also need to think about how information systems structure our lives. Eubanks writes, "Our holistic viewpoint revealed, for example, that women's relationship to the social service system is deeply mediated by IT [information technology]" (2012: 126). In this way, collaborating with students to critically examine technology in everyday life can help teachers learn both about the technical aspects of devices and software and about the social use of that technology.

The possessive pronoun Eubanks employs here ("*Our* holistic viewpoint") marks a set of values she shares with the students who were part of several projects in which Eubanks was involved. The first was the creation of a YWCA Community Technology Laboratory. Other efforts included developing online resource collections for local area women and helping to create a poverty simulation video game. Each project required a lot of planning and discussion. The terms and goals had to be defined clearly (which often was a long, complicated process), and the work to complete the project had to be broken down into multiple steps. Some projects went more smoothly than others, and Eubanks had to deal with her students' and her own frustrations when things didn't work out the way they thought they would. Moreover, Eubanks and the students needed to check in to see if the goals they began with were still appropriate and, if not, how to change direction. It is clear that collaborating with these students shaped Eubanks's sense of her own pedagogy as well as her critiques of the economic system to which the projects were responding. Her professional development thus was tied directly to work that she was doing with her adult students. This is not simply reflective practice, in which a teacher conducts a class with students and then gains insight by reflecting on how the lesson went. That is certainly valuable. Instead, the teacher and the students shared a desire to connect an exploration of technology with a communal, polyvocal analysis of women's experiences of poverty. In such efforts, there is no way of knowing ahead of time what the "answers" or outcomes will be; there is no preset body of knowledge to be acquired by the students. In this way, it is not the case that professional development by necessity happens *before* working with students, as a kind of preparation; instead, it can happen while collaborating *with* students on projects that continue to grow and evolve.

Stressing the importance of collaborative learning in professional development helps call attention to the social construction of knowledge, too. One of the built-in limitations of most in-service and workshop experiences is that they begin with fixed collections of ideas and information that are expected to be conveyed from an expert to attendees. During the workshop, teachers may be asked to share their perspective on or insight into the topic (e.g., preparing learners to take high school equivalency tests), but by and large the topics to be addressed have already been identified and prepared. This does not leave much room for extended analysis of the framework itself (e.g., questions about whether or not high-stakes standardized tests are the best way to evaluate student development). As with the concept of self-directed learning, collaboration *with* students can be seen as simply an effective pedagogical technique (e.g., dialogue that facilitates lesson delivery) or as an explicitly political stance. If we hope to prepare adult students to develop their ability to critique taken-as-natural situations and problem solve in technology-rich environments, it is essential we hear from them about how they define technology, how they experience their environment, what problems they want to solve and what they consider to be appropriate solutions. This kind of collaborative analysis helps align teachers' professional development goals with the goals of the learners with whom they are working and is much more likely to be of use to them in making productive changes in their own lives.

FACILITATED EXPLORATION

To engage in self-directed learning or to participate in collaborative projects does require a certain amount of self-efficacy, especially with regard to the use of technology. For this reason, Vanek (interviewed for this chapter) suggests we need to identify ways to scaffold the experiences of teachers who would like more guidance in their exploration of technology. However, this does not mean offering the kinds of one-shot technology workshops that many people seem to want to avoid. Rather, a different option is a *facilitated project* in which participants start by working within a pre-designed structure but then gradually take over responsibility for their own problem solving and learning. In this kind of facilitated exploration, a more experienced technology user can highlight questions the field has been wrestling with and introduce models and projects that demonstrate ways to use technology that are consistent with different pedagogical approaches. After this introduction, participants explore technology on their own, with ongoing learning support in addition to strictly technical advice.

I recently coordinated an adult education project in New Jersey (working with Literacy New Jersey). The main goal was for participating teachers and tutors to design their own technology-related project, which could include developing materials or resources to use directly with students or developing materials for other teachers' benefit. The participating teachers varied with regards to their experiences with digital technologies. They were all adept at searching the web to find websites relevant to their own teaching, but only a few had created new resources. They knew what blogs were, but only one teacher had created one. One teacher was already using Google Drive in their teaching, but the rest were generally unaware of how Google Documents or Maps could serve as classroom resources. The one thing they all had in common was a desire to move beyond their current level of experience with digital technologies. In order to provide structure while allowing for individualized exploration, I created the following six-step sequence for the project.

1. Introduction

Teachers participating in the project came from different programs in different parts of the state, so scheduling face-to-face meetings was difficult. We conducted this first meeting via videoconferencing and used it as a way to introduce ourselves, to set the goals for the project as a whole, and to talk about how best to manage communicating with each other.

2. Reviewing Technological Resources

Our next meeting was held in the computer lab of a community college. The meeting began with people talking about the kinds of technology they already use in their daily lives and with their students. I then gave an overview of different types of resources (blogs, Google Maps, video editing software, etc.) and how they have been used in the classroom. The second half of the meeting was given over to the teachers experimenting with different technologies, with the goal of identifying helpful resources. I circulated around the room, talking with teachers about what they were finding and thinking about.

3. Initial Individual Exploration and Experimentation

For two weeks after the in-person meeting, the teachers spent more time exploring technology and thinking about how it could address needs in their own classrooms and programs. During this time I remained in email contact with participants, providing encouragement, answering technical questions when I could, and acting as a sounding board with regard to a personal project they each would work on as part of participating in this group.

4. Working on the Project

At this fourth step of the process, participants identified what projects they wanted to take on. During a synchronous online meeting they articulated their ideas and got feedback from each other and from me. Then they began working in earnest to complete their project, with the goal of presenting their work after a month's time. As they moved forward, they shared their work in progress, asking for and receiving additional feedback from the group.

5. In-Person Presentations

After working on their projects for a month, the group came back together to share their work in person. Most had completed projects (e.g., one class of adult basic education students completed a Google map that tracked where they originally came from), but few teachers were still finishing up. During this meeting, participants shared what they learned about the resources they worked with and about their own process of becoming more comfortable with using technology. The discussion focused on implications for teaching and learning in relation to their own students and for their own professional development.

6. Presentation at a Conference

Several members of the group volunteered to give a presentation at a local conference. In keeping with the approach of the project, rather than presenting particular technologies in a decontextualized manner, they shared insights into the processes of their own professional development (e.g., how they set learning goals for themselves, what they did to get the information they needed, what they did when they got stuck). This encouraged them to reflect on their experiences and articulate what they had learned. Presenting at the conference gave these teachers a chance to obtain feedback from those outside the group, and since they had never presented before, it also introduced new voices into the conference setting.

As noted above, the idea here was to facilitate exploration rather than to direct it.

I wanted to initially provide some structure so that participants could get started, and so I introduced a few different resources and sample projects. However, I steadfastly refused to define their projects for them. In the beginning, this was a struggle for some of the teachers. They would say, "I don't know what to do, do you have any recommendations for technology that I should work with?" Each time I would state that I didn't know their class and I didn't know what kind of professional development path they had in mind. I repeated, "What do you need it for? Let's start with the problem and the task and then think about the tool that might be helpful." After some time, I believe the message was understood. At the end, one participant noted, "You may provide tech resources, but [the] teacher has to try it out with their own students." More than that, participants grew to understand and value the open-ended nature of the project. Another teacher wrote, "I liked the freedom to choose the technology, the use of the webinars and occasional in-person meetings. I recommend using a similar flexible format for other professional developments."

Although the freedom and flexibility were positive for most participants, the open nature of the project certainly created hurdles for some. One noted that it "[c]an take a long time to find what you need" when exploring on your own. Indeed, part of the task was to develop research strategies and persistence necessary to engage in that kind of self-directed learning. Similarly, another teacher noted that "Not being able to get full resolution" to a problem was frustrating. It is true that sometimes there are no clear answers to problems when working on technology projects, both in technical terms ("How can I get this to work?") and in terms of value ("Is it worth it to keep using this tool?"). A facilitator can address some, though not all, technical concerns, but only teachers themselves can answer questions about value within their particular teaching context.

One of the participants said about her project: "It wasn't awe inspiring, but it gave me confidence and I want to be able to do the same thing for my students." I would suggest that while the desire for awe-inspiring projects may be natural for many people, I do not think it is particularly helpful. Epiphanies are by definition rare. We understandably do not expect them while sitting in workshops, but we also should not expect them in other contexts, either. We also should not expect each isolated experience of professional development–related activity to produce sudden growth—that is the logic of the provision or banking model of professional development. The teacher above noted a growth in her confidence, which I took as a positive outcome that cannot be attributed to simply being in the project. Development is a longitudinal phenomenon, accruing over long periods of time and through the interplay of various influences and experiences.

In addition, Eubanks (2012) reports how disappointing it was for people when their working groups dissipated over time. I have heard from others who lament that their own communities of practice were not sustained. Although I think it is natural to mourn the passing of communities, it may be that this is part of the natural waxing and waning of shared interests. Some communities of practice may falter because of structural problems, but others fade away once they have accomplished their goals (as was the case with the original group that established and built the ALE Wiki). We may devote our energies to the communities we are currently in, but in the end we are engaged in serial professional development projects. We can certainly work to maximize the experience of our current project (whatever it may be), but if we are honest and humble about it, we can keep the goals to an appropriate scale.

IMPLICATIONS

Moving forward, I believe that professional development around technology within adult basic education should prioritize the following.

1. Building on the Progressive Heritage of Adult Basic Education

Although those within the field should continue to advocate for states and other systems to provide more resources for professional development, we also can continue to build on the adult basic education tradition of teachers, students and others moving forward even when authorities do not. Teachers engaged in self-directed learning projects, the folks working collaboratively at the YMCA in Troy-Cohoes, and all the participants who built the 1,000-page Adult Literacy Education Wiki found inspiration in the Do-It-Yourself ethos the field has long evinced. In fact, providing opportunities for professional development that lie outside of the formal education system usefully allows for critiques of that very system. Access to state resources comes at the cost of participating in accountability regimes that may not be consistent with more emancipatory views of education and development.

In addition, adult basic education has been tied increasingly to the notion of workforce development. Certainly jobs matter, especially since many adult learners enroll in programs as part of a plan to seek employment or secure better work. However, the history of adult basic education demonstrates a broader sense of the goals of study. Programs often have conceived of literacy as a way for adult students to document the conditions of their lives, speak their own truths, and organize for change (Greene 2015; Ramdeholl 2014). Although changes in technology affect how adult basic education can be provided and what the content of courses might be, the more fundamental project of seeing education as a way to make the world more just and humane remains in place.

2. Expanding Notions of Professional Development

Brookfield and Holst (2011) believe that adult education should help learners develop a "structuralized" worldview, which interprets "individual experiences in terms of broader social and economic forces" (p. 60). This is consistent with the goal of helping learners identify and act against the causes of their oppression instead of internalizing rhetoric that places blame on their supposed lack of skills or culture. I would suggest professional development opportunities for teachers should likewise promote the ability to analyze the larger forces that shape education and pedagogy. The phrase "teach me something I can use on Monday" highlights teachers' desires for practical resources, and purely technical skills are certainly important (e.g., how to work with PDF files), but professional development should not be framed in strictly functionalist ways. Teachers need opportunities to explore and consider the implications of particular technologies for their students, themselves, and society as a whole.

As noted above, professional development can take on the form of self-directed learning, collaborative projects and facilitated explorations (among others). All of these focus on an open-ended learning process rather than a fixed time period (such as with workshops). Professional development can occur whenever teachers are self-consciously exploring aspects of their pedagogy or content knowledge that they would like to expand or modify. Rather than only happening when they are in the presence of "experts," teachers' professional development can be informed by many parties and, most importantly, by their students. For this reason, teachers should receive more recognition for the professional development they already take on and be encouraged to experiment with new ways of learning, even if these ways cannot be easily quantified.

3. Problem Posing in Technology-Rich Environments

As noted above, adults' abilities to work with technology are now being evaluated as part of the Programme for the International Assessment of Adult Competencies' international survey of adult skills. The notion of *problem-solving in technology rich environments* was developed in part to capture the ways in which technology has redefined everyday life for many people around the world. The Programme for the International Assessment of Adult Competencies document (2009: 10) explains:

> The ability to solve problems with digital technologies is tightly related to the achievement of personal, civic and work-related purposes, which, in turn, take the form of concrete, practical tasks. Examples include shopping, learning about laws and regulations, and organizing teamwork through online agendas and reservation systems.

With an eye towards the ideological nature of education, several questions immediately come to mind. Do learners in adult education programs get to define the problems that occur within (and possibly because of) technology-rich environments? Do these learners get to generate and evaluate possible solutions to those problems? A real danger here is that work on technology will focus primarily on tasks that are labeled "functional," like online shopping and managing employment-related responsibilities. However, learners identify a host of other types of problems that they have to solve via (and because of) technology. For example, in the September 2013 issue of *The Change Agent*, a newspaper devoted to social justice and adult education, adult learners wrote about a range of technology-related topics, including creating music with technology, how to use Twitter for social justice efforts, using text-to-speech software to deal with the effects of cerebral palsy, managing their children's use of technology, and the negative impact that the production of technology has on the environment. These stories arose because the editorial board and participating teachers took a problem-posing approach (Freire 1970), working with learners to foreground issues they are concerned about. Here the tasks included using technology to be creative, to fight for social justice, and to be a parent in the 21st century. Each task required different sets of skills to problem solve, rather than a general facility with technology. Shopping online never once featured as a problem that kept these adult learners awake at night.

If teachers are to help adult students develop the ability to problem solve in technology-rich environments in ways that move beyond generic, functional concerns, professional development activities should include an emphasis on *problem posing* around technology. Together with our students we need to think about how we conceptualize technology and how we use it to act on the world. What is it that we want from technology? This also means asking questions about how technology is used to act on us. What are we willing to trade or give up in order to receive the benefits of certain technology? How do we coordinate our connectivity and manage privacy? As suggested above, it does not make sense to suggest that fixed or definite answers can be provided—we all have to make decisions about these issues for ourselves.

Shifting the focus from short-term technical training to extended analysis and critique may create opportunities for adult basic education teachers to transform their own understanding of technology, their teaching practice, and the world.

REFERENCES

Bell, S, Ziegler, M. and McCallum, R. (2004). What adult educators know compared to what they say they know about providing research-based instruction. *Journal of Adolescent and Adult Literacy*. 47(7): 542–563.

Belzer, A. (2006a). Less may be more: Rethinking adult literacy volunteer tutor training. *Journal of Literacy Research*. 38 (2): 111–140.

Belzer, A. (2006b). What are they doing in there? Case studies of volunteer tutors and adult literacy learners. *Journal of Adolescent and Adult Literacy*. 49(7): 560–572.

Berger, J. (2005). Perceived consequences of adopting the internet into adult literacy and basic education classrooms. *Adult Basic Education*. 15(2): 103–121.

Brookfield, S. and Holst, J. (2011). *Radicalizing Learning*. San Francisco: Jossey-Bass.

Eubanks, V. (2012). *Digital Dead End: Fighting for Social Justice in the Information Age*. Cambridge, MA: The MIT Press.

Fogg, N. and Harrington, P. (2013). *Labor Market Underutilization Problems Among College Educated Immigrants in the United States*. Philadelphia, PA: Center for Labor Markets and Policy, Drexel University.

Foster, M. (2012). *Adult Education Funding Levels and Enrollment*. Washington, DC: Center for Law and Social Policy.

Freire, P. (1970). *Pedagogy of the Oppressed*. (Myra Bergman Ramos, Translation). New York: Seabury.

Freire, P. (1985). *The Politics of Education*. (Donald Macedo, Translator). New York: Bergin and Garvey.

Greene, D. (2015). *Unfit to Be a Slave*. Boston: Sense Publishers.

Jacobson, E. (2008). The adult literacy education wiki as a virtual community of practice. In P. Hildreth and C. Kimble (eds), *Communities of Practice: Creating Learning Environments for Educators*. Charlotte, NC: Information Age Publishing, 325–343.

Jacobson, E. (2012). *Adult Basic Education in the Age of New Literacies*. New York: Peter Lang.

Joyce, B. and Showers, B. (2002). *Student Achievement Through Staff Development*, 3rd edn. Alexandria, VA: Association for Supervision and Curriculum Development.

Knowles, M. (1988). *The Modern Practice of Adult Education*, 2nd edn. New York: Cambridge

Moriarty, M. (2011). *Finding our Way: Digital Technologies and E-learning for Adult Literacy Students, Educators and Programs*. Toronto, ON: AlphaPlus.

New York State Professional Development Standards. (2015). Available: http://www.highered.nysed. gov/tcert/resteachers/pd.html Downloaded 21 September, 2015.

Perry, K. and Homan, A. (2015). "What I feel in my heart": Literacy practices of and for the self among adults with limited or no schooling. *Journal of Literacy Research*. 46(4): 422–454.

Programme for the International Assessment of Adult Competencies. (2009). *Problem Solving in Technology-Rich Environments: A Conceptual Framework*. Paris: OECD Publishing.

Ramdeholl, D. (2014). *Adult Literacy in a New Era: Reflections from the Open Book*. Boulder, CO: Paradigm.

Senge, P. (1990). *The Fifth Discipline: The Art and Practice of the Learning Organization*. New York: Currency/Doubleday.

Smith, C. (2010). The great dilemma of improving teacher quality in adult learning and literacy. *Adult Basic Education and Literacy Journal*. 4(2): 67–74.

Smith, C., Bingman, M., Hofer, J. and Medina, P. (2002). *Connecting Practitioners and Researchers: An Evaluation of NCSALL's Practitioner Dissemination and Research Network*. Cambridge, MA: National Center for the Study of Adult Learning and Literacy.

Smith, C. and Gillespie, M. (2007). Research on professional development and teacher change: Implications for adult basic education. In J. Comings, B. Garner and S. Smith (eds), *Annual Review of Adult Learning and Literacy, Vol. 7*. Mahwah, NJ: Lawrence Erlbaum, 205–244.

Snow, C. and Strucker, J. (1999). Lessons from preventing reading difficulties in young children for adult learning and literacy. In J. Comings, B. Garner and S. Smith (eds), *Annual Review of Adult Learning and Literacy, Vol. 1*. San Francisco, CA: Jossey-Bass, 25–73.

Strawn, C. (2008). *The Relationship Between Literacy Proficiency and the Digital Divide Among Adults with Low Educational Attainment: A Technical Report from the Longitudinal Study of Adult Learning*. Portland, OR: Portland State University.

Tough, A. (1971). *The Adult's Learning Projects*. Toronto, ON: Ontario Institute for Studies in Education.

Webster-Wright, A. (2009). Reframing professional development through understanding professional learning. *Review of Educational Research*. 79(2): 702–739.

Wenger, E. (1998). *Communities of Practice: Learning, Meaning and Identity*. Cambridge: Cambridge University Press.

CHAPTER TEN

#PD: Examining THE Intersection OF Twitter AND Professional Learning

CARLY BIDDOLPH AND JEN SCOTT CURWOOD

INTRODUCTION

Learning is a life-long process—it is essential for understanding and responding to the ever-changing world (Hammerness et al. 2005). It is particularly important for teachers, who are not only expected to instil the value of life-long learning in their students, but who are also faced with the challenges of developing their pedagogy in response to the rapidly changing social, cultural, and economic environment in which they live and work (Duncan-Howell 2010). For this reason, it is essential that teachers update their skills and knowledge through professional learning and development (Organisation for Economic Co-operation and Development 2009). For the purpose of this chapter, we draw a distinction between *professional development*, which understands learning as a progression through stages and a series of learning opportunities designed and administered by an "outside-the-school" expert, and *professional learning*, as an active, self-directed, iterative, and ongoing process based on a learner's needs (Easton 2008).

Professional development is perceived as a high priority in schools, and a substantial financial investment is made each year in school inservice development and external conferences (Australian Institute for Teaching and School Leadership 2012; The New Teacher Project 2015). It is considered particularly important within Australia, and the recent implementation of the *Great Teaching, Inspired Learning Initiative* (Board of Studies Teaching and Educational Standards NSW 2013) has placed increased pressure on schools to enhance teacher quality. However, despite this investment, compulsory school-funded professional development has long been described as "boring" (Wilson and Berne 1999: 176), "ineffective" (Walshe and Hirsch 1998: 11), and "irrelevant" (Lieberman and Mace 2009: 77).

Scholars and teachers alike have criticised traditional approaches to professional development for being decontextualised, didactic, and failing to provide teachers with opportunities to interact and collaborate with their colleagues or actively participate in the construction of knowledge (Walshe and Hirsch 1998). The prevalence of teachers seeking their own professional learning, separate from their school and not required as part of accreditation, suggests that there is a need to re-think the way professional development is approached in schools, so that it is more relevant to the individual needs and interests of teachers (Forte, Humphreys and Park 2012). The social media platform Twitter has given rise to new ways of engaging in professional learning and has become increasingly popular among teachers around the world (Alderton, Brunsell and Bariexca 2011; Forte, Humphreys and Park 2012; Grosseck and Holotescu 2011).

While there has been a growing body of scholarship on the participation of teachers in online communities (Duncan-Howell 2010; Forte, Humphreys and Park 2012; Mills and Chandra 2011), there is limited research into how teachers learn within these spaces. This is particularly the case with social media like Twitter. Consequently, this presents opportunities for further research into how content area teachers use Twitter for professional learning. In response to this gap, we drew on multiple data sources, including a survey, interviews, and tweets, to explore the intersection of Twitter, English teaching, and professional learning. Specifically, we asked: How and why are English teachers using Twitter for professional learning? In what ways does participating in professional learning through Twitter influence teachers' professional practices?

THEORETICAL FRAMEWORK

Theoretical and empirical studies in the field of education have highlighted the situated and social nature of learning (Brown, Collins and Duguid 1989; Greeno 1997; Vygotsky 1978; Wenger 1998). This has challenged previous theories that conceptualised cognition as an individual and internal process of knowledge acquisition (Greeno 1998). For many people, learning is synonymous with schools and universities, conjuring up images of classrooms and lecture halls, yet sociocultural and situated perspectives emphasize that learning is an integral part of everyday life and influenced by an individual's social and cultural context (Wenger 1998). For this reason, it is important that learning occurs through authentic activities within real-world contexts (Lave and Wenger 1991). For instance, teachers may find it difficult to sustain engagement when reading an academic article on pedagogical approaches, yet they will readily engage in discussion about the strategies they use in the classroom because it is personally meaningful and situated in an authentic setting.

This theoretical framework has influenced the way many educators support the learning of their students. However, despite the shift away from passive, teacher-centred approaches to student learning toward more interest-driven, collaborative and interactive forms, these theories are often not applied to the education of teachers themselves (Putnam and Borko 2000). In recent years, scholars have drawn attention to the importance of applying a sociocultural approach to teacher professional development. For instance, Wenger (1998: 4) described learning as a process of "social participation" within various "communities of practice." These same kinds of communities are evident in spaces of teacher professional learning, as teachers engage in authentic dialogue to develop their knowledge and practice (Curwood 2013; Desimone 2009).

Putnam and Borko (2000) argue that professional learning is most effective when it is situated in a specific context, social in nature, and distributed across people, resources, and tools. This perspective recognises that professional learning occurs in multiple contexts that include formal conferences and meetings, brief conversations with colleagues, and interactions in online spaces. Borko (2004: 4) suggested that in order to understand teacher learning, "we must study it within these multiple contexts" and acknowledge both the individual teachers and the social environments in which learning takes place.

Our study examined Twitter as a context of professional learning. Taking a sociocultural and situated approach was particularly relevant for this study due to the interactive, participatory, and social nature of Twitter (Cho, Ro and Littenberg-Tobias 2013; Fuchs 2014). Moreover, as social media sites are a part of everyday life for many teachers, Twitter situates professional learning in an authentic context (Forte, Humphreys and Park 2012).

LITERATURE REVIEW

Much of the scholarship related to the professional learning of teachers takes a sociocultural and situated perspective by considering the way an individual's context influences what, how, and why they learn (Lankshear and Knobel 2007). Here, we examine this scholarship to place our study within the wider context of the academic literature and identify critical gaps in this knowledge base. This literature review firstly investigates research on effective professional development and the move towards more collaborative and participatory models. It then examines teacher professional learning in online communities. Finally, it considers the ways that Twitter can be used for professional learning.

Professional Learning

A substantial body of literature suggests that effective professional learning has five core features: a focus on content, opportunities for active learning, coherence with previous professional experiences, involvement with colleagues from the same subject area, and significant contact hours (Borko 2004; Curwood 2011; Darling-Hammond 1997; Desimone 2009; Wilson and Berne 1999). Despite the importance of interaction, collaboration, and active participation for effective professional learning, many scholars have drawn attention to the prevalence of traditional models of professional development in schools (Butler et al. 2004; Curwood 2014a; Duncan-Howell 2010; Wilson and Berne 1999).

Recent studies have argued that traditional models, such as in-school workshops, are often decontextualized, of short duration, and typically are run by outside experts who spend a relatively brief amount of time interacting with teachers and have little knowledge of the school (Avalos 2011; Hur and Brush 2009; Little 2012). Darling-Hammond and Sykes (1999), writing over fifteen years ago, argued that this model of professional development is problematic because it does not provide teachers with the opportunity to engage in dialogue, collaboration, or curricular innovation, all of which are critical components of effective professional learning. More recently, Butler and colleagues (2004) conducted a two-year case study across four Canadian schools and found that, at the time, in-school workshops still favoured a top-down, one-size-fits-all approach to learning. Likewise, Duncan-Howell (2010) argued that these compulsory, school-based workshops often have limited impacts on pedagogy.

Prior studies highlight that there is often a disjunction between sociocultural theory, which advocates for conceptualising learning as social and contextual, and the professional development offered in schools (Cochran-Smith and Zeichner 2010; Curwood 2014b; Roth and Lee 2007; Webster-Wright 2009). They emphasise the importance of re-thinking the way professional development is approached, so that it is more relevant and tailored to the needs of individual teachers and local schools (Borko 2004). While these studies provide valuable insight into compulsory, school-based professional development, interest-driven, technology-mediated, and self-directed forms of professional learning are generally under-researched. This presents an opportunity for further research into contemporary forms of professional learning that draw on sociocultural and situated theories of learning.

Learning in Online Communities

The proliferation of digital tools in the 21st century has affected the way information is produced and the way people engage with knowledge (Fuchs 2014; Jewitt 2008). New technologies, such as online forums and social media, have created new spaces for professional learning (Grosseck and Holotescu 2011). Professional learning in these spaces may be formal, such as master's degrees or accredited courses, or informal, such as reading or commenting on another teacher's blog (Desimone 2009).

In an online survey, Duncan-Howell (2010) found that teachers generally regarded participation in online communities as a meaningful and relevant form of professional learning. The survey provided insight into the positive attitudes of participants towards online learning communities, as these spaces encourage conversations between like-minded teachers from different schools. Alderton, Brunsell, and Bariexca (2011) suggested that the support teachers receive when engaging in dialogue online may give them the confidence to try new and innovative strategies in their own classrooms. Skulstad (2005) examined the interactions of pre-service teachers in an asynchronous forum. As part of a compulsory task, the pre-service teachers posted their work online to be critiqued by their peers. The study found that by giving advice and praise, the participants utilised the online forum to improve their writing by learning from and with each other. Similarly, Mills and Chandra (2011) researched pre-service teachers in an Australian university and found that using the social networking platform Edmodo to collaborate on assignments established a supportive community of learners within this particular online space. Hur and Brush (2009) conducted a case study of eight K-12 teachers in three online forums, which were created specifically to support and encourage collegiality. Through interviews and an analysis of archived posts to the forums, they discovered that teachers were motivated to participate in these online communities because they provided a space to explore ideas, share emotions, and establish a sense of camaraderie (Hur and Brush 2009).

This body of research suggests that online communities provide a space for teachers to share resources and explore ideas (Hur and Brush 2009), overcome isolation by providing support and guidance for each other (Alderton, Brunsell and Bariexca 2011; Mills and Chandra 2011; Skulstad 2005), and can be a meaningful and relevant form of professional learning (Duncan-Howell 2010). While these studies have described some of the reasons teachers participate in online communities, there has been limited investigation into how teachers use these spaces for professional learning. Much of the research is also concerned with forums that were specifically created for professional discussions rather than social media, like Twitter. For this reason, the implications of online learning communities for teachers have yet to be extensively explored, which presents a critical gap in the literature.

Twitter and Professional Learning

Social media sites have become popular among educators as a complement to more traditional forms of professional development (Lloyd and Duncan-Howell 2010). Social media refers to online applications that include, but are not limited to, Facebook, Twitter, Instagram, and Tumblr (Grimes and Fields 2012). Scholars have suggested that Twitter, in particular, has the potential to foster opportunities for authentic professional learning (Cho, Ro and Littenberg-Tobias 2013; DeCosta, Clifton and Roen 2010; Khan 2012). O'Connell (2008: 23) described Twitter as a "powerful, ongoing learning community" that encourages collegial interaction, reflection, and sharing. Cho, Ro, and Littenberg-Tobias (2013) and DeCosta, Clifton, and Roen (2010) suggested that the interactive nature of Twitter allows teachers to engage in personalized and distributed professional learning with colleagues from around the world, both asynchronously and in real time.

While the impacts of Twitter on professional learning have been relatively unexplored, there have been some small-scale empirical studies of Twitter as a tool for developing teachers' practice. Forte, Humphreys, and Park (2012) conducted a study of how teachers participate in Twitter chats as a form of professional learning. Twitter chats are public conversations that take place at a designated time by using a common hashtag. Hashtags categorise messages about specific topics and are searchable within Twitter (Cho, Ro and Littenberg-Tobias 2013). A study by Forte and colleagues (2012) triangulated findings from a survey, interviews, and the content analysis of 2,000 tweets with the American-focused hashtag #edchat and found that many teachers regarded Twitter as a valuable platform for discussing classroom practices and sharing resources.

Alderton, Brunsell, and Bariexca (2011) examined the way a group of American teachers used Twitter to communicate and collaborate with each other. An analysis of their tweets and the data collected from a survey revealed that 62 per cent of the group's tweets provided evidence of dialogue between teachers, and nine out of ten participants provided examples of how they used Twitter as a tool for collaboration. At the same time, the study found that the 140-character limit per tweet restricted communication, with teachers explaining that they moved to other platforms such as Facebook and email for more in-depth discussions. Khan (2012) agreed that while Twitter chats encouraged professional dialogue, the constantly updating stream of information could be overwhelming, making it difficult for some teachers to engage in discussions in depth.

Although there have been some studies into why teachers use Twitter for professional learning, these were primarily with American teachers and focused on Twitter chats across multiple subject areas. Consequently, studies looking at how and why content area teachers use Twitter for professional learning in international contexts would be a beneficial addition to the current knowledge base, as research has shown that professional learning is most effective when it is situated and discipline specific (Darling-Hammond 1997; Desimone 2009).

METHODOLOGY

Context

Our study draws on data from the popular social media platform Twitter.com. Launched in 2006, Twitter allows users to read and write 140-character messages, called tweets, to communicate both in real time and asynchronously. Tweets can contain text, images, and links to external pages, articles, and websites (Greenhow and Gleason 2012). In addition, tweets can be linked to or shared on other social networking sites, as well as through email. Figure 10.1 provides a screenshot of the standard website interface of Twitter. Running across the top is a navigation bar that includes icons for Home, Notifications, Messages, and a search bar that can be used to search keywords, usernames, and hashtags.

The top left corner of the screen shows the profile information of the user, including their name, profile picture, number of tweets, number of followers, and the number of people they are following. Followers are people who subscribe to a user's tweets. In other words, a user chooses to see a person's tweets by "following" them. These tweets appear as a constantly updating list down the centre of the interface and can be replied to, favorited or retweeted (Cho, Ro and Littenberg-Tobias 2013). A "favorite" is used to like or praise another user's tweet and can also save the tweet for access at a later time. A retweet refers to the reposting of another user's tweet to demonstrate agreement with it or provide validation (Khan 2012). Users can write and post tweets by clicking on the button in the top right corner.

Figure 10.1: Twitter Interface.

Participants

The participants were recruited for our study by posting a link to a survey we had designed, using the English teaching hashtags #engchat and #ozengchat, as well as via Facebook, where the link was posted to the English Teachers Association of New South Wales, National Council of Teachers of English, and Australian Association for the Teaching of English pages. Despite the global audience of Twitter and Facebook, the 64 survey respondents were primarily from an Australian context. Table 10.1 further illustrates the survey demographics.

Table 10.1: Survey demographics

		Number of participants
Country	Australia	49
	USA	12
	New Zealand	1
	Singapore	1
	Ireland	1
Age	20–24	5
	25–30	8
	31–35	5
	36–40	14
	41–45	10
	46–50	7
	51–55	8
	56–60	6
	61–65	1
Years Teaching Experience	Pre-service	3
	1–5	8
	6–10	15
	11–15	16
	16–20	7
	21–25	7
	26–30	2
	31–35	6

Survey respondents were given the opportunity to express interest in participating in an interview. These eight self-nominated teachers were selected as representative of #ozengchat, as they were varied in terms of their years of teaching experience and their activity on Twitter. All participants worked in secondary schools with students in Grades 7 to 12, with the exception of Leah, who worked as a university lecturer. All were Australian and based in New South Wales, with the exception of Hannah, who taught in South Australia, and Leah, who taught in Queensland. Table 10.2 summarises the relevant demographic information and shows the participants' varied degrees of Twitter use, including the number of tweets they have posted, number of followers, and number of people they were following at the time of data collection.

Table 10.2: Interview participants

Name*	Role	Age	Years of teaching experience	Years using Twitter	Number of tweets posted	Number of followers	Number following
Jackson	English teacher	25–30	4	6	37K	1,495	1,259
Whitney	English and ESL teacher	36–40	16	3	21K	1,885	1,461
Kat	English teacher and Head of Professional Learning	31–35	10	6	49.9K	4,428	1,316
Hannah	Head of Library, and an English teacher prior to this study	36–40	13	3	8,585	413	213
Elise	Head of English	36–40	11	3	2,726	1,036	1,722
Jill	Head of English	51–55	30	5	12.8K	1,627	1,132
Ryan	Head of English	31–35	10	6	570	104	444
Leah	University lecturer of English Curriculum	31–35	10	6	10.7K	3,044	2,633

* All names are pseudonyms

Data Collection

To answer our research questions concerning English teachers and their use of Twitter for professional learning, we collected multiple data sources. This included: (a) an online survey of 64 teachers about their professional learning and Twitter use, which included Likert scale and open-ended questions; (b) hour-long semi-structured interviews with eight focal participants that were conducted via Skype; and (c) an analysis of the content of 530 tweets that included the #ozengchat hashtag. These tweets were taken from four archives that were identified by the creator of #ozengchat as representative of the hashtag. Tweets were collected from #ozengchat because all of the interviewees had used it and because of its Australian focus.

Hashtags are created by including the # symbol before a word or phrase. They are searchable within Twitter, and, as such, can be used to broaden the scope of a tweet by reaching a larger audience that extends beyond one's "followers" and can serve to highlight a particular topic, and also turn a topic into a "trend" (a topic that is popular at a particular time). Some popular education-themed hashtags include #engchat, #edchat, and #aussieed. A screenshot of the #ozengchat hashtag is shown in Figure 10.2. This particular hashtag was created in 2012 for Australian English teachers to interact, share resources, and reflect on their practice. The chat is moderated by several members of the community, which assists in maintaining #ozengchat as a space for professional learning that is relevant to English teaching. While the hashtag can be used and accessed publically at any time, a live chat occurs fortnightly on Tuesday nights.

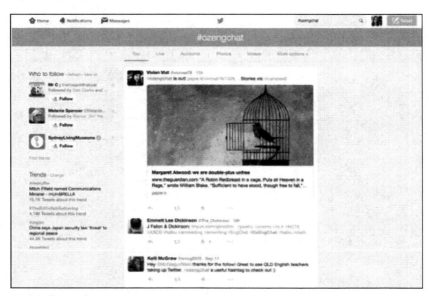

Figure 10.2: #ozengchat.

Data Analysis

The interviews and tweets were analysed concurrently through a process of thematic analysis. This involved closely reading the data and separating it into salient fragments or themes, which were then used to infer meaning (Saldaña 2013). With the surveys, multiple-choice and Likert scale data were analysed quantitatively, and frequently used terms were identified in the open-ended questions.

The interviews and tweets were analysed thematically using first-cycle and second-cycle coding methods (Miles, Huberman and Saldaña 2014). During the first cycle, we analysed the interview data line by line and labelled meaningful fragments with *in vivo* codes, which use the participants' own words as codes. This showcased the unique voices of the interviewees and situated the data within an authentic context. "On your own" is an example of an *in vivo* code we used to label data that described a perceived lack of support and instances of self-initiated learning. Each tweet was attributed a process code such as "sharing resources" to reflect *how* Twitter was used by educators by describing observable action (Saldaña 2013). Only one code was applied to each tweet, which are described in Table 10.3 below.

During the second cycle of coding, we identified patterns across data sources and reduced the number of codes by removing those that occurred less frequently, as well as those that shared the same meaning with another code. *In vivo* codes were changed to descriptive codes to summarise and clarify their meanings. For example, the *in vivo* code "on your own" became the descriptive code "self-directed learning." Codes were then cross-referenced with the quantitative data from the survey to highlight salient themes and determine key findings (Denzin and Lincoln 2000). By triangulating the data from the survey, interviews, and tweets, the study provided a holistic understanding of why and how eight teachers used Twitter for professional learning.

FINDINGS AND DISCUSSION

Our study investigated how and why English teachers use Twitter for professional learning, and it also examined Twitter's influence on their professional practice. The findings are organised into four sections. We first explore the reasons for the popularity of self-directed and voluntary forms of professional learning. Second, we discuss Twitter as a global professional learning network. Finally, we describe participants' changing roles and varied levels of participation within the Twitter community before considering the implications for classroom practice.

Trending: The increasing popularity of self-directed professional learning

We get told so much… sometimes it's nice for people to be able to pick. (Kat)

Agency was a recurring theme throughout our study, with participants emphasising the importance of having choice and control over what they learn and how they learn it. When asked in the survey to identify a valuable experience of professional learning, a significant number of teachers cited voluntary learning opportunities such as TeachMeets, Google Hangouts, and Twitter chats. Examples of these include the Literacy Research Association's Research to Practice Show via Google Hangouts, Sydney-based TeachMeets, and #ozengchat on Twitter. These professional learning opportunities provide teachers with a sense of agency over their own learning because they have the chance to select activities that are relevant to their classroom practice (Alderton, Brunsell and Bariexca 2011; Pluss 2008). With Twitter, teachers can join a Twitter chat that addresses a topic in which they are personally interested. For example, #pbl has a focus on project-based learning, while #ozengchat emphasises English curriculum and pedagogy. Interestingly, data from the survey suggested that school-based professional development often does not differentiate between teachers, with only 4 out of 64 respondents strongly agreeing that the professional development offered by their school was tailored to their individual needs and interests.

The perception among interview participants was that school-based professional development was often generic, repetitive, and provided teachers with limited agency over their own learning. Kat described her frustration with the decontextualised and pre-packaged approach to professional development in her school: "We don't really get a choice… it's just this thing that someone else implemented in another school and then it's been brought over to our school." Leah elaborated on the generic nature of school-based professional learning: "You would be doing something [in a professional development workshop]…really broadly, not specifically for that in the English classroom."

Issues of accessibility also influenced teachers' use of Twitter. While most survey respondents found external conferences to be a valuable form of professional learning, many of the interview participants expressed that due to cost and location, these conferences are often inaccessible. Whitney explained, "I enjoy going to conferences, but… my time to go to them is limited because of teaching commitments and because there is not enough funding." Jill described her difficulty in accessing "good professional development" in a rural setting, as "we don't have the money for travel and accommodation." Twitter, on the other hand, offers free, just-in-time professional learning that is not restricted by geography or money, as it can be accessed from any device with an internet connection (Cho, Ro and Littenberg-Tobias 2013). This is especially important for connecting teachers in schools with limited funds, as well as schools in rural or remote Australia.

Voluntary and self-directed forms of professional learning are becoming increasingly popular among teachers because they provide opportunities for interaction, collaboration, and active participation, all of which are core features of effective professional learning (Borko 2004; Darling-Hammond 1997; Desimone 2009). Hannah explained that she finds it "really useful to be able to talk to people… about areas that I'm passionate about," and Jackson explained that he is motivated to participate in Twitter chats because of the "ongoing dialogue" with other teachers. This is in contrast to Kat's experience of school-based professional development, where teachers had no choice or active involvement in their learning but instead "had this woman talking at us for two and a half hours. We were sitting at circular tables, which I thought was amusing, because at no point were we invited to talk to each other or to do an activity."

This passive style of knowledge transmission is problematic considering the substantial research base that emphasises the importance of learning through social interaction (Gee 2004; Lave and Wenger 1991; Moll 1992; Street 2014; Vygotsky 1978; Wenger 1998). The attitude among several of the interview participants was that due to the lack of agency and the often repetitive, decontextualized nature of school-sponsored learning, teachers have a responsibility for pursuing their own professional learning. It is for this reason in particular, it seems, that self-directed and digitally mediated platforms such as Twitter are becoming increasingly popular among teachers. As Jill explained, "If you weren't active in terms of finding your own [professional learning], then you wouldn't learn anything new."

Follow me: Finding support within a global professional learning network

> Twitter is the staffroom that you'd really like to have. (Jackson)

Twitter is unique because it enables teachers to freely access professional learning and to communicate at any time with colleagues from around the world (Cho, Ro and Littenberg-Tobias 2013). This means that professional learning networks are not limited to school staffrooms, as teachers are able to seek support and share their experiences with a global audience (Pluss 2008). Jackson explained that by expanding his professional learning network through Twitter, he can interact with "great educators…. that are willing to share ideas and resources… while in schools people aren't that forth coming." Elise further described the benefits of Twitter's global reach: "Once you say, 'Can I have help with this or does anyone have any ideas for this?', you get retweeted a couple of times, and your audience ends up being unlimited." At the same time, this unlimited access to information can be overwhelming. As Kat explained, "Sometimes there's so many people in there, you can't open all those links and you can't favourite everything." Leah conveyed her frustration over resource sharing on Twitter that can become repetitive, as "everyone will share, share, share, and then the same question comes up again in six months' time."

Through Twitter, teachers are engaging in reciprocal learning as they share resources and ideas within a global professional learning network. Whitney explained that Twitter gives her access to innovators and experts in the field, and she also has the opportunity to see beyond her classroom "to other things that are happening in Australia and in the world." Ryan further described the advantage of Twitter for networking and collaborating with people with different perspectives to his own: "I interact with the English teachers at my work all the time and we often think pretty similarly... if everyone in a school all thinks the same way... you can shut down opportunities to grow and improve." In this way, knowledge and information are distributed across the Twitter community, with each member bringing diverse perspectives, skills, and areas of expertise. This, in turn, enables teachers to learn from and with each other (Gomez et al. 2010; Putnam and Borko 2000).

The analysis of tweets from #ozengchat highlighted how teachers use Twitter for professional learning. During analysis, we categorised each contribution to the hashtag into one of the following codes: sharing resources, reflecting on experiences, describing practice, asking a question, offering ideas, responding to a question, and networking. These codes are explained in further detail in Table 10.3.

Table 10.3: Tweet Codes

Code	Description	No. times code occurred
SHARING RESOURCES	Links to external resources such as websites and articles that inform teaching practices or can be used in the classroom. Example: "OK, straight off the bat is the top two Shakespeare links I give to my students: nfs. sparknotes.com & shmoop.com/shakespeare/ #ozengchat"	122
REFLECTING ON EXPERIENCES	Reflecting on personal experiences they have had as a teacher. This can include sharing successes and failures and reflecting on their teaching philosophy. Example: "Hurley is interesting for me personally. I feel it's a bit dry for students. Lots of interesting idea of disc. through #ozengchat"	77

Code	Description	No. times code occurred
DESCRIBING PRACTICE	Tweets that describe strategies that have been implemented in the classroom. Example: "#ozengchat I did a Macbeth/GoT lesson re: regicide + kingslayer, doubletrust + red wedding, and Lady Macbeth + Cersei ..."	75
ASKING A QUESTION	These were in the form of open questions that were directed towards everyone, as well as direct questions that were specifically targeted towards individual users. Example: "#ozengchat I need some help Language, Learning and Literacy Does anyone have any information that's not on the intranet?"	71
OFFERING IDEAS	Suggestions and inspiration for classroom practice. Example: "Engaging with poetry - get students to illustrate a selected poem #ozengchat"	70
RESPONDING TO QUESTION	Directly responding to or answering a question posed by another user. Example: "we do insults as well! And idioms that we use today from Shakespeare #ozengchat #greatminds"	51
NETWORKING	Networking includes making plans to collaborate with other users and personal conversations unrelated to professional practice. Example: "We should do some collaborative projects w my ESL classes then! :) #sokeen #ozengchat #authenticlearning"	47

We found that teachers most commonly contributed to the #ozengchat hashtag by sharing resources, reflecting on their experiences, and describing their classroom practice. This was consistent with the survey data, which indicated that teachers use Twitter predominantly for professional purposes. Notably, while the code "sharing resources" occurred most frequently, 57 out of 122 of these instances occurred outside of the designated time of #ozengchat. In fact, the overwhelming majority of tweets that occurred asynchronously were links to resources. This suggests that asynchronous participation on Twitter is more about sharing ideas and resources than about seeking advice or expecting a response. This idea was supported by data from the interviews. For example, Elise explained that the benefit of asynchronous communication is that "you can go back and look at the conversations and add to it later." However, Jackson expressed that this can be problematic, because without understanding the context of a tweet, "you can really misinterpret other people's tone." Jill agreed that it can be difficult to communicate your ideas clearly "without going over 140 characters... so sometimes it's really nice to talk face-to-face."

Of further interest was the acknowledgement and social validation of teachers' ideas, which was apparent in both the interviews and the tweets. Several of the interview participants indicated the importance of having their learning and contributions acknowledged by other teachers, yet this was often absent within their schools. As Kat explained, "We don't get report cards, and we don't get test results that say we've done well." We found evidence of teachers affirming the contributions of others within the #ozengchat tweets. These affirmations were either direct in the form of praising someone through a reply or indirect by a favourite or a retweet. From 530 tweets, we counted 228 favourites, 143 retweets, and 12 instances of direct praise. This means that on average, 72 per cent of the contributions to #ozengchat received some form of validation. This finding reinforces teachers' perception of Twitter as a supportive and collegial network where their learning and contributions are socially recognised. As Kat elaborated, "Twitter was about establishing myself within a community of educators who value me."

From lurker to leader: Changing roles and the importance of participation

> When you think of birds up in a tree going tweet, tweet, tweet, if they're not actually tweeting, if they're not actually saying little 140 things to each other quite quickly and continuously, nothing is twittering. (Leah)

A community of practice refers to a group of people with common interests and goals who learn from each other by sharing information, knowledge, and experiences (Lave and Wenger 1991). Studies related to adolescents' contributions and interactions in affinity spaces and online forums, reflected the importance of participation within communities of practice (e.g., Ito et al. 2013; Margerison 2013). Our survey asked several questions related to the way teachers participate in professional learning through Twitter. Respondents were asked to identify how often they read, retweet, and post original tweets related to their professional practice. The results are illustrated in Figure 10.3.

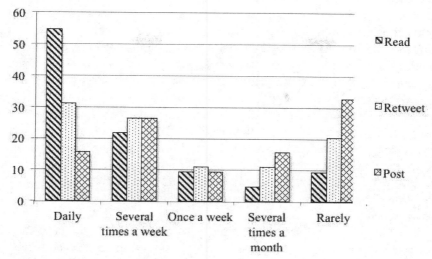

Figure 10.3: Frequency of participation.

While the majority of participants indicated that they read tweets on a daily basis, only 15.6 per cent reported that they post original tweets daily. We explored this idea further by asking interview participants how they use Twitter for professional learning. We found that participation takes multiple forms, including posting an original tweet, retweeting or favoriting another person's tweet, and reading what other people have contributed. With this in mind, the survey highlights that teachers are largely participating on Twitter by reading, which arguably is a valid and often under-valued form of participation (Wenger 1998).

Jackson considered the multiple possible types of participation as one of the advantages of Twitter over other forms of professional learning. This is because participation "doesn't necessarily mean you have to be present. It's the nature of Twitter that you can be an observer…you can just watch… you aren't forced to participate." Hannah explained that she only participates directly when the topic is something she is passionate about or when she feels she can add something of value to the conversation. This quality of Twitter is something that Ryan, a self-described "lurker," also finds advantageous. He elaborated, "I lurk a little bit sometimes and read through a few discussions that happen on #ozengchat, but I rarely contribute."

The concept of lurking describes the process of being present in the Twitter community through observation rather than actively contributing to the conversation. This idea is consistent with Lave and Wenger's (1991) theory of legitimate peripheral participation, whereby participation includes both active involvement and observation. Moreover, legitimate peripheral participation holds that newcomers to a community of practice need the opportunity to participate in low-risk ways. As individuals become more familiar and experienced within the community, they often move from the periphery to take on a more central and active role (Lave and Wenger 1991). Jill described her changing level of participation in this way. "In the first few months you just sit back and you take, you favourite and you follow the links. Then you become brave and start sharing what you know." Similarly, Jackson began using Twitter as a pre-service teacher mostly to find resources and ideas that he could implement in the classroom. As he gained more experience as a teacher, his role and use of Twitter changed from seeking advice and resources to sharing resources and ideas of his own. He explained, "When I first started I was desperate for any ideas... But now that I've been teaching for a couple of years, I'm starting to feel like I can offer something."

These changing degrees of participation also provide opportunities for teachers to establish themselves as leaders within the community. Both Whitney and Leah assumed leadership roles within the #ozengchat community. Whitney is the creator and moderator of the chat, while Leah also assists with moderation. Leah and Whitney described the responsibility of leading the chat as more challenging than simply participating in it; according to Whitney, the role of the moderator is to "keep the flow going…. Asking the questions and responding to what people are saying." Interestingly, Whitney explained that despite her role, she does not consider herself "the provider of professional development." Instead, she believed that as a moderator, she facilitates the conversation in which educators learn from and with each other.

On the other hand, Kat and Ryan explained that as they become more experienced in their careers, they are contributing less often to Twitter. While Kat acknowledged the importance of having more experienced teachers on Twitter "to help the new people," she explained that she is not interested in having that role. Ryan believed that ultimately, the ideas and resources shared on Twitter are "superficial," because while they provide inspiration, they need to be adapted for the unique context of his classroom and school. For this reason Ryan prefers to learn through self-selected workshops, conferences, and research, and he uses Twitter to complement and support this learning. These varied degrees of participation on Twitter are a reflection of the agency teachers have over their learning within this online space. This again suggests that Twitter is not a provider of professional development per se but, rather, is a valuable tool that can be used by teachers to support their professional practice and complement other forms of professional development.

IMPLICATIONS FOR PROFESSIONAL PRACTICE

Our survey found that 81 per cent of respondents believed that participating in Twitter chats was a meaningful form of professional learning. The interviewees elaborated on this belief by providing examples of how Twitter influenced their practice as English teachers. Two prominent influences emerged: Twitter as a source of inspiration and Twitter as a tool for learning.

The resources and ideas shared on Twitter seem to inspire teachers. As Jill stated, they influence "day-to-day activities, assessments, and the way technology is used to engage students in the classroom." Elise explained that through Twitter she was provided with "links, programmes, and examples" that assisted her implementation of the flipped classroom strategy with her students. Jill stated that a "key part of her work with iPads" was inspired by an idea she found on Twitter, where students create movie trailers for books they are studying in class. She also explained that from a link on Twitter she learned about new feedback models, which influenced her implementation of a student reflection task. Similarly, Jackson described the "medals and missions" feedback strategy that was shared by a colleague on Twitter and how it "has totally changed" the way he approaches marking.

Twitter is also a valuable tool for supporting teachers' and students' learning. Hannah, who teaches in an all-girls' school, described tweeting authors to engage students in the novels they were studying. "When I was reading Claire Zorn's book to Grade 8, I was tweeting her the responses the girls were having, and she was tweeting back... I would then share that with the students." Kat used Twitter in her classroom to provide an authentic audience for her students to share their work. She explained that this significantly changed her practice because it allowed her to "see that my students are composers, more than just responders." She said, "Twitter has made me a better English teacher" because, rather than asking her students to write about texts that other people have created, she also encourages students to create their own. She further shared her plans, as head teacher of professional learning, to embed Twitter within her programmes as a way of encouraging her colleagues to share their learning with an "audience outside of the school." Elise also used Twitter for this reason, as she believed that retweeting, favouriting, and sharing her experiences with a global audience influenced her practice as a teacher, because they allow "me to reflect on my ideas, values, what I teach, how I teach... and this is really important."

Despite this rich evidence to suggest that Twitter influences the practice of English teachers in positive ways, many teachers are reluctant to embrace Twitter as a platform for professional learning. As Jackson put it, "They think it's Justin Bieber talking about combing his hair... they have got no idea." The attitude among the interview participants was that there is a need for a shift in the way Twitter is perceived by educators, so that instead of viewing it as a social media platform for celebrity gossip, it is seen as a valuable and authentic space for professional learning. As Jill emphasised, "I have learned more about my craft and my subject in the six years I've been on Twitter than I did in the 24 years of teaching before then."

CONCLUSION

Previous studies considered the potential of Twitter for professional learning (Alderton, Brunsell and Bariexca 2011; Cho, Ro and Littenberg-Tobias 2013; Forte, Humphreys and Park 2012; Grosseck and Holotescu 2011; Pluss 2008). Adding to the research, this study highlighted three key factors that influenced teachers' use of Twitter: *agency* in how, what, and why teachers engage in professional learning; *accessibility* in terms of funding and location; and *reciprocity* in how learning occurs and is socially validated. The findings indicate that Twitter is an effective form of professional learning because it is self-directed, and teachers can select Twitter chats that are relevant to their unique needs and interests, while school-sponsored professional development is often generic and decontextualised. Moreover, while professional development can be expensive and often requires teachers to travel, Twitter offers free professional learning that is accessible from any location and at any time. Scholars argue that teaching needs to move away from being a solitary activity and instead, emphasise the importance of reciprocal learning, dialogue, and collaboration (Kedzior and Fifield 2004). By sharing resources, reflecting on experiences, and engaging in dialogue with passionate and like-minded colleagues, learning through Twitter is social, distributed, and situated in an authentic context. In this way, Twitter fosters a supportive professional learning community, where teachers' ideas are acknowledged and valued. This was evident through the high frequency of favorites and retweets within #ozengchat.

Twitter also has a significant influence on pedagogy, with all teachers in the study providing examples of using Twitter as a source of inspiration, and as a tool for learning. However, the extent of Twitter's influence varied among study participants, with some becoming more active and assuming leadership roles and others becoming less engaged and seeking professional learning in other forms over time. This suggests that Twitter is most effective when complemented by other forms of professional learning and adapted to the social and cultural contexts of individual teachers and schools.

While this study provides valuable insight into how and why English teachers use Twitter for professional learning, there are several limitations. Due to the opportunistic sampling method of the survey, the participants were predominantly from Australia and primarily from New South Wales. For this reason, the findings are not representative of all English teachers using Twitter. Future studies can broaden the scope of the research to include teachers from more diverse contexts. The case study methodology bounded the research context within the #ozengchat hashtag. Future research could assess the transferability and repeatability of the findings by comparing a variety of educational hashtags through a multiple case study design (Merriam 2009). In addition, longitudinal or ethnographic studies that explore how content area teachers use Twitter over a substantial period of their career would provide a more in-depth understanding of the long-term impacts Twitter has on their practice.

The findings clearly show that Twitter, as an online community of practice, embodies the characteristics of effective professional learning. This includes a focus on content, active participation, and an ongoing dialogue with teachers of the same subject area (Desimone 2009). Consequently, this study advocates for the acknowledgement of Twitter as a powerful complement to recognised and certified professional development. Furthermore, as agency and reciprocity were crucial factors that influenced teachers' use of Twitter, this study suggests that schools allow teachers to choose their professional development activities and incorporate the participatory, interactive, and reciprocal attributes of Twitter into the professional development programs they offer to teachers. In doing so, school-based professional development can become more relevant, engaging, and have a long-lasting influence on the practice of teachers. We know that our students are motivated when they have agency and when they have access to an interest-driven community; it is time we apply this knowledge to teacher professional development.

REFERENCES

Alderton, E., Brunsell, E. and Bariexca, D. (2011). The end of isolation. *The Journal of Online Learning and Teaching.* 7(3): 1–16.

Australian Institute for Teaching and School Leadership (AITSL). (2012) Australian Teacher Performance and Development Framework. Available at: http://www.aitsl.edu.au. Downloaded 8 October, 2015.

Avalos, B. (2011). Teacher professional development in teaching and teacher education over ten years. *Teaching and Teacher Education.* 27(1): 10–20.

Board of Studies Teaching and Educational Standards NSW. (2013) Great Teaching Inspired Learning. Available: http://www.nswteachers.nsw.edu.au/great-teaching-inspired-learning Downloaded 8 October, 2015.

Borko, H. (2004). Professional development and teacher learning: Mapping the terrain. *Educational Researcher.* 33(3): 3–15.

Brown, J., Collins, A. and Duguid, P. (1989). Situated cognition and the culture of learning. *Educational Researcher.* 18(1): 32–42.

Butler, D., Lauscher, H., Jarvis-Selinger, S. and Beckingham, B. (2004). Collaboration and self-regulation in teachers' professional development. *Teaching and Teacher Education.* 20(1): 435–455.

Cho, V., Ro, J. and Littenberg-Tobias, J. (2013). What Twitter will and will not do: Theorising about teachers' online professional communities. *LEARNing Landscapes.* 6(2): 45–62.

Cochran-Smith, M. and Zeichner, K. (eds) (2010). *Studying Teacher Education: The Report of the AERA Panel on Research and Teacher Education.* Washington, DC: Routledge.

Curwood, J. (2011). Teachers as learners: What makes technology-focused professional development effective? *English in Australia.* 46(3): 68–75.

Curwood, J. (2013). Applying the design framework to technology professional development. *Journal of Digital Learning in Teacher Education.* 29(3): 90–97.

Curwood, J. (2014a). Between continuity and change: Identities and narratives within teacher professional development. *Teaching Education*. 25(2): 156–183.

Curwood, J. (2014b). English teachers' cultural models about technology: A microethnographic perspective on professional development. *Journal of Literacy Research*. 46(1): 9–38.

Darling-Hammond, L. (1997). *Doing What Matters: Investing in Quality Teaching*. New York, NY: National Commission on Teaching and America's Future.

Darling-Hammond, L. and Sykes, G. (1999). *Teaching as the Learning Profession: Handbook of Policy and Practice*. San Francisco, CA: Jossey-Bass.

DeCosta, M., Clifton, J. and Roen, D. (2010). Collaboration and social interaction in English classrooms. *English Journal*. 99(5): 14–21.

Denzin, N. and Lincoln, Y. (2000). *Handbook of Qualitative Research*. Beverly Hills, CA: Sage.

Desimone, L. (2009). Improving impact studies of teachers' professional development: Toward better conceptualizations and measures. *Educational Researcher*. 38(3): 181–199.

Duncan-Howell, J. (2010). Teachers making connections: Online communities as a source of professional learning. *British Journal of Educational Technology*. 41(2): 324–340.

Easton, L. (2008). From professional development to professional learning. *Phi Delta Kappan*. 89(10): 755–759.

Forte, A., Humphreys, M. and Park, T. (2012). Grassroots professional development: How teachers use Twitter. *Proceedings of the International Conference on Weblogs and Social Media*. Presented at the International Conference on Weblogs and Social Media, Dublin, Ireland: Association for the Advancement of Artificial Intelligence, 106–113.

Fuchs, C. (2014). *Social Media: A Critical Introduction*. London: SAGE.

Gee, J. (2004). *Situated Language and Learning: A Critique of Traditional Schooling*. New York, NY: Routledge.

Gomez, M., Schieble, M., Curwood, J. and Hassett, D. (2010). Technology, learning, and instruction: Distributed cognition in the secondary English classroom. *Literacy*. 44(1): 20–27.

Greenhow, C. and Gleason, B. (2012). Twitteracy: Tweeting as a new literacy practice. *The Educational Forum*. 76(4): 464–478.

Greeno, J. (1997). On claims that answer the wrong questions. *Educational Researcher*. 26(1): 5–17.

Greeno, J. (1998). The situativity of knowing, learning, and research. *American Psychologist*. 53(1): 5–26.

Grimes, S. and Fields, D. (2012). *Kids Online: A New Research Agenda for Understanding Social Networking Forums*. The Joan Ganz Cooney Center at Sesame Workshop. Available: http://www. joanganzcooneycenter.org Downloaded 8 October, 2015.

Grosseck, G. and Holotescu, C. (2011). Teacher education in 140 characters: Microblogging implications for continuous education, training, learning and personal development. *Procedia - Social and Behavioral Sciences*. 11(1): 160–164.

Hammerness, K., Darling-Hammond, L., Bransford, J., Berliner, D., Cochran-Smith, M., McDonald, M. and Zeichner, K. (2005). How teachers learn and develop. In L. Darling Hammond and J. Bransford (eds), *Preparing Teachers for a Changing World: What Teachers Should Learn and Be Able to Do*. San Francisco, CA: Wiley & Sons, 358–389.

Hur, J. and Brush, T. (2009). Teacher participation in online communities: Why do teachers want to participate in self-generated online communities of K-12 teachers? *Journal of Research on Technology in Education*. 41(3): 279–303.

Ito, M., Gutiérrez, K., Livingstone, S., Penuel, B., Rhodes, J., Salen, K., Schor, J., Sefton Green, J. and Watkins, S. (2013). *Connected Learning: An Agenda for Research and Design.* Irvine, CA: Digital Media and Learning Research Hub.

Jewitt, C. (2008). Multimodality and literacy in school classrooms. *Review of Research in Education.* 32(1): 241–267.

Kedzior, M. and Fifield, S. (2004). Teacher professional development. *Education Policy Brief.* 15(21): 76–97.

Khan, S. (2012). Getting started with Twitter: A "why and how" for teachers. *English Australia Journal.* 28(1): 55–60.

Kress, G. (2003). *Literacy in the New Media Age.* London: Routledge.

Lankshear, C. and Knobel, M., (eds) (2007). *A New Literacies Sampler.* New York, NY: Peter Lang.

Lave, J. and Wenger, E. (1991). *Situated Learning: Legitimate Peripheral Participation.* Cambridge, UK: Cambridge University Press.

Lieberman, A. and Mace, D. (2009). Making practice public: Teacher learning in the 21st century. *Journal of Teacher Education.* 61(1–2): 77–88.

Little, J. (2012). Professional community and professional development in the learning centered school. In M. Kooy and K. van Veen (eds), *Teacher Learning That Matters: International Perspectives.* New York, NY: Routledge, 22–46.

Lloyd, M. and Duncan-Howell, J. (2010). Changing the metaphor: The potential of online communities in teacher professional development. In J.O. Lindberg and A. Olofsson (eds), *Online Learning Communities and Teacher Professional Development: Methods for Improved Education Delivery.* Hershey, PA: IGI Global, 60–76.

Margerison, J. (2013). Online discussion forums in the classroom: Can the principles of social media benefit literacy and enhance engagement with learning? *Literacy Learning: The Middle Years,* 21(2): 19–28.

Merriam, S. (2009). *Qualitative Research: A Guide to Design and Implementation.* San Francisco, CA: Jossey-Bass.

Miles, M., Huberman, A. and Saldaña, J. (2014). *Qualitative Data Analysis: A Methods Sourcebook.* Thousand Oaks, CA: Sage.

Mills, K. and Chandra, V. (2011). Microblogging as a literacy practice for educational communities. *Journal of Adolescent & Adult Literacy.* 55(1): 35–45.

Moll, L. (1992). *Vygotsky and Education: Instructional Implications and Applications of Sociohistorical Psychology.* Cambridge: Cambridge University Press.

The New Teacher Project. (2015). *The Mirage: Confronting the Hard Truth About Our Quest for Teacher Development.* Available at: http://tntp.org/publications/view/the-mirage Downloaded 8 October, 2015.

O'Connell, J. (2008). What's that sound? Tweet: New perspectives on leadership and learning. *Access.* 22(4): 23–25.

Organisation for Economic Co-operation and Development (OECD). (2009). Creative Effective Teaching and Learning Environments: First Results from TALIS. Available: http://www.oecd.org Downloaded 8 October, 2015.

Pluss, M. (2008). Twitter: Viral professional development and networking. *Teacher: The National Education Magazine,* November: 58–60.

Putnam, R. and Borko, H. (2000). What do new views of knowledge and thinking have to say about research on teacher learning? *Educational Researcher.* 29(1): 4–15.

Roth, W. and Lee, Y. (2007). "Vygotsky's neglected legacy": Cultural-historical activity theory. *Review of Educational Research.* 77(2): 186–232.

Saldaña, J. (2013). *The Coding Manual for Qualitative Researchers.* Thousand Oaks, CA: Sage.

Skulstad, A. (2005). Competing roles: Student teachers using asynchronous forums. *International Journal of Applied Linguistics.* 15(3): 346–363.

Street, B. (2014). *Social Literacies: Critical Approaches to Literacy in Development, Ethnography and Education.* New York, NY: Routledge.

Vygotsky, L. (1978). *Mind in Society.* Cambridge, MA: Harvard University Press.

Walshe, J. and Hirsch, D. (1998). *Staying Ahead: In-service Training and Teacher Professional Development.* Paris, France: OECD.

Webster-Wright, A. (2009). Reframing professional development through understanding authentic professional learning. *Review of Educational Research.* 79(2): 702–739.

Wenger, E. (1998). *Communities of Practice: Learning, Meaning, Identity.* Cambridge, UK: Cambridge University Press.

Wilson, S. and Berne, J. (1999). Teacher learning and the acquisition of professional knowledge: An examination of research on contemporary professional development. *Review of Research in Education.* 24(1): 173–209.

CHAPTER ELEVEN

Connected Learning Professional Development: Production-Centered AND Openly Networked Teaching Communities

CHRISTINA CANTRILL AND KYLIE PEPPLER

INTRODUCTION

Committed to helping youth develop powerful ways of seeing and acting in the world, learning scientists and educators came together in 2010–2013 to imagine how to support production-centered ways of engaging in systems thinking. Conceived as a collaborative design research project between Indiana University, DePaul University, the Institute of Play in New York City, and the U.S.'s National Writing Project (NWP), the idea was to learn from curriculum designed for the Quest to Learn (Q2L) School in New York City that used systems and gaming pedagogy as a way for schools to be organized around core "Connected Learning" principles (Ito, et al., 2012). Connected Learning, a new approach to education that directly engages the interests, social capital, and future opportunities of students, served as a compelling framework for harnessing the innovations of the digital age to best support production-centered, interest-driven learning. Organized around a set of learning principles that outline how learning opportunities can be academically oriented, interest powered and peer supported, Connected Learning also includes design principles for linking learning across school, home and community. Our goals were to adapt these Connected Learning designs for schools, classrooms, and afterschool programs where there was an interest in these same topics but not necessarily the same whole-institutional support infrastructure as that underpinning the Quest to Learn school.

One result of this work has been the creation of a set of curricular materials called *Interconnections*, which is a series of four scalable modular toolkits that promote engagement in design and systems thinking in young people by means of designing with new media (e.g., Peppler, Salen-Tekinbas, Gresalfi and Santo 2014). This work was meant to support youth in becoming the designers of systems using new tools and digital media in interest-driven ways. (We elaborate on what we mean by "design" later in this chapter.) What we discovered in the process of co-creating this curriculum, however, had far greater implications, owing to the power of Connected Learning principles, to shine new light on our understanding of how to shape effective professional development experiences.

Our discoveries first came when we began offering professional development for teachers who would pilot the *Interconnections* curriculum. Using an approach called Design-Based Research (Brown 1992) that positions both researchers and practitioners as active learners, we tested and tinkered with the *Interconnections* modules alongside a number of expert teachers across the United States affiliated with the National Writing Project (NWP), the largest teacher professional development network in the country taught by and for teachers. In one of the workshop "camps," which took place over the course of four weeks in the summer of 2011, National Writing Project teachers piloted the modules with more than 100 youth from Chicago. In the two weeks before the camps began, National Writing Project teachers received training from the research team on the tools (e.g., e-textiles, game design, coding software) as well as the concepts (e.g., design, systems thinking, circuitry, crafting) in this new curriculum that were also new to most of them. As the teachers engaged in the same production-based activities that they soon would be asking youth to do, they reported making a number of realizations that directly informed their feedback on the curriculum in the form of insights and mods. One of the educators, Laura Lee Stroud, was a secondary teacher, an English language arts instructional coach in the Round Rock Independent School District, and a member of the Central Texas Writing Project. Even while facilitating one of the production-centered modules with students, Stroud saw herself as a learner:

> As the youth entered the camps, for the most part not one teacher assumed the comfortable position of "expert" with our novice youths learning under us. Instead, we were positioned as learners alongside our campers. In some cases, our campers knew more about the content than did we, the teachers. We had to remember our new value of supporter, encourager, observer, and researcher… When we teachers had group time to reflect on our experience, we found that we all struggled in one way or another, and as a result, we had a newfound level of respect for our youths' learning processes and struggles, as well as a wonderful glimpse into our own learning process. (Peppler, Salen Tekinbaş, Gresalfi and Santo 2014: xix–xx)

Comments by teachers like Laura help remind us that improving the way we teach is often dependent on deeply engaging with what it means to be a learner again. The act of co-design—not only teachers creating the same projects as their youth, but also educators and researchers working collaboratively to create a supportive ecosystem of connected professional practices—is what we describe as a Connected Learning approach to professional development. This chapter outlines our approach, emphasizing production-centered design and openly networked teaching communities. This work connects Make-to-Learn practices (Peppler, Resnick, Eidman-Aadahl and Ito, in preparation) and constructionist theory (Kafai 2006; Papert 1980) with what National Writing Project educators know about writing to learn and writing-as-making (Lieberman and Wood 2001; Shipka 2011; Smith, West-Puckett, Cantrill and Zamora, under review; Whitney 2008) alongside peer-supported professional development and networked community building (Lieberman and Wood 2003; McDonald, Buchanan and Sterling 2004).

Expanding young people's access to learning opportunities in the home, community and social spheres, Connected Learning occurs when a young person's passions and interests (a) are cultivated and supported by their peers and adult mentors; and (b) translate into academic achievement, career opportunities and civic involvement. This chapter highlights the design opportunities of Connected Learning and calls forward the need to continue to create supportive ecosystems that move us, as educators, from spaces of externally designed professional development into spaces where we practice our profession as co-designers and colleagues.

TEACHING AND DESIGNING IN THE CONNECTED LEARNING CLASSROOM

Today, teachers often are positioned as passive recipients of policy and curriculum efforts to standardize education. We have found that in contrast, the principles of Connected Learning can provide both language and a needed spotlight on the agency that teachers have in the classroom as designers. On a daily basis, teachers make and design the classroom learning experience, deciding on everything from the placement of the desks to the moment-to-moment shaping of classroom dialogue—all the intangibles that we know are actually consequential to learning. Moreover, we're coming to recognize that the more teachers fluidly connect students to the outside world, the more relevant and impactful they make the learning experience. This, by its nature, is not easily scalable, nor should we strive for it to be. Teachers need to broker and connect the everyday experiences of their students to the curriculum, often within contexts of high-stakes testing and lock-stepped curriculum, requiring an intense amount of knowledge and improvisation.

In *Teaching in the Connected Learning Classroom*, Colorado State University Writing Project leader Antero Garcia argues that Connected Learning provides a vocabulary from which teachers can argue for what is best for the students in their classrooms and communities (Garcia, et al. 2014).

> I believe connected learning principles can provide a vocabulary for teachers to reclaim agency over what and how we best meet the individual needs of students in our classrooms. With learners as the focus, teachers can rely on connected learning as a way to pull back the curtain on how learning happens in schools and agitate the possibilities of classrooms today. (p. 7)

Bringing together many examples of practice where teachers are exploring ways to balance various mandates with students' passions and interests as well as learning goals, Garcia co-curates this collection not as a set of "best practices" but instead as a set of vignettes with related commentary meant to spur dialogue and inspire context-specific pathways among educators. "Context drives practice," he writes, and the language of connected learning is encouraged as a way to make meaning within those contexts while also facilitating the sharing of practice and expanding or developing practice across contexts as we go.

We know from Connected Learning research that forging learning opportunities between academic pursuits, youth's digital interests, and peer culture is not only possible but also positions youth to adapt and thrive under the ever-shifting demands of the 21st century. Students regularly seek coherence across the boundaries of school, out-of-school, and today's workplace (Peppler 2014). We find, too, that teachers regularly seek a similar coherence and that Connected Learning can provide some meaningful ways to design learning to that end. In order to access and effectively use these design principles, teachers themselves also need to challenge their ordinary practices, bringing their private acts of teaching into public performances within supportive communities (McDonald, Buchanan and Sterling 2004).

"MAKING" PROFESSIONAL DEVELOPMENT: THE NATIONAL WRITING PROJECT

Connected Learning in many ways reflects core beliefs and social practices held by National Writing Project educators and their local writing projects (Ito, et al., 2012; Lieberman and Wood 2002) with an emphasis on making and designing as integral to their founding vision for professional development. The National Writing Project began in 1974 when educators came together—across grades and disciplines from Kindergarten through to university—to dig into their passion for supporting literacy learning for youth with a particular focus on writing and teaching writing. This self-organized peer-supported group of writing project teachers emphasized youth as producers, not just consumers and, because of this, invested in themselves as "makers" and started their own kind of maker movement. Thus, within these writing projects, a core theory of action is that if you are going to teach writing, you also need to write, or make, as well (Lieberman and Wood 2002; Whitney 2008). This is both a means of exploring a discipline and a key way in which National Writing Project educators turn their practice into shared public performances that foster community building and learning (McDonald, Buchanan and Sterling 2004).

McDonald, Buchanan and Sterling frame this as a situation of mutual risk taking which, when supported in a shared community of mutual benefit, allows for further risk taking and change:

> In facing the first two risks, writing and sharing, teachers experience the relief and exhil-aration that comes from discovering that they too are writers and that writing is difficult for everyone—though no harder for themselves. In the process, they become open to the equally risky step of sharing their teaching of writing and of opening themselves up to both collegial critique and collegial learning. (p. 11)

Learning through writing and/or making, situated in social contexts, is a produc-tion-centered way of working that has been continually fostered as the network has grown, connecting nearly 200 writing projects' sites, colleges, and universities, as well as partners and educators outside the project, through work such as the National Writing Project-powered Educator Innovator Initiative. As a research and profes-sional development network, the National Writing Project serves educators across the curriculum while continuing to encourage educators to make, share, and risk take across more traditional boundaries in education and learning. This means bringing together educators who work both in and out of schools, as well as constantly blur-ring and reimagining the lines between theory and practice, teacher and learner, researcher and designer. The National Writing Project catchphrase, "teachers teach-ing teachers," for example, underscores a set of shared social and participatory prac-tices of learning from and alongside peers and colleagues that then extends into classrooms and teaching spaces where writing project teachers continue to learn from and alongside the youth with whom they work (Lieberman and Wood 2003).

Learning alongside one another is also fueled by the process of inquiry, or "inquiry as stance" in teaching (Lytle and Cochran-Smith 2009; Lieberman and Wood 2003). Inquiry becomes a means by which writing project educators con-stantly reflect on, share, and develop practice (Córdova, Kumpulainen and Hudson 2012). These inquiry-driven practices are connected to ongoing making and pro-ducing that writing project teachers do, which in turn has profound implications on what it means to teach writing as well as on notions of professional learning. Elyse Eidman-Aadahl, executive director of the National Writing Project, notes, "the very notion of what it means to write today is being influenced by the kinds of composing possibilities that are available to youth" (Bradley, Douillard, Eidman-Aadahl, Oh and Paraiso 2014). Therefore an iterative, inquiry-driven approach supports National Writing Project educators in keeping abreast of the possibilities of these changes by continually tapping into the knowledge and experience of youth as well as networked colleagues.

Elyse also describes National Writing Project professional development as an opportunity for play and experimentation: "It might seem counterintuitive," she says, "for busy people like teachers to slow down, play, and experiment, but the insights we learn when we do are what help us teach for depth of understanding" (DeVoss, Eidman-Aadahl and Hicks 2010: 119). This way of approaching the design of professional learning opportunities within writing projects supports that continual sharing of inquiry through making and has been key to maintaining a "healthy technological ecology" for writing as it has become increasingly digital over time (DeVoss, Eidman-Aadahl and Hicks 2010). The framework of Connected Learning then provides the shared purpose and language from which to learn and design this kind of context-specific, inquiry-driven, and production-centered classroom experience across learning environments and among extended groups and networks of educators.

THE IMPORTANCE OF PRODUCTION-CENTERED DESIGN

Design—whether it be writing a story, designing an app, sewing a T-shirt, or building a robot—is an essential activity for learning because it positions the learner as an active agent in the creation process. As learners construct an artifact, they externalize their mental models and iterate on them throughout the design process (Kafai 2006; Papert 1980), revisiting prior understandings and refining them in a self-directed way. In contrast to prescriptive design tasks, where everyone constructs the same artifact in parallel or arrives at an idealized solution, production-centered design strikes a balance between structure and free exploration (Colella, Klopfer and Resnick 2001). For example, in working on a set of materials, one might encourage reflection upon the range of options available because of those materials as well as the constraints and parameters the materials cause within a design-task without determining what exactly is to be designed; in the same way, building a sharing process in a design cycle could support cross-design inspiration and connection among designers, further encouraging iteration and development. Such reflexivity is not only emblematic of youths' engagement with production-centered design, but it is also a trademark of the work classroom teachers undergo when designing classroom experiences.

In our work, we draw closely on Resnick's (2007) design spiral that describes the creative process of design as an idea that is realized by iteratively imagining, creating, playing, sharing, and reflecting on the work. One can see how the act of *imagining* is central to the activities of both student and teacher, involving the open exploration of materials to ignite creativity and take work in personally meaningful directions. The next step in Resnick's design spiral, *creating*, describes the act of designing and constructing, which not only provides opportunities to develop and enrich creative thinking but also presents designers with the chance to experience disciplinary content through hands-on reconstruction of their prior knowledge. *Play* is where playful experimentation with ideas is done in a low-risk environment to explore the boundaries of the materials. The *sharing* of work is also critical to learning and motivation, for this is where many designers find new inspiration through the feedback they receive from an audience. Resnick also argues for systematic *reflection* on both the design and learning process—the discussions and meta-reflection that are so central to the classroom experience. Finally, Resnick describes this pathway through the design process as a spiral that is then iteratively repeated.

The realities of teaching allowed us to surface two additional steps in this design cycle which we found to be important to openly networked teaching and learning: *researching* and *publishing*. *Research* encapsulates the inquiry and related information-gathering that is critical to high-quality teaching and learning: the introduction of vocabulary and key concepts and the activities used to gather this information (including the use of videos, diagrams, and other information sources) based on the needs and questions that arise within a particular context. We also disentangle the sharing of the final product, a step that we call *publish* (i.e., posting to social media, podcasting, etc.), from more informal moments where sharing is done within the local community to assist in iteration. Current research has demonstrated that this is an important moment for learning and community building and that there are some crucial differences in who is likely to post in the informal, interest-driven hours (Lenhart and Madden 2007).

In sum, when people design, they envision new solutions to open-ended problems, work through multiple versions of any idea, integrate ongoing feedback into the learning process, and identify the strengths and weaknesses of both their processes and solutions. In this regard, it's easy to see how designing is not only a powerful activity for youth to shape their learning but also a mindset for teachers to work from when reflecting on our own teaching practice.

INTERCONNECTIONS: NEW CURRICULAR TOOLKITS AND ASSESSMENTS

An increasing number of kids in the 21st century have new opportunities for learning as a result of the ever-developing technological landscape, one that continues to change the way students read and write. Youths' stories and modes of expression now tend to be filled with media-rich, interactive, and multimodal texts that integrate our digital and physical realities. Linking design to digital media tools expands the potential of production-centered learning even further: digital tools often make it easier, faster, and less risky to test ideas. There is no need to worry about wasting expensive materials, and erasing a mistake is as easy as clicking a mouse. There are a host of compelling tools that support their design efforts in the out-of-school hours—Scratch, Gamestar Mechanic, and Arduino Robotics, to name a few—yet the challenge for today's educators is finding a fluid and robust way to integrate these tools in the classroom when we lack curriculum to support these tools. Oftentimes there is a misconception that a new tool can be easily picked up and integrated into the classroom environment; this is simply not true. A guiding theoretical approach, pedagogical goals, guiding questions, and related means of assessment are necessary when introducing a new tool into the school day. In addition, standards alignment and related curricular connections are often also necessary, making the introduction of any new tools and technologies require a complex set of decision making.

The *Interconnections* series was intended to address these complexities, providing robust curricular activities that are well aligned with disciplinary and cross-cutting teaching objectives as well as standards, assessment, and other built-in professional development for production-centered learning. For example, in the process of learning how to design and program a solar-powered backpack, youth come to understand the systemic nature of energy and other targeted systems thinking, circuitry, and programming concepts. To facilitate this learning, the curriculum includes embodied role-play activities, opportunities to test how solar energy accumulates in different light sources and circuit configurations, and explorations of how to strategically design backpacks with circuitry and power in mind. Youth reflect on their process in various stages of learning before ultimately publicly posting their designs. Teachers are supported in this process with custom assessment techniques, tips, and suggestions for preparing the activities, descriptions of the Common Core and Next Generation Science Standards with which these activities align, an overview of materials required, and a series of handouts and related classroom resources (e.g., reference cards.) Lessons are also populated with "Voices From the Field," tips and reflections from National Writing Project teachers who have taught the activities before. *Interconnections* is a collection of four books created to introduce an innovative new way to support design thinking in young people that allows them to see how systems are at play in the digital contexts with which they regularly engage. Specifically, these modules put students in the position not only to use those systems but also to become designers of systems themselves.

Each book approaches the task in a different way. One focuses on teaching design thinking using game design, another uses digital storytelling, and two utilize "e-textiles" and other circuitry projects, which involve making physical computing projects based in fabrics, paper, and other everyday materials. The volumes incorporate design-based pedagogy with digital media and robust curricular resources for use in a variety of educational settings.

For example, one volume utilizes the Gamestar Mechanic game design platform (gamestarmechanic.com) to orient readers to the nature of games as systems, how game designers need to think in terms of complex interactions between game elements and rules, and how to pull out systems concepts in the design process. Another volume, on digital storytelling, focuses on how stories offer an important lens for seeing the world as a series of systems, and its curricular resources utilize the Scratch visual programming environment (scratch.mit.edu) as a means to tell stories about how to effect change in youths' local communities. The final two books cover the fields of e-textiles and physical computing from differing perspectives, offering readers insights into the systemic nature of electronics and circuitry. Each outlines a series of curricular challenges that result in the creation of a variety of electronic projects, one focusing on textile-based digital puppets and DIY flashlights that incorporate LEDs, while the other takes on the world of e-fashion through LED cuffs, t-shirts, and solar-powered backpacks. The Interconnections series has a relationship with electronics retailer, SparkFun (sparkfun.com/interconnections), to simplify the act of procuring the tools and materials featured in the e-textiles design challenges. Educators can purchase off-the-shelf toolkits, either for individual users or group kits for 20 learners.

In developing the volumes, we wanted to ensure that while we tied the work into insights found in the academic research, we also wanted to ground the volumes in the lived experiences of educators. The research team included a number of members that had worked as educators for many years in both formal learning contexts like public schools as well as informal ones like afterschool programs, libraries, and museums. Most importantly, though, the initiative's partnership with the National Writing Project meant that the kind of educators interested in the sort of innovative approaches we were developing were kept at the center of the project. Through this partnership, we hoped that the *Interconnections* volumes would be useful to educators in a wide variety of settings to engage youth in design activities in ways that would encourage them to become design thinkers, thereby positively transforming the world we live in today.

Each of the partners was involved in a broader movement started by the MacArthur Foundation in 2006 to investigate the ways that digital media was changing how youth learned and how these technologies might be leveraged to create new opportunities for learning that might have been previously unimaginable. To date, the Digital Media and Learning (DML) initiative has provided over $80 million USD in grant funds to research and to developing innovations in digital learning. It has focused on youth interest-driven activity in digital spaces as a source of inspiration for creating new learning environments that incorporate the kinds of engagement and higher-order skill development found in places like massively multiplayer online (MMO) games or do-it-yourself (DIY) online creative communities like those centered around fanfiction, video blogging, and myriad other forms of making, tinkering, and designing. The Quest to Learn school, as well as the Gamestar Mechanic platform utilized in the game design module of *Interconnections*, were two examples of learning environments that came out of the Digital and Media Learning initiative, both aiming to build on youths' interests that they brought with them into school as well as focusing on the kinds of 21st-century skills they will need in order to thrive in the world.

PRODUCTION-CENTERED PROFESSIONAL DEVELOPMENT

Building on our new classroom materials (i.e., the new *Interconnections* curriculum and associated toolkits), we moved to thinking about how to make this kind of curriculum accessible to large numbers of teachers. Several professional networks, including the National Writing Project, have annual conferences targeted at sharing practices and engaging in hands-on professional development. For this project, we sought to create high-quality teacher professional development experiences to give new audiences tangible experiences with the newly designed curricular materials. Core to our approach is a belief that professional development should parallel student learning experiences, so that teacher-learners consciously experience being learners themselves, as well as see for themselves the facilitation strategies and classroom learning experiences modeled during the professional development. In other words, we strove to demonstrate the guiding theories and associated design work by engaging teachers in sample workshops from the curriculum.

Sample Interconnections Professional Development Workshops: Scratch & e-Puppetry

In one workshop, offered to around 60 practitioners at an Annual National Writing Project gathering, we put together a production-centered event where participants had to write a short story and create an e-puppet representing one of the characters. The workshop combined content from the first two Design Challenges in the Interconnections volume on e-puppetry, *Short Circuits: Crafting e-Puppets with DIY Electronics* (Peppler, Salen-Tekinbas, Gresalfi and Santo 2014). *Short Circuits* explores the field of electronics and "e-textiles," which involves making wearable (and washable) computing projects that employ microcontrollers and conductive thread alongside fabrics and other everyday materials in order to delve into literacy, puppetry, and storytelling. The production-centered professional development was faster paced than what would be experienced in the classroom, but it offered a chance for teachers to learn the cross-disciplinary content—science content around circuits, writing content around storytelling—and modeled the pedagogical strategies and guiding theory for the participants, all within the context of a single project.

At the start of the workshop, participants were given a watch battery, LED lights, and wired alligator clips and were told to create a working circuit from these materials. Once they achieved a functioning circuit, they were tasked to add an increasing number of lights to the circuit, exploring the various configurations (i.e., series or parallel) required to make all LEDs illuminate successfully. For some without any background in electronics or circuitry, this was challenging because, while participants may have understood the components of a circuit, they didn't have a fundamental understanding of how they interacted with each other; namely the direction of the current and how this related to the polarity (positive or negative) of the watch battery and how the components of the circuit were connected together. In the next phase of the work, participants were challenged to add a switch to the circuit and to really think through how circuits work (i.e., switches open and close the circuit like a gate that allows the electricity to pass through or interrupts the current from flowing to turn off the light). This was all done with materials that allowed participants to create physical models that were snapped together before moving to the basics of sewn circuits. This free-exploration activity, intentionally lacking in direct instruction, was based on the principles of constructionist learning (Papert 1980). Here, participants were expected to learn by doing and, by confronting where any of their misconceptions lay about circuitry and energy, evolving and deepening their understanding of how circuitry operates. This allowed the participants to understand the big ideas of circuitry (Peppler and Glosson 2013) before moving into applying this understanding in a new context.

In sewn circuits, the participants at the National Writing Project Annual Meeting were asked to replace the insulated wiring and alligator clips with conductive thread, which looks and feels like traditional thread but has conductive qualities. The ultimate design goal of the workshop was to creatively use the sewable circuit materials to make an electronic puppet that had a light (or two) that would work when you turned on the switch (or made a connection that closed the circuit and turned on the light). Participants each received two pieces of felt cut out in a puppet shape, a sewable battery holder, one or more LEDs, and two small pieces of conductive material to create a DIY switch along with a host of buttons, ribbons, fabric, yarn, and other materials to use to decorate the puppet and create their character. As educators worked through their plans and settled into sewing their circuit, the room hushed and you could see the intensity of engagement (see Figure 11.1).

Figure 11.1: National Writing Project practitioners focusing on creating their e-puppets at the professional development workshop. (Photo by Kim Douillard, 2014)

An interesting aspect of multimodal making such as this is that each participant comes with a unique set of prior knowledge—we found the most simple or most challenging part of the production process was different for almost every individual. One of the participating teachers reflected "for some the sewing was the hardest part, for others it was working through the circuitry, and for others it was totally about creating the puppet character they had in mind" (Douillard 2013). To complete the project, participants needed to apply an understanding of circuitry, think about how to leverage various materials to create unique characters (e.g., a red LED placed on the nose of the puppet would suggest a "Rudolph" character but when placed in the heart region may suggest "love" instead), and accomplish various design goals (e.g., how to hide or reveal the sewing lines). Teachers sitting side by side took note of the various approaches and designs in their midst and were inspired by their peers' novel uses of the materials and interesting gestures to facilitate closing circuits. The beauty of production-centered design work like this is that no two projects look alike.

To begin this design process, participants began by tracing their puppet on paper and creating a circuitry diagram, which outlined where they would sew their battery holder, LED light(s), and switches. As they were working, we asked them to draw and label the sewing lines to think about the directions of the circuit as well as to avoid short circuits (shorts). One of the main challenges that stretched thinking was moving between the 2D representations of the circuit diagram to creating the design in 3D. To accomplish this, many participants mapped physical materials to the surface of the puppet, as well, to aid in the visualization of the design and to "check" to see if things worked. Participants could then test and physically trace how the connections should flow as they drew their circuit diagram (see Figure 11.2).

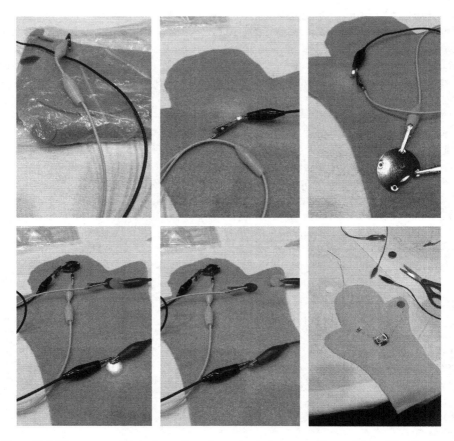

Figure 11.2: The process of designing and creating a circuit documented by participant Kim Douillard. (Photos by Kim Douillard, 2014).

Despite being able to get fairly complicated circuits involving multiple LEDs lighting up, it was thought provoking for participating educators to brainstorm how to translate the mess of insulated wiring into a sewn circuit that wouldn't short. Puppets, for example, necessitate that the fabric bends and moves in a range of directions with the handling of the puppet. This quality also makes it possible to put switches in interesting places (e.g., one half of the open switch on each of the two hands of the puppet to light up when touched together) but also easily introduces unanticipated problems in the circuitry design (e.g., when the two hands of the puppet touch, they might obscure the goal of the system if the completion of the circuit results in an LED illuminating near the puppet's "heart").

Kim Douillard, a co-teacher at Cardiff Elementary School in San Diego and director of the San Diego Area Writing Project, reflected on this professional development session in terms of how the systems content encouraged new ways of thinking about the world in general, but also how the act of designing her e-puppet (see Figure 11.3) made her think differently about her teaching practice (Douillard 2013):

> I find that I have a better grasp of how to explain some of the approaches I use in my classroom. Like why design is so important to student learning, why mistakes are valuable to learning … if you take the time to work through what you did and figure out a better outcome, and why students need space to create their own plans and work through the spaces where things are not working the way they intend … I'm worried when we make things in the classroom too "neat" that we are working harder and learning more than our students. That's one of the things I love best (and hate the most) about teaching writing. When it's at its best, it's messy. I can have an overall plan in mind for the outcome, but my students benefit from getting 'just right' instruction along the way. And not all my students need the same instruction … and some benefit from learning by watching and listening to their classmates.

Figure 11.3: Kim Douillard's e-puppet. The heart lights up when the hands touch. (Photo by Kim Douillard, 2014).

The design process made visible the importance of "messy" learning, which allows for multiple points of entry and divergent goals. In our own research, we are beginning to find that this approach to learning allows for lots of simultaneous and interconnected learning about disciplinary content, the rules of design, the materiality of our world (how things work), among a host of other inter- and intrapersonal skills. Such opportunities for collaborative learning and serendipitous discoveries along the way are hallmarks of production-based design, which benefit students as well as teachers.

A similar appreciation for the spontaneous inspiration, open-ended exploration, and peer-to-peer learning affordances of production-based design was echoed by other practitioners at the conference, many becoming involved in an informal remixing trope across a number of digital platforms. For example, two attendees started a "#twitcatastrophe" game, involving an open call for people to tweet funny twists on themes from the meeting, which would then in turn be tweeted back as illustrations, pictures, Vines, digital creations, or more. Kevin Hodgson, a sixth-grade teacher at William E. Morris Elementary School and technology liaison with the Western Massachusetts Writing Project, described in his blog how his concept for a #twitcatastrophe—a "close read" (i.e., the concept in literary analysis involving the careful, methodical interpretation of a short passage of text) that involves a book literally closing on the reader's nose—was tweeted back first as a hand-drawn illustration, then reincarnated as a Scratch project, which he then remixed with additional technical capabilities, then shared back out as a Vine (Hodgson 2013):

> It was a blast, and reminded all of us how iteration and inspiration and creativity are at the heart of the remix culture. Each step—from creating the twitter game to the reader/artist response to the gameplay and remixing of the game—are different points on the compositional spectrum that we need to nurture and value.

This example highlights the benefit of production-centered professional development as being capable of drawing several participants into the activity using playful and engaging means. It is important that the participants used Twitter not just as a forum for commentary but as a place to share texts produced and elaborated on by multiple people. The resulting artifacts used humor to deepen the pedagogical goals around remixing and learning how to utilize the openly networked aspects of new media in effective ways for the classroom.

THE IMPORTANCE OF OPENLY NETWORKED LEARNING

Based on the idea that "[l]earning is most resilient when it is linked and reinforced across settings of home, school, peer culture and community" (Ito et al. 2012), being openly networked in one's learning is a key principle of Connected Learning. This can mean many things, however, and in *Connected Learning: An Agenda for Research and Design* (Ito et al. 2012: 76), openly networked learning is described as both a matter of on- and offline design.

> In online space, this means maintaining transparent and open standards that allow for people and institutions to connect and extend infrastructure across diverse settings (home, community, school) and technical platforms (mobile, PC, game devices, traditional media). In physical space, this means maintaining an open-door policy and using online infrastructures to extend beyond physical boundaries to allow greater access to resources, and connect across institutions and communities.

The importance of being networked in open ways, both online as well as face to face, is key to the professional practices that we have been able to develop together as co-designing researchers and practitioners. Playful games like #twitcatastrophe grow in these open spaces as well as thoughtfully shared documentation and reflection on the process and implications for making and thinking about systems via the *Interconnections* work. These abilities to "see" each other's work and grow and develop it, whether playfully or seriously, is an essential skill as networked technologies support the distribution and curation of knowledge. Given that knowledge can be accessed, curated, as well as produced by individuals, communities, and networks in increasingly distributed ways (Juhasz and Balsamo 2012; Williamson 2013), the capacity to form these connections, and to find patterns within those connections is required for learning today (Siemens 2005).

Networks like the National Writing Project, with established practices of being publically accessible, with practice alongside colleagues and across institutions and systemic boundaries a key characteristic of network activities, have historically been referred to as "third spaces" where knowledge could be shared and distributed across contexts and communities (Eidman-Aadahl 1996; McDonald, Buchanan and Sterling 2004). In our *Interconnections* project, similar practices of sharing, remaking, and reflecting supported networked educators as they ventured onto the early web (DeVoss, Eidman-Aadahl and Hicks 2005); Bud Hunt, known online as @budtheteacher and a member of the Colorado State University Writing Project, calls this work "'openly networked' reflective practice":

> I soon became one of those teachers, writing frequent blog posts and sharing podcasts—which I often recorded from my car as I commuted back and forth to my classroom—that discussed issues from my work as a high-school language arts teacher. I began to conduct lots of lesson planning on my blog, explaining my way through complex challenges for the people who may have been (or likely, were definitely not) reading along. But the audience for my contributions was complicated. I wasn't writing just for others, and I wasn't writing only for me. I was engaged in ... "openly networked" reflective practice. (in Garcia et al. 2014: 71)

Outside our project, experiments in open online learning continue among individual educators as well as within and across institutions and organizations alike, raising conversations about what is possible for learning on the open web, along with questions and concerns. Mia Zamora, director of the Kean University Writing Project, writing in connection to connectivist-oriented MOOCs such as Connected Courses and the National Writing Project's CLMOOC, explains:

> [I]n this day and age—with the dynamism of open online technologies—learning can be driven by self-interest, research can be conducted with powerful global collaboration and crowdsourcing, and teachers and students can discover alongside each other as they break down old hierarchies that have limited the production of new knowledge. (Zamora 2014: no page)

Whereas scholars such as Juliet Schor, a professor at Boston College and a member of the Connected Learning Research Network, who look across the field of open learning and shared economies, writes that "new institutions and new practices, as they arise in a highly unequal and stratified society ... will take on those [same] inequalities unless they are actively combated" (Watkins and Schor 2013). Learning in openly networked ways, we know, is no exception. And critiques of open learning will question the extent to which opening is actually fostering access for many or replicating access for those already networked into these extended communities.

Professional networks like the National Writing Project are designed to continually involve a greater and greater network of educators over time into its participatory communities of practice (Lieberman and Wood 2003; Wenger and Lave 1991). And even so, we are aware that not every educator, or even everyone from the network, can have the kind of hands-on open experience with production-centered design and systems thinking alongside other colleagues in a supportive face-to-face setting described above. Nor can we simply just move work online without thinking about the ways that we are explicitly opening up production-centered opportunities and inviting those who might not otherwise have access, for a variety of reasons, to actively participate and create through their participation.

What we have found, however, is that when we bring a production-centered focus into open spaces focused on inquiry and design, we begin to see how inequities might be shifted by allowing for co-construction of the open spaces themselves (Seely Brown, Shah and Schmidt 2013; Smith, West-Puckett, Cantrill and Zamora, under review). National Writing Project educators like Laura, Kim, Kevin, and Bud have over time become leaders through making their practices and reflections on practice visible to others in online spaces such as their own blogs and at forums such as National Writing Project Digital Is (digitalis.nwp.org). These same educators also have begun to imagine ways in which to actively open the invitation to work in openly networked ways with others on production-centered inquiries and experimentation. Among these experiments is CLMOOC, a Connected Learning Massive Open Online "Collaboration" facilitated by National Writing Project educators during the summer months as part of the Educator Innovator Initiative.

CLMOOC: FROM PROFESSIONAL DEVELOPMENT TO PROFESSIONAL PRACTICE

CLMOOC began in the summer of 2013 and attempts to provide interest-driven, production-centered, and openly networked experiences for educators—both in and outside schools—to spark new ways of thinking about learning and about teaching. Being interest driven and production centered has meant that participants start by making things—whether physical or digital, text based or multimodal—and then share what they have made, as well as thoughts, questions, and reflections about what they made, with the larger community. It is designed to engage an increasingly extended group of colleagues in connected learning and National Writing Project social practices through playing, making, and inquiry-driven design iterations.

Tapping into the parallels between writing, composing, and making, participants in CLMOOC engage, as young people might, in tinkering and experimentation. This allows them to play with habits of mind that foster the kinds of agency and creativity they look for in the youth they work with while practicing cycles of design, making/remaking, play and reflection with a wide range of tools, both digital and analog (Smith, West-Puckett, Cantrill and Zamora, under review). CLMOOC is also an opportunity for participants to tap into a connected community via open networks in support of their making and their learning. In this networked context, participants access what George Siemens describes as "specialized information sets" which offer their own possibilities for learning beyond any single person's "current state of knowing" (2005).

CLMOOC runs over the course of six weeks and is organized as "make cycles" that are open-ended invitations to make, compose, play, learn, and connect. So whether educators are making an interactive map in a tool like Thinglink.com (an image that gets poetically remade/recaptioned over and over) or are inspired one evening to create something new in their kitchen and document it for the community, we see the key role that "making"—that is, creating and contributing, sharing and responding, as well as remixing, leading, and remaking—plays in the ways that participants socialize and build connections. And when we reflect on this as educators, considering implications such as peer-to-peer learning and community critique for our classrooms and spaces of learning, then we start to see the importance of production in learning for the youth we work with, as well as us as adults—supporting our collective ability to be not just knowledgeable and critical consumers of information but also its producers.

Stephanie West-Puckett, associate director of the Tar River Writing Project, describes this work as moving from "professional development to professional practice." Influenced by participation in CLMOOC, she created a local openly networked learning opportunity called #trwpconnect with her colleagues at Tar River. In sharing this work at the National Writing Project Digital Is website, she writes that since the structure of this opportunity was new to most participants, "[they] were unsure what to expect ... and were surprised to learn that they would not be moving through content delivery modules and completing quizzes to assess their mastery at the end. Instead, #trwpconnect would become both an exercise in and a study of Connected Learning and the habits of mind and body (new literacies) that are necessary for collaborative writing, learning, and participation in academic and civic spaces" (West-Puckett 2014: no page).

CREATING SHARED ECOSYSTEMS FOR LEARNING: LEARNING ALONGSIDE EACH OTHER AS MAKERS IN TEACHING

Learning alongside each other as connected teachers and learning scientists, we have come to understand that the production-centered design activities we have described are not just isolated approaches to teaching, but, rather, are key parts of a larger movement to rethink learning in a digital age. There is an incredible amount of innovation happening at the edges of what we formally know as "education" and in places that people tend not to count as learning spaces, including homes, libraries, sport fields, community spaces, and so on. In these spaces we see youth learning in new ways connected to pursuing their interests, engaging deeply, and solving problems through engagement with technology and networked communities. It is this learning that we seek to know better as formal educators and researchers.

Taking our cues then from the youth-derived learning and design principles of Connected Learning, alongside what we know from design research and from working within inquiry-driven communities of practice as educators, CLMOOC and projects like *Interconnections* inform our rethinking of teaching and professional learning. No longer are production-centered and networked ways of learning optional for educators—instead these experiences are essential to learning and teaching and a core part of what it means to practice as a professional. What then are the implications for design-based research and teacher professional development?

Returning to Resnick's design spiral, we see that imagining, playing, sharing, and publications, research, and reflection are critical mindsets and actions that support teachers and researchers in a range of practices. And we can also see how these practices can be supported in a range of ways, from the playful opportunities to explore a range of ideas and materials in interest-driven, production-centered ways on the open web at CLMOOC as well as through very deliberately designed and dedicated over-time collaborations as was experienced in the *Interconnections* project. What we see cutting across these two otherwise very different professional opportunities are educational professionals engaging alongside each other within the full design spirals, supporting an embodied experience of Connected Learning design and learning principles while making throughout.

We know that we're not alone in our desire to reimagine learning and teaching in more production-centered and openly networked ways; many educators, in fact, bring these interests and experiences with them into teaching, even if the actual context of their teaching is not currently as conducive as we might wish to these more connected principles and practices. The pressure is on, however, to reimagine learning opportunities and outcomes for a contemporary world (Thomas and Seely Brown 2011).

When we shift our focus from teaching to a focus on learning, we can start to engage deeply with what it means to be a learner, which ultimately guides us in rethinking what are the implications for teaching. This is what we describe as a Connected Learning approach to professional development or, picking up on the words of Stephanie West-Puckett, connected professional practice. And within this process of practice, and because of the production-centered, constructionist nature of the work, educators, researchers, and youth are working alongside each other and consequently building the exact right tools, knowledge base, and resources that are needed. We therefore call forward the continued development of creative supportive ecosystems of connected professional practices where educators, learning scientists, and the like can practice as co-designers and colleagues in order to build what's needed to support youth learning in connected and networked ways across their homes, communities, and social spheres.

Education can be done differently. Youth can engage in problems that are meaningful for them, connected to their lives, and that prepare them for lifelong learning in a changing and complex world. Toward that end, professional development can also be done differently, supporting adults and educators that youth work with to learn alongside each other, thereby coming to understand and embody the changes and complexities of a rapidly changing world.

REFERENCES

Bradley, L., Douillard, K., Eidman-Aadahl, E., Oh, P. and Paraiso, J. (2014). Making space and time for student agency and voice [Webinar]. In *Educator Innovator* series. Available: http://

educatorinnovator.org/webinars/making-space-and-time-for-student-agency-and-voice-an-educator-innovator-webinar/ Downloaded 25 October, 2015.

Brown, A. (1992). Design experiments: Theoretical and methodological challenges in creating complex interventions in classroom settings. *The Journal of the Learning Sciences*. 2(2): 141–178.

Cochran-Smith, M. and Lytle, S.L. (2009). *Inquiry as Stance: Practitioner Research for the Next Generation*. New York, NY: Teachers College Press.

Colella, V., Klopfer, E. and Resnick, M. (2001). *Adventures in Modeling: Exploring Complex, Dynamic Systems with StarLogo*. New York: Teachers College Press.

Córdova, R., Kumpulainen, K. and Hudson, J. (2012). Nurturing creativity and professional learning for 21st century education: Responsive design and the cultural landscapes collaboratory. *Learning Landscapes*. 6(1): 157–180.

DeVoss, D., Eidman-Aadahl, E. and Hicks, T. (2010). *Because Digital Writing Matters: Improving Student Writing in Online and Multimedia Environments*. Hoboken, NJ: Jossey-Bass.

Douillard, K. (2013). Systems thinking. *NWP Digital Is* [Web log post]. Available: http://digitalis. nwp.org/site-blog/systems-thinking/5813/. Downloaded 25 October, 2015.

Eidman-Aadahl, E. (1996). *My Third Spaces: From Sharkey's Cove to the USN*. Cityscapes: National Writing Project.

Garcia, A., Cantrill, C., Filipiak, D., Hunt, B., Lee, C., Mirra, N. and O'Donnell-Allen C. (2014). *Teaching in the Connected Learning Classroom*. Irvine, CA: Digital Media and Learning Research Hub.

Hodgson, K. (2013). More NWP annual meeting: Circuits, systems, coding, remix. *Kevin's Meandering Mind* [Weblog post]. Available: http://dogtrax.edublogs.org/2013/11/23/more-nwp-annual-meeting-circuits-systems-coding-remix Downloaded 26 October, 2015.

Ito, M., Gutierrez, K., Livingstone, S., Penuel, B., Rhodes, J., Salen, K., Schor, J., Sefton-Green, J. and Watkins, S. (2012). *Connected Learning; An Agenda for Research and Design*. Irvine, CA: Digital Media and Learning Research Hub.

Juhasz, A. and Balsamo, A. (2012). An idea whose time is here: FemTechNet—a distributed online collaborative course (DOCC). *A Journal of Gender, New Media and Technology*. 1(1). Online. Available: http://adanewmedia.org/2012/11/issue1-juhasz/ Downloaded 26 October, 2015.

Kafai, Y. (2006). Constructionism. In K. Sawyer (ed), *Cambridge Handbook of the Learning Sciences*. Cambridge, MA: Cambridge University Press, 35–46.

Lave, J. and Wenger, E. (1991). *Situated Learning: Legitimate Peripheral Participation*. Cambridge, MA: Cambridge University Press.

Lenhart, A. and Madden, M. (2007). Teens, Privacy and Online Social Networks: How Teens Manage Their Online Identities and Personal Information in the Age of MySpace. *Pew Internet & American Life Project*. Available: http://www.pewinternet.org/files/2013/05/PIP_TeensSo cialMediaandPrivacy_PDF.pdf Downloaded 26 October, 2015.

Lieberman, A. and Wood, D. (2002). *Inside the National Writing Project: Connecting Network Learning and Classroom Teaching*. New York, NY: Teachers College Press.

McDonald, J., Buchanan, J. and Sterling, R. (2004). The National Writing Project: Scaling up and scaling down. In T. Glennan, S. Bodilly, J. Galegher and K. Kerr (eds), *Expanding the Reach of Education Reforms: Perspectives from Leaders in the Scale-up of Educational Interventions*. Santa Monica, CA: The RAND Corporation, 81–106.

Papert, S. (1980). *Mindstorms*. New York, NY: Basic Books.

Peppler, K. (2012). Scratch: Digital art making. *ChildArt Magazine*. 12(1). Available: http://www. academia.edu/8078679/Scratch_Digital_Art_Making Downloaded 26 October, 2015.

Peppler, K. (2014). *New Creativity Paradigms: Arts Learning in the Digital Age*. New York, NY: Peter Lang Publishing.

Peppler, K. and Glosson, D. (2013). Learning about circuitry with e-textiles. In M. Knobel and C. Lankshear (eds), *The New Literacies Reader*. New York: Peter Lang Publishing, 139–150.

Peppler, K., Resnick, M., Eidman-Aadahl, E. and Ito, M. (in preparation). *Make-to-Learn: Broadening Participation and Deepening Learning Through Making*. Boston, MA: MIT Press.

Peppler, K., Salen Tekinbaş, K., Gresalfi, M. and Santo, R. (2014). *Short Circuits: Crafting E-puppets with DIY Electronics*. Cambridge, MA: MIT Press.

Peppler, K., Santo, R., Salen Tekinbaş, K. and Gresalfi, M. (2014). *Script Changers: Digital Storytelling with Scratch*. Cambridge, MA: MIT Press.

Resnick, M. (2007). All I really need to know (about creative thinking) I learned (by studying how children learn) in kindergarten. Paper presented to the ACM Creativity & Cognition Conference, Washington DC, June.

Salen Tekinbaş, K., Gresalfi, M., Peppler, K. and Santo, R. (2014). *Gaming the System: Designing with Gamestar Mechanic*. Cambridge, MA: MIT Press.

Seely Brown, J., Shah, N. and Schmidt. P. (2013, September 27). Reclaiming open learning: A stake in the ground [Webinar]. In *Reclaim Open Learning Symposium*. Available: https://www.youtube.com/watch?v=RhlwvdNgYEo Downloaded 26 October, 2015.

Shipka, J. (2011). *Toward a Composition Made Whole*. Pittsburgh: University of Pittsburgh Press.

Siemens, G. (2005). Finding our way: Better understanding the needs and motivations of teachers in online learning. *International Journal of Instructional Technology and Distance Learning*. 2(1). Online. Available: http://www.itdl.org/journal/jan_05/article01.htm Downloaded 26 October, 2016.

Smith, A., West-Puckett, S., Cantrill, C. and Zamora, M. (under review). Remix as professional learning: Fostering transformative teacherly identities in CLMOOC.

Thomas, D. and Seely Brown, J. (2011). *A New Culture of Learning: Cultivating the Imagination for a World of Constant Change*. Charleston, SC: CreateSpace.

Watkins, C. and Schor, J. (2013). Connected learning as pathway to equity & opportunity [Webinar]. In *Connected Learning TV*. Available: https://www.youtube.com/watch?v=mr8YxLuKNG0 Downloaded 26 October, 2015.

West-Puckett, S. (2014). From professional development to professional practice: The SEEDs of connected learning in a high need middle school. *NWP Digital Is* [Weblog post]. Available: http://digitalis.nwp.org/collection/professional-development-professional-practice-seeds-connected-learning-high-need-middle Downloaded 26 October, 2015.

Whitney, A. (2008). Teacher transformation in the National Writing Project. *Research in the Teaching of English*. 43(2): 144–187. Urbana, IL: NCTE. Available: http://iawp.ucr.edu/files/teacher_support/teacher_transformation.pdf Downloaded 26 October, 2015.

Williamson, B. (2013). *The Future of the Curriculum: School Knowledge in the Digital Age*. Cambridge, MA: MIT Press.

Zamora, M. (2014, March 14). Some thoughts on open learning: Ode to the dandelion. *NWP Digital Is* [Weblog post]. Available: http://digitalis.nwp.org/site-blog/some-thoughts-open-learning-ode-dandelion/6005 Downloaded 26 October, 2015.

Contributors

Carly Biddolph recently completed a Bachelor of Education (Honours) and a Bachelor of Arts at the University of Sydney, Australia. During her five years of study, her professors and peers inspired her teaching of secondary English and history, as well as her interest in educational research. As part of a class about youth and digital culture, Carly was encouraged to use Twitter to share her thoughts with a public audience. This was a highlight of her professional learning, and it has significantly influenced her passion for using social media to teach and learn.

Susi Bostock is currently a fourth-grade teacher at Vanderbilt Elementary School in Dix Hills, New York. During her tenure as a classroom teacher, she has been involved in professional learning and is committed to providing Thirdspace teaching and learning in her classroom that fosters learning and idea sharing. She is the author of the article, "Thirdspace: A perspective on professional development" (*Language Arts*, 2012), in which she shares her personal experience of teaching and learning with first graders. Susi's research interests include early childhood reading, writing, and play. She has worked as an adjunct faculty member in literacy studies at Hofstra University, where she recently earned her doctorate in education. You can follow Susi on Twitter @drsusiq.

Benjamin de Buen was born in Mexico City in 1980 and is a writer, editor and translator. In 2008 he completed a Masters of Creative Writing at the RMIT University in Melbourne, Australia. He is currently assistant editor at *Thin White*

Line: Football Culture Magazine (thinwhitelinemagazine.com) and has translated a number of nonfiction books and academic articles.

Christina Cantrill is Associate Director for National Programs at the National Writing Project. She has been a teacher fangirl since the early '90s, when she began working alongside writing project educators and exploring the emerging possibilities of the internet and networked technology. Christina leads national digital media and connected learning programming and the National Writing Project Educator Innovator Initiative. Christina brings a background in curriculum studies as well as participatory arts practice. She was the former chair of and a longtime volunteer at Spiral Q Puppet Theater, a community-based social justice organization based in Philadelphia, and currently is teaching in a new Connected Learning Certificate program she helped design at Arcadia University. Her philosophy of professional development has been shaped by Philadelphia Writing Project teachers, who learn from portfolios of student work through processes of descriptive review.

Melissa Collucci is a full-time doctoral student at Montclair State University, New Jersey (USA), in the Teacher Education and Teacher Development program. Her research interests include preparing general education teachers to teach all students, with a particular focus on English language learners in early literacy classrooms. Melissa was a primary-grade teacher for 10 years as well as a Literacy Coordinator for a K-6 school before working in higher education. As an early childhood educator, Melissa was part of several grassroots efforts—teacher book clubs, parent-teacher partnerships, cross-age tutoring programs, peer coaching collaborations—that developed out of a desire among her partners to infuse more developmentally appropriate, research-based literacy practices into a traditional didactic curriculum. Melissa continues to value the input of teachers, students, parents, and colleagues as together they do what is best for kids.

Jen Scott Curwood is a senior lecturer in English education and media studies at the University of Sydney, Australia. Her research focuses on literacy, technology, and teacher professional development, and her work has appeared in the *Journal of Literacy Research*, *Journal of Adolescent and Adult Literacy*, *Asia-Pacific Journal of Teacher Education*, and *Teaching Education*. She also co-authored the book *Conducting Qualitative Research of Learning in Online Spaces* (SAGE, 2016). As a high school English teacher in Wisconsin, Jen researched her students' engagement with digital poetry. Her experiences with action research were instrumental to her professional learning, and they shaped her current work as a teacher educator and literacy researcher.

Inés Dussel is a researcher and professor at the *Departmento de Investigaciones Educativas del CINVESTAV-IPN*, Mexico City, Mexico. Before moving to Mexico, she served as the director of the Education Research Area at FLACSO (Latin American School for the Social Sciences) in Argentina from 2001 to 2008. She has been involved in teacher education for two decades, creating programs on new literacies, media literacy, and visual pedagogy for Argentinean teachers. She is interested in recent changes brought about by the use of digital media in classrooms and how they are transforming what counts as school knowledge and how pedagogical authority is produced. Her work has appeared in *Journal of Curriculum Studies, European Journal of Educational Research, Paedagogica Historica, Educational Policy Analysis Archives, Gender and Education, Cadernos de Pesquisa*, among others.

Ola Erstad is Professor and Head of Department at the Department of Education, University of Oslo, Norway. He works within the fields of media and educational research. He has published on issues regarding technology and education, and especially on media literacy and digital competence. Recent publications include: *Identity, Community, and Learning Lives in the Digital Age* (Erstad and Sefton-Green 2012, Cambridge University Press) and *Digital Learning Lives* (Erstad 2013, Peter Lang). From the first time Ola entered a classroom as a researcher, he has been struck by the complexity of classroom activities that teachers have to deal with on a daily basis. Working with substantial content and bonding with a diverse group of students can be challenging tasks, and he has built appreciation for the complexity and challenge of everyday classrooms into how he approaches supporting teachers' development and learning.

Stephanie Fisher is a PhD candidate within the Language, Culture and Teaching Program in the Faculty of Education at York University, Toronto, Canada. She has been involved in several research initiatives that support inservice teachers' professional development in the area of digital and multimodal learning through long-term classroom-based projects, including the collaborative action research project discussed in Chapter 4 in this volume, which was conducted at Joyce Public School. This work garnered municipal and provincial recognition for project and team excellence.

Oscar Hernández Razo is Associate Professor in the Cultural Studies Department at the Autonomous Metropolitan University, Campus Lerma, in Mexico City. He is a member of the Education, Technology and Society Lab in the Department of Educational Research, CINVESTAV (Mexico City), where he recently completed his doctoral studies. Oscar has participated in research projects focused on the use of digital technologies and teacher development in basic, middle and higher education, particularly in social sciences and Spanish language arts. As part of his doctoral dissertation, his research focused on the social appropriation of digital technologies in contexts of urban marginalization, as well as on digital literacy and youth and adult education. Oscar has published books, articles and papers related to the use of digital technologies in teacher training, educational uses of digital technologies in basic education, and models of youth and adult education that use information and communications technologies.

Marcea Ingersoll, formerly an SSHRC Postdoctoral Fellow at McGill University, is an Assistant Professor in the School of Education at St. Thomas University (Canada). Her professional development experiences have been as a participant and workshop leader with pre-service teachers and students in Canada, Malaysia, and Morocco. Building on her experiences as an international teacher and a teacher-educator, her scholarly work is situated at the crossroads of methodology, identity, multimodality, new literacies and digital spaces. Her publications explore literacy practices and identity within Canadian schools and around the globe.

Erik Jacobson is an Associate Professor in the Early Childhood, Elementary and Literacy Education Department of Montclair State University, New Jersey (USA). He is the author of *Adult Basic Education in the Age of New Literacies* (Peter Lang, 2012). When he began working in adult basic education he taught a variety of classes, often finding himself over his head and relying upon conversations with veteran teachers to understand what was happening. Since that time his most memorable professional development experiences have involved ongoing dialogues with people whose work he respects. A highlight is time he spent with the late Toshiro Osawa, who led adult literacy classes in a day laborer's neighborhood in Yokohama, Japan. He still reflects on Osawa's disposition in the classroom, finding it to be an enduring source of inspiration.

Jennifer Jenson is Professor of Pedagogy and Technology and Director of the Institute for Research on Digital Learning at York University, Toronto, Canada. She has published on technology implementation and integration and professional development opportunities and needs for teachers in K-12 education in Canada (*Policy Unplugged*, 2007, McGill-Queen's University Press), as well as on gender, games and technologies, games and learning, player experience in massively multiplayer online games, and technology policy and policy practices in K-12 education in numerous journals. She has worked with teachers and university faculty for the past 20 years to theorize and enact pedagogical and learning transformations in digital and ludic environments.

Judy Kalman is a professor at the Departamento de Investigaciones Educativas (DIE) of the Centro de Investigación y Estudios Avanzados del IPN

(CINVESTAV) in Mexico City, Mexico. Her work centers on the social construction of literacy, everyday literacy use, new literacies, and reading and writing in school settings. She has authored articles in Spanish, English and Portuguese in academic research journals, as well as in practitioner-oriented publications. She has collaborated with the Secretaría de Educación Pública in Mexico on programs designed for creating learning opportunities for adult learners, evaluating new curricular proposals, and writing materials for language arts programs for students in rural secondary schools. In 2002 she was the recipient of an International Literacy Research award given by the UNESCO Institute of Education for her literacy work with unschooled and underschooled women. She has been a member of the Mexican Academy of Science since 2004. Her current work centers on literacy and ICT in and out of school. In 2008 she co-founded the Laboratorio de Educación, Tecnología y Sociedad (LETS), where she is currently Director of LETS at the CINVESTAV South campus.

Michele Knobel is Professor of Literacy within the Department of Early Childhood, Elementary and Literacy Education at Montclair State University (USA). She has been involved in supporting preservice and inservice teachers' literacy and digital technology learning in the U.S., Australia, Mexico and Canada. Her publications include *New Literacies* (Open University Press, 2011, 3rd edn; with Colin Lankshear), *A New Literacies Reader* (Peter Lang, 2013; edited with Colin Lankshear) and *A Handbook for Teacher Research* (Open University Press, 2004; with Colin Lankshear), among others. As a first-year teacher, Michele was part of a local branch of the Australian Literacy Educators' Association. Monthly events were run by teachers for teachers, and even though these sessions tended to focus on different topics or problems each time, the group instilled in her an ongoing, strong appreciation for teachers coming together of their own accord and unstintingly sharing their ideas, strategies, suggestions and resources.

Reijo Kupiainen is University Lecturer of Media Education within the School of Education at University of Tampere (Finland) and Adjunct Professor within the Department of Education and Lifelong Learning at the Norwegian University of Science and Technology in Trondheim, Norway. He is involved in preservice teacher education in the field of media and digital literacy and learning technology and develops learning environment and learning scenarios for pre- and inservice teachers in an e-media education lab (e-MEL) in Europe. His recent publications include *Media and Digital Literacies in Secondary School* (Peter Lang, 2013). He has learned much from children and young people in different projects focused on media literacy, and, lately, in online groups, communities and networks where teachers share their thoughts, experiences and experiments with each other.

Hanna Leinonen is an elementary school teacher who holds a Masters of Education degree from the University of Tampere, Finland. While participating in co-writing Chapter 6 in this book, she was writing her master's thesis. Today she is responsible for the use of digital technologies in her school. While interviewing teachers for her master's thesis, she noticed how difficult it is to combine technological and content knowledge. Choosing the best technological application for teaching particular content is something that she struggles with in her current position, as well.

Laura Mae Lindo (PhD) is the Director of the Diversity and Equity Office at Wilfrid Laurier University, Waterloo, Canada. She has been involved in various programs aimed at integrating critical approaches to diversity and equity education for educators in traditional and non-traditional learning environments. Her work aims to encourage the ongoing development of powerful pedagogical strategies, and she has taught technology integration and critical approaches to social justice education for elementary through to post-secondary students with this in mind. She has published in award-winning books in the area of social justice education, advanced the use of humour and comedy as a pedagogical tool to more effectively advocate for social change, and she has encouraged alternative designs for equity, diversity, and social justice education more generally.

Kathy Lisi-Neuman has taught for 30 years and is currently a fifth-grade teacher at Warren Point School, in Fair Lawn, New Jersey (USA). During Kathy's tenure as an educator, she has been involved in a myriad of professional learning activities, including action research with colleagues. She is dedicated to providing Thirdspace opportunities for her students that foster a love of learning and their sharing of original ideas. Kathy was named Warren Point School's Teacher of the Year in 2012 and has co-authored the parent/teacher resource book *Engaging Parents as Literacy Partners* (Scholastic, 2014). Kathy also teaches adult English language learners as an adjunct faculty member of the American Language Program at Bergen Community College, NJ.

Heather Lotherington is Professor of Multilingual Education at York University, Toronto, Canada, where she is appointed to the graduate programs in Language, Culture and Teaching (Faculty of Education) and Linguistics and Applied Linguistics (Faculty of Liberal and Professional Studies). She has been involved in language and literacy teacher education in Canada, Australia, England, Germany, and Fiji, focusing on contextually oriented, linguistically inclusive education; multimodal, digitally mediated literacies and pedagogical innovation. She spearheaded the collaborative research venture between York University and Joyce Public School described in Chapter 4, in which researchers and teachers co-designed multimodal literacies projects over a decade. The results of their award winning research have been published widely. Heather's most recent book is *Pedagogy of Multiliteracies: Rewriting Goldilocks* (Routledge, 2011).

Marita Mäkinen is Professor of Education (Teacher Education) in the School of Education, University of Tampere, Finland. She has been involved in developing interventions for children with literacy disorders and enhancing inclusive education reform in Finland. She has conducted multi-faceted research related to teacher education, including a pedagogy of multiliteracies and teaching in and for the future learning environments. Currently she is leading the research group Higher Education in Transition. One of the subgroups of this initiative is focusing on multiliteracies and teacher education for transformative teaching and learning.

Claudia Mitchell is a James McGill Professor in the Faculty of Education, McGill University, in Montreal, Canada, where she directs the Participatory Cultures Lab, and an Honorary Professor in the University of KwaZulu Natal (South Africa). While she has worked with inservice and preservice teachers in Canada and South Africa, particularly in relation to professional identity, her current work is with inservice education in South Africa and focuses on what she terms "digital voices" and self-study through the use of participatory video and cellphilming to address critical issues linked to addressing HIV and AIDS and gender-based violence. Her co-authored and co-edited publications related to teachers and teaching include the following books: *That's Funny You Don't Look Like a Teacher: Interrogating Images of Identity in Popular Culture*; *Reinventing Ourselves as Teachers: Beyond Nostalgia*; *Just Who Do We Think We Are?*; *Methodologies for Autobiography and Self-study in Teaching*; *Making Connections: Self-study and Social Action*; *Teaching and HIV/AIDS in the South African Classroom*; *School-University Partnerships for Educational Change in Rural South Africa*; and *Memory and Pedagogy*. In her work as an English teacher in rural Nova Scotia in the 1970s, she recalls the openness at that time and places for teachers to engage in innovation and experimentation, particularly through film and other arts-based approaches. It is this work which sustains her belief in the potential for professional development to be liberating for teachers.

Kylie Peppler is an Associate Professor of Learning Sciences in the School of Education at Indiana University, Bloomington (USA). An artist by training, Kylie engages in research that focuses on the intersection of arts, technology, and interest-driven learning. Her early work with notables in the field like Mark Warschauer, Yasmin Kafai, Mitchel Resnick, and James Catterall instilled in Peppler an interest in how to leverage and design new technologies for high-quality teaching and learning experiences, which led to combining her passions in art with new technologies. She has conducted preservice and inservice training in making, e-textiles, and systems thinking across the U.S., Russia, Belarus, and other countries. Her publications include *Interconnections: Understanding Systems through Digital Design* (2014), a four-volume set that combines professional development and curricula rooted in constructionist learning theory. Peppler works to capture youths' pre-existing interests in areas such as new media, fashion, and design while supporting learning and creativity in arts, design, and STEM areas.

Victor J. Rendón is a doctoral student in the Department of Educational Research, CINVESTAV, part of the Instituto Politecnico Nacional, in Mexico City. He completed his master's studies at the same institution, and has an undergraduate degree in psychology with a specialty in education from the National Autonomous University of Mexico. He is currently a member of the Laboratory of Education, Technology and Society, CINESTAV. His research interests include the use of digital technologies in the socio-historically situated activities of high school youth.

Teresa Strong-Wilson is Associate Professor in the Faculty of Education at McGill University, Montreal. She is editor-in-chief of the *McGill Journal of Education*. She has research interests in memory, literacy/literacies, stories, early childhood, children's literature, social justice education, Indigenous education, and teacher learning and professional development. She has published extensively in peer-reviewed journals, has authored *Bringing Memory Forward: Storied Remembrance in Social Justice Education with Teachers* (2008), co-authored *Envisioning New Technologies in Teacher Practice* (2012) and co-edited *Memory and Pedagogy* (2011), *Productive Remembering and Social Agency* (2013) and *The Emperor's New Clothes?: Issues and Alternatives in Uses of the Portfolio in Teacher Education Programs* (2014). The importance of relevant, contextualised professional development (formal, informal, non-formal) that teachers could take up and use and that can simultaneously enhance their growth as members within a wider community of teachers—along with non-teachers (viz., community members, parents etc.)— was first impressed upon her from her experiences of teaching in the First Nations community of Bella Bella (Canada). It became a thread that has persistently followed her into research, in which she tries to develop projects in collaboration with teachers and/or that are designed so as to maximize opportunities for teacher sharing and growth, most recently around the digital.

Angela M. Wiseman is an Associate Professor of Literacy Education in the Department of Teacher Education and Learning Sciences at North Carolina State University in Raleigh, USA. Angela's teaching and research have been guided by the concepts of social justice and the importance of recognizing students' "funds of knowledge." As a former elementary school teacher and literacy specialist, her understanding of literacy learning is grounded in classroom experiences and interactions with students in diverse urban and suburban settings. Research projects have focused on children's responses to social issues, such as bullying or racism—through multimodal texts—which include books, film, videos, and photographs. Her research, which has been published in journals such as *Reading Writing Quarterly, Language Arts,* and *Children's Literature in Education,* demonstrates how responses that build on students' understanding and engagement lead to deeper and more complex learning. Angela's professional development experiences as a participant in the Literacy Through Photography program at the Center for Documentary Studies (documentarystudies.duke.edu/projects/past-projects/literacy-through-photography) have been influential in her understanding of multimodal and visual learning.

Name index

Subject index

U

V

W

Y

Colin Lankshear & Michele Knobel
General Editors

New literacies emerge and evolve apace as people from all walks of life engage with new technologies, shifting values and institutional change, and increasingly assume 'postmodern' orientations toward their everyday worlds. Despite many efforts to take account of such changes, educational institutions largely remain out of touch with the range of new ways of making and sharing meanings that increasingly mediate and shape the lives of the young people they teach and the futures they face. This series aims to explore some key dimensions of the changes occurring within social practices of literacy and the educational challenges they present, with a view to informing educational practice in helpful ways. It asks what are new literacies, how do they impact on life in schools, homes, communities, workplaces, sites of leisure, and other key settings of human cultural engagement, and what significance do new literacies have for how people learn and how they understand and construct knowledge. It aims to challenge established and 'official' ways of framing literacy, and to ask what it means for literacies to be powerful, effective, and enabling under current and foreseeable conditions. Collectively, the works in this series will help to reorient literacy debates and literacy education agendas.

For further information about the series and submitting manuscripts, please contact:

Michele Knobel & Colin Lankshear
Montclair State University
Dept. of Education and Human Services
3173 University Hall
Montclair, NJ 07043
michele@coatepec.net

To order other books in this series, please contact our Customer Service Department at:
(800) 770-LANG (within the U.S.)
(212) 647-7706 (outside the U.S.)
(212) 647-7707 FAX

Or browse online by series at:
www.peterlang.com